THE PROBLEM OF DISTRACTION

THE PROBLEM OF DISTRACTION

Paul North

STANFORD UNIVERSITY PRESS

STANFORD, CALIFORNIA

Stanford University Press
Stanford, California

© 2012 by the Board of Trustees of the Leland Stanford Junior University.

This book was published with the assistance of the
Frederick W. Hilles Publication Fund of Yale University.

Printed in the United States of America on acid-free, archival-quality paper

Library of Congress Cataloging-in-Publication Data

North, Paul, 1971– author.
    The problem of distraction / Paul North.
        pages cm
    Includes bibliographical references and index.
    ISBN 978-0-8047-7538-0 (cloth : alk. paper)
    ISBN 978-0-8047-8687-4 (pbk. : alk. paper)
        1. Distraction (Philosophy)   2. Philosophy, Modern.   I. Title.
B105.D58N67   2011
128'.3—dc22

2010051611

For my parents

In te, anime meus, tempora mea metior. Noli mihi obstrepere; quod est, noli tibi obstrepere turbis affectionum tuarum.

In you, O my mind, I measure my times. Do not interrupt me; that is, do not interrupt yourself with a disturbance of your affections.

—AUGUSTINE, *Confessions*

Contents

Acknowledgments

Peter Fenves, Werner Hamacher, and Samuel Weber provided indispensible insights and criticisms during the research and writing of this book. I am deeply grateful to them for their guidance. I am also beholden to people who shared thoughts on distraction in innumerable conversations: Anthony Adler, Giorgio Agamben, Carolina Baffi, David Ferris, Paul Fleming, Janet Frigo, Rodolphe Gasché, Eckart Goebel, Roshen Hendrickson, Andrew Libby, Avital Ronell, Robert Ryder, Thomas Schestag, Kenneth Schwarz, and Friese Undine. Critical comments on individual chapters by Corinne Bayerl and Barbara Cassin were invaluable in revising. Accuracy in the French, Ancient Greek, German, and Latin quotations and translations is due to the careful attention of Benjamin Hoffmann, Maya Gupta, and Thomas Stachel.

Primal Distraction

There is no distraction today, even though one often hears there are too many distractions. Yes, this is the age of distraction; many have called it that. For a hundred years or more (in actuality fifteen hundred, since Augustine), the disintegration of attention has been lamented, and every new decade and discipline seems to offer a new explanation and remedy for the loss. Education calls out the attention brigades to fight the shifty figure that steals away our focus. Have we won the war on distraction? A more primary question would be: have we found the enemy we are hunting? Commerce wrestles over the splinters of awareness that technology has shattered. Psychology struggles to get a hold on concentration, mainly against children, even though these same children will soon be required to "multi-task" and are already clicking and scanning and surfing. Why cure them of what is surely a timely habit? Statistics and politicians battle drivers' lapses; new media gather up the shards of culture from the broken cult. Drugged up, warned off, lured in, and made to swallow theories about a society in distraction, few have the presence of mind left to ask: what is this pervasive evil? What is the meaning of the word, the truth of the phenomenon, and moreover, who will tell the story of its arrival in this history and its fetishization in reasonable discourse?

Who can say they understand distraction?

The English word calls up several images: a mathematics of division; a morality of bad choices; a movement of dispersion across a grid of more and more disparate points; a diminishment of strength, quality, or purity; vices or quasi-vices that produce pleasure without work: amusement, diversion, entertainment. All these are practiced by notorious figures, by sidetracked workers, bored students, and dissolute citizens, by the day-dreamer, the sleeper who doesn't dream, the absentminded one. At the farthest limit, the least collected, the least "with it," lie the dead, who are permanently elsewhere. Which one or more of these do we mean when we say distraction? Burdened with the label, occupants of an age named for our chief failing, we mean, almost inevitably, when we say distraction, the lack of attention. And we know it is a fundamental thing we are lacking. Today we lack that which makes us most fundamentally ourselves, and so we credit the force that could steal the fundament from us with great powers, such that powerful acts are needed to contain it.

This furtive and destructive force, a distraction not only equal to but possibly also stronger than attention, is not the subject of this book. It must be—it is—the starting point for a prologue to the problem of distraction, but only insofar as we can quickly move through the common understanding before arriving at a different distraction, beyond the anxieties about attention that appear to determine it fully.

Disciplines cling to attention; they desire it as one desires a solution to a problem even when the outlines of the problem are still fuzzy. They write about it, lament its perversion or breakdown, and act with uncommon urgency to bring it back when it is not at hand. This is the most common circumstance in which attention appears. When it makes itself unavailable, attention becomes the object of an anxious search. Attention intensifies most, you might say, in its loss; it becomes itself when one goes in search of it. Producing itself out of fear of its unavailability, through this fiction, it must be pulled back continually from an unknown place to which it has slipped away. In this way, attention depends on an internal reference to distraction. But this reference, in turn, never seems to produce its referent. Attention constitutes itself by saving itself from a distraction whose meaning or image is even less articulable than the attention we say distraction is not.

A tautology seems to block our inquiry here. The non-attention whose negation forms the most common origin for attention can only be specified from the perspective of attention. So let us start again, taking our departure from what is presumed to be the primary term. Although it is often described on analogy with vision, attention has other attributes worth noting. Attention is patient; it has fortitude, is obsessive even, about its activity and its objects, and, continuing in this direction, the content of its patience and the object of its obsession is greed. This is its self-referential core: it holds greedily onto greed. The hand of attention stretches out, *ad-tenere*, toward the things it wishes to take and possess, and it compels itself to do so again and again. Attention is a name for a will to possession that is comparable to vision only insofar as vision is also thought of as willful and possessive. One idea of sight co-originates with attention in this will. The more restrictive of the two is clearly attention—there can be attentive and non-attentive vision. Above all, at least in the common understanding, attention always possesses a unit, even if the unit is a conjunction of a few objects. And it possesses the unit alone, abandoning other units to other faculties or disciplines (to handle in the same way, greedily, administering their ownership defensively against other disciplines). Only to its own thing does attention give the gift of undividedness, and the gift often brings with it a share of defensive violence. The opposite of this possessiveness, we are led to assume, is distraction. Distraction either does not appropriate or impedes appropriation. Perhaps it is not even greedy about its own tendencies; it shifts, undervalues itself, gives itself away. Thus, when a discipline—a *Wissenschaft*, a methodical, repeatable relation to sanctioned objects, an institutionalized attention—restricts itself to its objects, it excludes not only other objects and disciplines but also, and more importantly, other acts or non-acts that would include them, even though they are unrelated and even if they are not properly sanctioned as objects. Reception of the human genome and a fruit fly and three hundred years of American military history and the concept of the proper name is simply not attention. Attention's conjunction is "or," not "and."

It would seem then, that the answer to the tautology or near-tautology—attention is not non-attention—is to describe the positive contents of the concept and the act, to derive the concept of attention from what it is and does, and to define distraction as the negation of this. Yet, by this argument alone attention cannot definitively be said to be attentive. Its will to possession cannot be derived from observation of its activity. This is because attention can possess anything but itself.[1] And for this reason attention may not be a unitary thing; there may not be a single unambiguous disposition called attention, or at least there is no way of verifying that there is. An argument *ex negativo* can perhaps demonstrate this problem. When the intellect is duly disciplined, the blinders on, so to speak—when it pays attention—what faculty remains to attend to it—to attend to the attention to objects? If attention is the only intellectual disposition that produces truth, this poses an enormous problem, akin to classical formulations of the problem of reflection. To attention attention cannot be paid. Franz Brentano made this impossibility a cornerstone of empirical psychology, and this insight had broad effects in twentieth-century philosophy and psychology. For Brentano, as well as for his students such as Husserl and Freud, the intellectual mode in which attentive thought can possibly come to be studied is not itself attention.[2] Insofar as attention is constitutively hidden from attentive thought, the scientist of attention is forced to work on an "oblique" path; the faculty by which she does this may best be called parattention, a sideward glance that targets its object somewhat like the eye sees its blind spots, less by seeing them than by registering non-seeing in a visual way. Where attentive thought is considered the prime condition for truth, where the attendable is the only candidate for the true (be the objects empirical, intellectual, or divine), this is tantamount to an admission that the nature of attention is neither verifiable nor unverifiable. Attention may be asserted by disciplines; they may even practice it or claim they are practicing it; nevertheless, it cannot be understood in a disciplined way, at least insofar as discipline is associated primarily with attentive thought.

Attention is not an attendable, and this is where its supposed opposite, distraction, begins to take on supreme importance. This is also where the problems we are dealing with cease to be only our problems; they are not recent, but lie at the heart of an old understanding of thought. For as long as a grasping, excluding, unequivocal attention has been desired as the fundamental human disposition, we have been living in an age of (potential) distraction. Most attempts to place cognition at the font of human life, from Aristotle to Descartes to Husserl, depend on it, however clandestinely.

For this reason, when we ask what we mean when we say distraction, we could answer: when faced with the crisis of the loss of attention, we mean attention's opposite, its determinate negation, the negation of the uncertainty that arises when we try to ground attention in itself. Distraction, according to this reasoning, means the disintegration or misdirection of a unified, stable, directional mental force for possession of sanctioned objects. In the most common understanding today, distraction means a divided or a diverted attention.[3] Here a third problem develops. The dialectic begins to break down, insofar as, in this picture, the two concepts, attention and distraction, are not opposites at all, but rather contraries, the one, distraction, consists in the other, attention, to the lowest degree. The age of distraction, it turns out, was always but the age of attention, and what it lacked more than anything was its eponymous phenomenon. There is no distraction, only an attention to the zero degree. What we call distraction is attentive thought degraded until it can do nothing but clamor for a return to its ideal. "Age of distraction" is a terrible euphemism, shibboleth for a posited utopia, and, at the same time, a mask behind which deep uncertainties teem. Naming itself thus, the age assures itself that attention awaits, before or after it. Its task is to find a way to it, whether the way runs back or forward.

Recent intellectual history has been written in accordance with this conceptual shell game. Theories of attention depend on distraction, since alone attention cannot be understood. Distraction is then defined as a divided or hugely degraded attention. In this way the tautological structure of the concept is preserved. One book that claims to critique the emphasis on attention nevertheless makes its unspoken commitment to an attention theory of distraction plain. The author describes his program in the introduction: "I am interested in how Western modernity since the nineteenth century has demanded that individuals define and shape themselves in terms of a capacity for 'paying attention,' that is, for a disengagement from a broader field of attraction . . . " (Crary 1). In the current fever for finding lost attention, Jonathan Crary's plan might seem like a change, a revolution even. It is true, as long as we think of it as the fundamental capacity of an eternal psyche, attention does not seem susceptible to historicization. Crary attacks this assumption, challenging the intellectual complacency that led to the concealment of the history of attention. Drawing his theory of history mainly from Foucault, in order to argue that the emphasis on attention has arisen recently and for political reasons, Crary writes a gene-

alogy of attention in which it appears as a mode of "perception," in order
to expose its hidden source not in God or the psyche, but in "other kinds
of forces and relations to power" (2). Behind the age's obsession with attention, Crary reveals an essential act of power, by which he means the power
of the state over "individuals." Domination is the hidden motivation for
the modern push toward attention. With this theory, however, Crary confines his inquiry to the very edifice he wishes to dismantle. What he calls
the "modernization of perception," that is, the increasing demand for control over the receptive capacity of "a subject," in order to insure that the
subject "is productive, manageable, and predictable, and is able to be socially integrated and adaptive," relies unreservedly on the terms, continually operative in his argument, "subject," "field of attraction," and even the
methodological motivation for his whole project, the unassuming phrase
"I am interested" (4)—each of which has already answered the question
of distraction in advance. Here a "subject," as a priori subjugated to its
outside, can only approach the world through an a posteriori "attraction,"
and although in modernity its scope may have narrowed from a field to,
say, a point, the ontological assumptions underlying the schema remain
the same.[4] Distraction is diversion, and diversion is a version of attention.[5]

How would distraction appear if it were released from its subordina-
tion to attention, to perception, to the subject? Few ask, and those who
do often cannot abide the peculiar conclusions to which the inquiry leads.
Another distraction that is not diversion, not a species or degree of attention, appears rarely in the history of the thought of thought. This is not
all that can be said about it, however. Its rarity seems to follow a pattern,
a pattern closely intertwined with the path of Western philosophy beginning in Greece, namely: banishment and return.

The specter of a non-attentional distraction haunted Aristotle in
his attempt to theorize the soul. Chapter 1 argues that what frightened
Aristotle was the image of an intermittent interruption of cognition. A
century and a half earlier Parmenides had already envisioned something
like this as the defining characteristic of mortals. It was also, Parmenides
demonstrated, the chief threat to the new discipline he was inventing: true
thought of what is. In the course of the movement from Parmenides to
Aristotle in which the intellect, *nous*, rose to prominence, the image, and

with it the problem, of a primal distraction beyond attention was banished in Ancient Greece. This banishment had a long life: even today it affects studies of Aristotle, where this distraction—not-always-thinking—is rarely mentioned. In the drive to understand what was meant by thinking, periodic non-thought, *to mē aei noein*, remains at the margins. Yet banishments prepare the way for returns. Even if the forces and events that led not-always-thinking to surface again in Europe in seventeenth-century France are too many and too multifaceted to be accounted for without oversimplifying, it is nevertheless the case that primal distraction appeared at the end of the *Grand Siècle* and there for the first time it gained a name and a face in Jean de La Bruyère's figure, later called "le distrait." Chapter 2 offers an ontological and political interpretation of this figure, in part by contrasting him with Pascal's famous concept of *divertissement*, a near-contemporary theological counterpart.

The path of not-always-thinking is full of leaps. Let us affirm this from the beginning. Banishment in Ancient Greek philosophy and a belated return in seventeenth-century French moralism became legible, perhaps for the first time, only after the conceptual problems surrounding distraction began to be theorized in the early twentieth century. German-speaking writers undertook this task for concrete intellectual-historical reasons. Reacting to the supremacy of the intellect in the phenomenological philosophies of Franz Brentano and Edmund Husserl, three quite different writers, widely considered revolutionaries in their spheres, endeavored to conceptualize a radical distraction outside the dialectic with attention. Franz Kafka in fiction, Martin Heidegger in philosophy, and Walter Benjamin in cultural criticism, the foci of Chapters 3, 4, and 5 respectively, made distraction central to their writing. And although each set out to exploit specific resources of the German word *Zerstreuung*— Kafka as something like diaspora, Heidegger as dissipation, Benjamin as entertainment, with significant areas of overlap among them and differences within them—each almost inadvertently stumbled upon the most extreme and most unintentional withdrawal of thinking.

There appear to be three moments in this pattern of appearance— banishment, return, and theorization—and this book attempts to come to terms with each and to show their interrelations.

The history of thought is itself not a unitary thing. Every finite thinker abbreviates another history of thought into an image that can be read. Aristotle does this, most famously at the beginning of the *Metaphysics*, where he sums up the arguments of his predecessors. Hegel makes this abbreviation into the very movement of philosophy. Some histories of thought are absorbed from books or other epochs or teachers. Some are elections of taste, some spring from deep convictions, some—perhaps most—slip into intellectual work through a scholar's inattention or the inattention of an age. Perhaps the greatest affront to thinking, however, is not the history or pseudo-history that is inevitably adduced, with more or less awareness, to support it, but rather the desire to present the syncretic, interested, and transient image of the history of thought as true. The truth of the relation between the most contemporary thinking and the past it claims in support of its meaning and procedure is its image-character.

The history of the thought of thought, or as Gilles Deleuze called it, images of thought, is already a dubious case, in which historical image and thought-act are extremely difficult to distinguish. Insofar as thinking routinely makes this difference, the difference between a now of present thinking and a history leading up to and preparing for it—whether by continuity or by a radical break, it matters little—insofar as thought demonstrates by means of this history that it is in fact thinking now, and to the extent that it privately calls upon its potted genealogy in order to separate "thinking" from "not-thinking" or "non-thinking," with all the urgency of a now, the thought of thought falls into an unexpected stupidity about its own provenance. How can thought call its history into question if it can only operate by relying upon such a history to assert that it is, once again, thinking? What we think we do when we think can hardly be separated from our implicit understanding of what it means to think, and this, the meaning of thought, corresponds to the image that we inherit, co-opt, or in much rarer cases willfully invent. Thinking, it seems, will never be thought through.

Phenomenology provides one important image of what it meant for the twentieth century to think, and much has been done to extend this image of thought, to correct it or imagine alternative modes for it with other models or precursors. Acts of thinking are historical in this sense. They call upon a history of what it means to think in order to distinguish themselves as thinking now, as current thinking, as truly thinking and often also as the truth of thinking, even while, in order to do this, they ground their contemporaneity in prior instances that, while rejecting them, they clutch ever more tightly. The "history of thought" affirms a continuous, changing reel of thought-images to which a present thinker adds a frame, altered, to be sure, yet holding passionately onto this chain of positive appearances that lurk in the verb "to think." In this way acts of *Geist* fall within a *Geistesgeschichte* that runs from Anaxagoras's world-mind to Hegel's absolute spirit and beyond. To say "I think" is to evoke this continuum, a retrospectively proleptic, self-correcting race toward the present. If we are able to admit that consciousness might not always meet itself in self-reflection, we are still not at ease dispensing with a history that has mind at its helm and as its destination.

The other case, the case of distraction, is at first glance less philosophical and more ridiculous. Can we produce a genealogy of not-always-thinking so that we can say we have thought distraction through? It is a fact that such a history has not yet been written. Someone might suggest, and rightly, that distraction's case is hardly comparable to the history of thought, with its grand successes and stimulating paradoxes; distraction is trivial, a side issue, and one triviality among many. Surely there are a multitude of unwritten histories of minor unstudied concepts. Moreover, the lack of prior study might not indicate anything more than scholarly oversight, an accidental inattention in an otherwise efficient and responsible profession. That it has not only recently but also repeatedly been neglected over the course of the West's intellectual history would not necessarily prove the urgency of looking into distraction now.

Something in the way it has fallen into neglect, however, hints to the contrary. Inattention, absentmindedness, *Geistesabwesenheit, Gedankenlosigkeit,* plus other words or technical jargon that lay claim to this concept or lack thereof are the very terms we use to describe its disappearance in intellectual history. The human sciences have left distraction unthought. Until now it has escaped scholarly notice. Clichéd as this may at first seem, the idea that inattention has escaped our notice or that absentmindedness has remained unthought or unthinkable in a conceptual history begs the question. A loop ensues when we begin to think of distraction: there must already be a concept and thus a history to be able to make the claim that it has not yet been thought, and yet unlike other hidden threads or nodes in Western intellectual history, this one describes its own historical disappearance. The tradition has been inattentive to inattention, and thus we can argue that there is no tradition of distraction, no history of it per se. The circle in which we find distraction is not a hermeneutic circle.

The idea that a history of thought is required in order to state what thinking might be, so that we may be sure to continue doing it, this self-replicating movement, recalls an early scene in which the bond between thinking and being was discovered, or rather compelled (Parmenides calls it bondage by "fate," "*moira*"), in the fifth century BCE. The bond between thinking and being envisioned there has survived in part due to empirical events that came after it. To mention just one: Aristotle adopted the bond of *noēsis* and *ousia*, and Aristotle was adopted by succeeding ages as master of their thought. Yet the bond also persists for internal reasons, because of an emphasis on mythical necessity, transmitted from Parmenides to Plato and beyond: *anthrōpos* is required to think and to think being; it is this being's lot, its fate. Being, in turn, means, among other things, what lasts. It is thus no accident that something like thought again and again survives the twists and turns of history. Being survives because since Parmenides "survival" is being's secret name. Thought survives along with it as its medium of preservation. Thus Parmenides' dictum bequeaths two unvarying principles: thought is bound to being by fate and fate means that being survives the death of beings. The two are eternally conjoined: it is just as important that thought (*noēsis*) continue beyond any thinker or single thought (*noema*) as it is that being (*ousia*) outlive singular beings (*ontes*). These principles work together to project a thought-being construct— *nous, intellectus activus, je pense, Geist,* thought, mind—that outlasts the passing of sentences, vocabularies, languages, texts, schools, sciences, and philosophizing beings. What's more, the perdurance of thought correlates precisely to the idea of historical change. Since thought is of what-is, changes in what-is bring along with them or follow from (it doesn't matter which) changes in thought. On this one point idealism and realism agree. Whatever happens (historically), there will always be being (and not nothing) and thought (and not non-thought); true to its fate, thought will always be attracted to what-is (despite particular differences) and what-is will display itself for and through thought. For this reason there is much less of a difference between "paying attention" and a "broader field of attractions" than Jonathan Crary assumes. The concept of change—that which happens to the attributes of a substance—does not threaten but in fact preserves the correspondence between thought and being, assuring that both remain intelligible through vocabularies, fashions, and changing institutions. In the phrase "the history of thought," history is quite obviously the subordinate term.

Not-thinking tells another story, a *Geistesabwesenheitsgeschichte,* history absent mind, which is forced to dispense with a controlling spirit or *Geist* and so is barely recognizable as history. In such an account—parable, legend, or yarn may be better names for it—it would not be clear how or whether being and thought could continue their fateful *pas de deux.* One can turn one's thought to not-thinking—or one can claim to do this—but one does so at the risk of severing the bond with being. And so, of course, distraction must be studied from within *Geistesgeschichte,* even though a history of the thought of distraction by rights falsifies its object. From the perspective of not-thinking, thought vanishes before it can gain even an inkling of its coming disappearance. Still, it is only reasonable to concede that unthought needs to be addressed from the perspective of thought; indeed—when we begin to wonder what it would look like if its history were written according to its own nature, by its own laws or by its anomy, the result is ludicrous. What would a history of distraction be if it refused to borrow stability and permanence from thought? What if it rejected thought's temporal signature, always—*aei?* Aristotle recoils from this intuition at a key moment in his late text *De anima.* We follow him in recognizing that, admitting the existence of unthought—and we must do this in order to study it, mustn't we?—if we admit its existence or at least its occurrence, we are forced to admit that *Geistesgeschichte* and its more technical nephew, *Begriffsgeschichte,* are inadequate to the task, or worse, that they will be drawn to pieces by their object. This is our dilemma: we must suspend our belief in the existence of the thing in order to study it, since if we believe in it, we must also believe that it will most certainly ruin the ideal intellectual act that we fantasize stands behind our study. Insofar as unthought exists it cannot be thought; insofar as it occurs it cannot be conceptualized; it affects *Geist* yet falls out of the usual history written by it about it.[6]

Many philosophers relegate this sort of distraction to the empirical realm. Kant addresses *Zerstreutheit*, "distractedness," in *The Critique of Pure Reason*, but for him it is an accident affecting only empirical consciousness;[7] neither understanding nor reason are susceptible to it, and so it has little importance within reason's critique.[8] From the perspective of reason, distraction—a phenomenon for which "what is it?" is the most desperate and also the most inappropriate question—could have no transcendental condition, and so it would be unseemly for philosophy to inquire into it. The continuity of consciousness—despite the limits that Kant places on our ability to intuit its sources—is maintained by banishing distraction to the sphere of accident and illness.[9] If the disturbance affects only empirical thinkers and not their transcendental faculties, it is an anthropological matter, and thus a minor aberrance, a contamination, an annoyance.

The frequency with which the question of unthought springs to mind in the philosophical tradition is low. It receives a long scene in Parmenides' poem, though barely a mention in Plato. Aristotle picks it up once or twice, obliquely, and then he treats it suddenly as an unanswerable question in his late treatise on the soul. Hegel, following Kant, assigns it to the empirical as a minor detraction from habit.[10] What is there to mark its reappearance in philosophical systems, however, and perhaps also to explain its infrequent treatment, is a worry about a nefarious nothing that steals away the empirical thinker's intellectual powers, and more importantly, her relationship to eternity. What good would thinking be if no thinker could trust her special instantiation of it? Such a limit would threaten the transcendental order. The worry about this threat goes further: the thought of unthought is often accompanied by a premonition that since it is neither a being nor a thought (reality's exclusive vectors, at least for Parmenides) it can have no cause and no origin; it remains a rumor, mere opinion, a ghost, and thus is not truly cognizable at all. How can we think about a causeless, trackless nothing that snuffs out the spark of human thinking, especially if we suspect that it is only an empirical event with no transcendental corollary?

It may be this very self-defeating aspect of the problem that enticed thinkers in the early twentieth century to rethink it. In the most general terms, for Franz Kafka, Martin Heidegger, and Walter Benjamin,

Zerstreuung—and related words and concepts—both belonged and didn't belong to the cultural and intellectual tradition they were watching—or so they thought—fall to pieces. Unthought kills thought, if only for an instant of unspecifiable length, and this suggests both the reason for which it had been neglected and at the same time why it held promise for these writers writing in and against the ductus of phenomenology in the early twentieth century.

I understand distraction as a parontological relationship of thought to non-being and its variants: not-quite-being, more-than-being, not-yet-being, no-longer-being. Allied with figures such as presentiment, sublimity, clairvoyance, and recollection, as the advent of a mental nothing or a principle of disappearance however, it tests the limits of even these marginal mental phenomena, tending away from phenomenology and ontology toward fantasy, literature, and art. It is difficult to isolate distraction as a philosopheme that emerged within a specific historical horizon, as though it were an empirical event in the history of thought. This seems to be because it acts as the mental corollary of historical horizons themselves, and so it has no history of its own. It is hard to catch because, as a tendency toward the limit of what is, distraction is nearest when it escapes notice and most remote when attended to. As the receding-approaching limit of thinking, it haunts the history of thought and raises doubts about its legitimacy. And although it haunts, it is not itself spectral; it is closer to a capacity to receive specters. When it speaks it says: here comes nothing—an excess or shortage of what we think is. A paradoxical capacity to receive non-beings, and at the same time, inversely, an incapacity to think (if thinking is thinking being), it resists becoming an object of thought. While thought's capacity to take itself as an object remains the central problem of philosophy, as well as its central hope—as reflection—the problem of receiving distraction attracts little philosophical interest.

That which disengages moments or epochs of cognition is not strictly mental. An irruption of the non-mental within the mental, the inexperienceable within experience, it can occur when a mind or an epoch releases its hold on cherished intellectual structures, being-determining categories, and beings. Although anti-historical, it is not therefore eternal, and yet it does not seem to go away (more correct might be to say that it brings "away" to mind). Formally, it repeats an intermission in which history dispenses with coherence. For beings and their relations this entails great risk. More than risk—it assumes an underlying discontinuum over which continuity has been draped like a shroud. Distraction is a reminder of the loose fit of historical life on the casket of its coherence.

Intimations of distraction occasionally disturb the tradition, beginning with Parmenides, that binds thought to being, although they never concentrate themselves into theories of it. One finds theories of marginal phenomena such as laughter, boredom, and forgetting, and of course of central concepts such as form, appearance, language, and so forth, but never a full-fledged "theory of distraction," notwithstanding Walter Benjamin's notes that bear this title. Primal distraction comes and goes yet no source can be found for its coming and going. This study presents three disturbances in this non-history of distraction: a panic within Aristotelian metaphysics, a risible scatterbrain at the edges of French moralism, and a set of attempts to bring distraction and its potentials into theoretical focus during the inter-war years of the twentieth century.

Aristotle establishes the paradigm of an intermittent phenomenon whose phenomenality remains in question because its being—which should, as the source of its on-again off-again appearance, be eternal— is intermittent as well. It comes toward us but lacks a "whence." This sourcelessness is the source of its incoherence as a concept and its duplicity as a word, and that is why Aristotle drops the issue. And yet, although it cannot be conceptualized, distraction can be illustrated. When it returns in the seventeenth century it comes back outside philosophical discourse proper. Temporal inconsistency, intrusion of the discontinuum into the seamless weave of the everyday, the unheard-of ability to receive what-is-not in an inability to think—these traits are given a human shape in La Bruyère's *distrait*. Then, in the twenties and thirties of the last century some aspects of primal distraction are conceptualized for the first time in literature, philosophy, and art criticism. Kafka emphasizes the thoughtless-one's ability to shake itself loose from the means-ends logic of willing; Heidegger points to the freedom that the dispersing one—Dasein—enjoys with respect to its own ground; and Benjamin imagines an internal dissipation that, brought about through new media, will lead to an uncommon politicization. Together these tentative and partial reports on distraction contribute to an understanding of human being as one whose highest capacity is not the synthesizing process of *noēsis* but rather the periodic dissolution of its faculties. What Kafka, Heidegger, and Benjamin—taken together—intimate is the following. Where philosophy, criticism, and art theory are traditionally concerned with principles for the formation of things, distraction is concerned with their deformation, disintegration, and ceasing to be. It posits a tendency toward not-thinking and a release from being.

Please note: All the translations from Ancient Greek, Latin, and German are my own, unless otherwise indicated. In Chapter 2 published translations from the French have been used and cited, and where occasionally modified, so noted.

CHAPTER I

Not-Always-Thinking / Aristotle

No one who wasn't already convinced that asking what thinking means counted as thinking would ask such a question. At the same time, no one who didn't also intend from the outset to suspend or abandon this conviction would bother to ask. Either the most profound question in thought is also the silliest, or else something essential about the constitution of thinking is revealed here, or both. Am I thinking when I think about thinking's meaning, or do I put the act, receptivity, or spontaneity—however I may mean it or will mean it—into suspension, in order to inquire into its sense? If I suspend the sense of it, can I trust the outcome? Won't the thought of thinking's meaning for all intents and purposes be illegitimate, a result of faulty method, fickle? In short, the thought of thinking's meaning is a tangle that produces something more like not-thinking. If thinking seems to stumble when it makes its act into a question, its approach to distraction should be even more precipitous.

How many understandings of this activity or passivity—thinking, *penser, noein, denken*—and its ambiguous seat or faculty—*mens*, mind, intellect, *nous, Geist, esprit*, and so forth—have been posited, and how various the attempts to cut through the tangle! The stubborn "problem of the moving principle of our thought," so Franz Brentano summed it up in his brilliant 1867 study of Aristotle's *De anima*. Brentano was struck by the large variety of responses to what he perceived as a single problem with a single solution. "How different the paths that different minds have traveled!" in order to arrive at thought thinking thought (*The Psychology of Aristotle* 157). How different indeed, and how strongly Brentano wanted to send the paths back to their origin, to minimize the confusion and show their primordial convergence, which could be found, he contended, in Aristotle's account of *nous*. Not returning to Aristotle had been the kernel of the problem. "How many of those who indignantly shunned this thought were driven to the most extravagant assumptions by the difficulties of the problem. . . . " Aristotle too likes to list errant paths taken by his predecessors. Brentano and Aristotle agree on this methodological ideal: there is one original and unified description of thinking, representing the only solution to the problem of thought, and the different thoughts of different minds on the subject, when taken together, although they apparently point away from the origin, in pointing away simultaneously point back to the primordial path from which their minds strayed. They share the assumption that thinking is in essence whole, transparent, stable, essentially separate from the variety of ways in which one might try to gain access to it, a complex unity, to be sure, yet despite its complexity lacking nothing; thought is, in short, eminently thinkable. Diverging articulations of the meaning of thought prove the underlying unity. Brentano accepts the multiplicity; he has a plan for it: "is there not rather more unity where one begins with a multiplicity of assumptions, but where layer is securely placed upon layer, and the uniformity of style and coherence of all parts is skillfully preserved from top to bottom?" (159). The history of thought can be peeled away to reveal Aristotle, the skilled preserver who pioneered the layering of parts (in the soul) to engineer their coherence. After an afterlife of further layering, Brentano returns the parts to their proper strata.

Under the last layer, following this logic, lies the active intellect, the *hen* and *haplos* beneath the manageable complexity. No doubt it too is layered, encrusted with the false opinions of philologists and interpreters. The Aristotelian image of *nous poiētikos* is riddled with conceptual problems that Brentano sets out to simplify in a reading of *De anima*, perhaps better than Aristotle did or could possibly have done. Aristotle, after all, does not use the phrase "productive thought," *nous poiētikos*, which nonetheless came to represent his thought of thought for millennia, up to and including in Brentano's study.[1]

We will also start from a problem in Aristotle's account of *nous*, although it doesn't seem to have become diverted or layered over with opinion, and so it may not be a problem in Brentano's sense. Like Brentano, we will return to a beginning in *De anima*, but instead of the lofty *archē* of a tradition that degenerates into extravagance after "this thought," Aristotle's pure thought of actual thinking, ours will stop short at a trouble that might have prevented him from beginning. In the beginning there is the beginning of something that would arrest him, but it is not carried through. Aristotle addresses the arresting trouble in his treatise on the *psuchē*, when he calls for an investigation into a peculiar disturbance in *noēsis*. "Of not-always-thinking the cause must be investigated" (*tou de mē aei noein to aition episkepteon*) (*De anima* 430a5–6). An urgency sounds in this phrase, a fury to pinpoint a cause, and yet at the same time the strangeness and precariousness of the demand is also audible. With this sentence Aristotle enjoins us to find insight into the cause of an irregularity in the concept or experience of *noēsis*. In the general order of the argument in this section of the text, the demand seems to come out of nowhere. Unlike other *problēmata* or *aporiai* in the theory of *nous*, this one is not contextualized; it is not integrated into the network of psychic capacities—perception (*aisthēsis*), comprehension (*dianoia*), imagination (*phantasia*), and intellection (*noēsis*)—nor does it find a proper place in the ontological schema—potential/actual (*dunamis/energeia*)—that operates here. A sign of the peculiar difficulty inherent in making this demand is its sudden appearance and its even more precipitous disappearance from the argument. Once the productive aspect of *nous* has been determined to be actual, one, apart, and unchanging, Aristotle forgets or ignores the demand just as abruptly as he announced it.

The demand hangs suspended without a response, and in this suspension, and suspense, questions arise: why would a thinking whose time signature was not always, *mē aei*, present itself to Aristotle as requiring, let alone being susceptible to, causal investigation? Why would it seem necessary—as the suffix "-teon" implies—for an inquiry into the intellectual aspect of the *psuchē*, which was in turn necessary to the *logos* of *anthrōpos*? Moreover, how could the emphatically necessary investigation then come to be abandoned by this most rigorous of philosophers?

Aristotle's Insatiable Demand

An understanding of non-attentional distraction could have been articulated in Ancient Greece; conditions were ripe. A strong theory of intellectual activity had developed in which *nous*, with *theoria* as its main mode and genre, had taken a stand against poetry and history, as well as, in another vein, against less centralizing modes of community. As its meaning changed and became fixed in texts by thinkers from Heraclitus to Aristotle, *nous* came to replace other principles for organizing cultural goods, while at the same time excluding and substituting for disorder and the lack of principles.[2] Needless to say, only in retrospect do pre-noetic modes appear as lacking principle and as negations of order. Not-thinking is an accusation made within the agora of thought. After the demise of Mycenaean palace culture, at roughly the same time as scattered rural communities on the Greek peninsula began collecting into *poleis*, *nous* began its rise to prominence. *Nous* and *polis* have been seen as historically parallel centralizing, stabilizing, and ordering processes. In their own ways responding and contributing to the turning point between the so-called eighth-century renaissance when the Homeric poems were most likely recorded and the "golden age" when the dalliance called philosophy came into its own, the two concepts provided guidelines for a novel commonality and predictability in anthropic things.

Alternative structures had been articulated, among other places, in the Homeric poems, although the consolidation of political community around something like a soul had already begun there. The wild caprices of the Olympian gods in the *Iliad*, for instance, are ultimately quashed by "The Will of Zeus," which transcends all other negotiations.[3] When, a few centuries after the Homeric poems became codified, Heraclitus wrote that the unified intellectual principle (*hen to sophon mounon*) was "both willing and unwilling to be known by the name Zeus," he was commenting on a process, well underway, by which transcendence was falling out of fashion and was gradually being replaced with an immanent force or will, though the necessity for a divine will would never wane (Kirk and Raven #228). An internal will can be found at work in almost every scene of the *Iliad*, a plan sprung from the father's head that renders mortal challenges moot. Achilles' resistance—to Agamemnon, to war in general, to the gods, as well as to his own finitude and fate—is but a reaction to the Zeus principle, the psychic principle of principles. In the codified texts left from the Homeric tradition the hero's resistance becomes the medium through which the gods' will exerts itself, crushing other forms of order and pointing the way toward a collectivity based on a central intellect that keeps the destiny of the group firmly in mind, despite the vicissitudes of experience.

An anecdote highlights the importance for Aristotle of *nous*'s independence from all that might change. His student Clearchus reports that Aristotle attended a public experiment in which *nous* was shown to be separable not only from the body but also from the rest of the *psuchē*. In the anecdote, someone strikes a reclining boy with a rod made for attracting souls (*psuchoulkos rabdos*). Upon being hit, the boy's soul slips out of his body and comes to hover in a corner of the observation room. To the amazement of the onlookers who have gathered to witness the event, including Aristotle, when the soul is slipped back into him, the boy can report all that happened as though he had experienced it without interruption (Clearchus 11).[4]

Although the story is apocryphal and surely originates in a confusion about Aristotle's desires in his study of the *psuchē* and its separable aspect, productive *nous*, on the part of a well-meaning but too empirically minded student, or perhaps on the part of Proclus, who records Clearchus's anecdote, it is nevertheless striking. Through the veil of distortion produced by a student on one hand and a scholar on the other, the story lets a secret be communicated: the philosopher's desire for direct experience of the highest aspect of thought. Throughout his natural-scientific investigations and even in his metaphysics, a direct view of the separability of *nous* eluded Aristotle. Unlike later generations of psychologists, the scientist did not think to experiment on himself; the subject here is a prostrate boy.[5] In contrast to later schools of thought—Cartesianism or phenomenology, say—Greek "philosophy of mind" is acted out within a resolutely social milieu. Here, in contrast to Plato's communal philosophizing, which proceeds by dialogue, the experimenter philosophizes with an instrument, the soul-attracting rod, which attracts *psuchai* not through *erōs*, as the figure of the prostrate boy might otherwise suggest, but by a blow (*plēxas*, "having struck him") (Clearchus 11). The philosophical quality of the soul-attracting rod seems to be the brusqueness with which it jars loose what only appears to be integrated into soul and body. The experimenter's skill at moving *psuchai* around is also to be noted. It is Aristotle's teaching, after all, that the intellectual part of the *psuchē* is actualized by the highest being, a god (*Metaphysics* 1072b19–30). He doesn't say in the *Metaphysics*, however, that violence is needed. In this anecdote, Clearchus confuses the empirical with the intelligible, confounding the inductive method of second philosophy with the deductive method of first philosophy. Or perhaps he is poking fun at the frustrated desire at the center of his teacher's teaching: to be able to demonstrate with the certainty of the senses that *nous* is separable and immortal. The joke is on the student then, since it is not in the realm of phenomena that the difference of *nous* can be demonstrated. As soon as it became a phenomenon it would no longer be separable. Passed on in the anecdote, then, is the problem in Aristotle's animating wish: he desires mastery over the special motion of *nous*, but he cannot demonstrate to himself that he has gained it.

Clearchus's anecdote also reveals a peculiar quality, necessary in order for *nous* to be separable from the senses, from the other higher parts of the soul (such as imagination and the locomotive principle), and from *phusis* in general. If the *psuchē* is not mixed with physical life in any way it must have an unnatural motility of its own, different in kind from the locomotion it produces in bodies. Given Aristotle's rejection of a "self-moving mover," this motion would seem difficult to imagine. But the anecdote gives a clue. The peculiar movement of the *psuchē* is a movement without place, if place is thought of as physical location. In effect *nous* would have to be placeless, where being placeless meant *nous* could at any time slip away from these psychic locales, the senses, the imagination, the body, the world. To become master over this exceptional noetic motion is what it means, according to the anecdote, to be a philosopher. And indeed, the stunned boy recalls the process by which one comes to philosophy in the Aristotelian *muthos*. According to *Metaphysics* Λ, a philosopher is the one susceptible to a blow of wonder—*thaumazein* (982b12–13), but also the one who can make use of this stunning blow to produce motion. Philosophizing moves the philosopher from potential to actual philosophizing, from trivial aporias to momentous ones (982b11–983a11). This anecdote, in contrast, goes further: the *psuchē* is struck out of place and is made to reveal its special movement.[6] In this student's misreading or joke, a philosopher's *psuchē*-moving rod, in one and the same blow, stuns a student, proves the separability, unity, and power of *nous*, and inadvertently gestures toward its innate slipperiness.

And yet the boy's *psuchē* continues to process perceptions while he is out of his senses. Slipping away, in this tale, does not alter the ability of *nous* to function as the productive principle of thought. This is the exoteric teaching that survives in the anecdote. In his epilogue, Proclus remarks that the experiment convinced onlookers about the *psuchē*'s independence from the body (Clearchus 11).[7] And so, the philosopher has succeeded in demonstrating that, even when separated from the organs of experience, *nous* never stops *noetizing*. It operates continually, unchangingly, and forever, independent of circumstances.[8] Whatever ephemeral forces appear to affect it belong to the body or the lower parts of the soul, and they only *appear* to affect it. Thus, on the surface, to be a philosopher means to demonstrate the total and continual disaffection of *nous*. No merely empirical violence can compel *nous* to cease its activity; through all violations, its motion remains inviolable, continuous, and perfect. And at the same time we also learn here that, in the desire for an absolutely separate, autonomous, eternal, and changeless *nous*, a certain looseness in the soul also has to be stipulated. From the outset, Aristotle needs and hates this looseness.

Separability is duplicitous. And so, when a particularly threatening looseness within *noēsis* itself—the mysterious on-again off-again not-always-thinking—raises its head at the end of *De anima* 3.4, it is already part of a demand to pinpoint a cause. To be sure, the main thrust of the treatise is to demonstrate that the *psuchē* is the determining principle (*archē*) of living beings (*De anima* 402a6–7). By this Aristotle means that *psuchē* determines life in two ways: it is the source of motion (*kinesis*, which includes locomotion, generation and decay, and all other forms of change) and it is also that which perceives and is thereby receptive to the forms of beings. Not until Book 3 does he give *nous* an extended analysis; there he first shows the exceptionality of this part of the soul.[9] Unlike the motive and perceptive aspects, the thinking part is unmixed (*amigē*) with body and therefore incorruptible (429a18). Furthermore it is capable of thinking everything-that-is by receiving the forms (*tous eidē*) of beings (429a15–16) and receptive to the more fundamental being of a being (429b10–22). It is the unity of all predications (430b5–6), indivisible (430b17), unchanging, and undying (430a23)—in a word, divine.[10]

The way "not-always-thinking" is broached here is a product of the desires that shaped the discovery of the highest intellect. Not-always-thinking, if it cannot be explained, threatens the position of *noēsis* as crown prince of the soul and metaphysical ground of *anthrōpos*.

Nous rose to the top in three texts that were most likely written toward the end of Aristotle's second sojourn at Athens, that is, in the last years of his productive working life.[11] Book Λ of the *Metaphysics*, Book 6 of the *Nicomachean Ethics*, and Book 3 of *De anima* show *nous* ruling over, respectively, theoretical comportment toward being qua being (first philosophy), access to the good life (ethics), and the capacities and activities of the *psuchē* (psychology). In sum, it becomes the fundamental principle in an essentially intellectualist understanding of *anthrōpos*, directing the activities of the first philosopher, the politician, and the psychologist.

The first philosopher studies the *psuchē* because, as it seems (*dokei*), *nous* is "the most divine of all phenomena" (*tōn phainomenōn theiotaton*) (*Metaphysics* 1074b16). The source for this *doxa* is relatively easy to find. First philosophy, the science that knows the basic principles of all regions of knowledge including its own, initially presents an enormous methodological challenge. In contradistinction to natural philosophy, it must know everything without the need to experience each and every thing. First principles (*archai*), causes (*aitiai*), and being (*ousia*) reduce the empirical multiplicity to a limited set of things with dominion over the manifold. The motif of dominion and domination appears frequently in discussions of *nous*. *Metaphysics* Λ describes the way the non-sensual aspect of the *psuchē* must "have authority," are *kurioi* with respect to its primary objects—principles, causes, and essences (primordial logical, physical, and ontological objects, respectively)—which condense the diversity of experience. While it is clear that for Aristotle intelligibles like cause and essence exist, and, what's more, preexist the act of intellection—they are not produced or projected by *anthrōpos*, nor are they contained in the *psuchē* from birth, as Plato thought— and nonetheless, through its ability to receive them, *nous* shares in their natural authority over the manifold. A few intelligibles dominate the diversity of beings; *noēsis* through royal privilege makes intelligibles available to *anthrōpoi.* In addition *nous* and the intelligibles bring change to a standstill. This is consistent with Aristotle's understanding of change in the *Physics*. To confront a difference and cognize it as a change means already to have applied *noēsis* in advance to an intelligible aspect of the cosmos. Cosmic intelligibility means just this: the presentation of the limits of some change. This is one of his fundamental differences with Plato. Change is the truth of the cosmos, not illusion. Yet change is true only insofar as its limits can be identified, and this is because Aristotle refuses to abandon his prejudice toward the indefinite. Aristotle reiterates this at the opening of *Metaphysics* Λ: change is always of something (matter, *hulē*) from something (potential, *dunamis*) to something (actuality, *energeia*, or target, *telos*), a progression each stage of which is fully intelligible. Thus the first philosopher studies *nous* and *noēsis* as the point of access, on one hand, to the origin, telos, and matter of any change, and on the other, to the web of similarities in an empirical manifold. To think the similar and the limit is the metaphysical task of *nous*.

"The student of politics," in turn, "must theorize [*theōrēteon*] the *psuchē*" (*Ethica Nicomachea* 1102a23). While much of the *Nicomachean Ethics* is concerned with *phronēsis*, also an intellectual activity to be sure, but one with practical ends (E.N. 6.5 gives an analysis of *phronēsis*), the *logos* of first principles, including the principles of *phronēsis* and of knowledge and technics (it lists the three together: *epistēmē*, *technē*, *phronēsis* [1140b34–35]), is the prerogative of *nous* (1141a7). The difference between true and false *phronēsis* or between *phronēsis* and *technē* could not be told without a higher instance, which is the prerogative of *noēsis*. Of the virtues then, although practical ones are the products of intellectual procedures as well, purely intellectual virtues are the highest of all and are products of the highest capacity. *Nous* "seems to rule and lead by nature" (*archein kai hegesthai*) (1177a14–15).[12] Its way is similar to the way of the Good: separate, autarchic, for the sake of itself, and the most continuous. Even if it falls short of the eternal activity that defines Aristotle's god, *noēsis* nonetheless comes to govern all aspects of practical life (1177a20ff.).

In the greater *Ethics* as in *Metaphysics* Λ, noetic activities have their own hierarchy. No other form of *noēsis* is superior to thought's thinking itself. The logic of this ranking is roughly the following. If doing first philosophy means thinking the *ousia* of beings—what it means to be this or that—then thinking first philosophy, that is to say, distinguishing it from second philosophy, means, according to its own principle, thinking *ousia* as *ousia*. It is not enough, thus, to celebrate the dominion of *nous* over the most intelligible things. *Nous* itself must be not only cognizable, but actually cognized; it must be susceptible to *noēsis*, while avoiding the epistemological pitfall that Plato's later dialogues demonstrate so vividly, namely, an infinite regress. For this reason, the sine qua non of an intellectualist understanding of *anthrōpos* is thought's dominion over itself, its self-subjugation, if you will. It must subjugate itself, moreover, without at the same time diminishing its standing by becoming a slave.

Enter the psychologist, whose studies culminate with *nous* qua *nous*, or the intellect as sovereign of the soul, in order to resolve its aporias. By rights there should be none; indeed, productive *nous* should be the most intelligible of intelligibles, save perhaps god. Here let us remember that an aporia is not just any difficulty, but an impasse in a specific line of thinking, arising either from overdetermination or underdetermination. In either case, when a line of thought becomes impassable, the impasse both blocks the thinker and lets him pass. An aporia, while blocking, acts at the same time as an index of a thought's telos. Aristotle makes this quite clear: *aporia* is the condition of possibility for *euporia* (995a31ff.). It should not come as a surprise, then, that in *Metaphysics* Λ, Aristotle cautions travelers on the path toward the intellect: "the things concerning *nous* hold certain aporias" (*Metaphysics* 1074b15). This is prima facie true, since we cannot immediately see the end of thinking about it, and it is also wishful thinking. Where the difficulties are in fact aporias, good passage, *euporia*, is assured; one only has to clear the obstacle. Despite Aristotle's optimism, however, the difficulties of *nous* are not all aporias, nor is it clear how they could be. An aporia in the thought of thought could not be aporetic, given that, in it, thought's arrest would not show the way; non-thought in thought on the way to thinking would obstruct the very operation by which thinking normally frees itself from aporia. To put it coarsely, if the proper response to all aporetic cases is "think better," in the case of thinking precisely this would not be possible. That Aristotle classifies the not-thinking in thinking about thinking as an aporia reveals his wish to blow away the clouds that drift in at this point. Instead they become yet thicker. The image with which Aristotle depicts aporia's effect on thinking in the *Metaphysics* is a man in chains (995a31ff.). And yet, you cannot hold a man with fetters if a) he does not normally travel forward, b) he does not travel, or c) he is not by nature free to go beyond where he is. In each of these cases a fetter is not a fetter, but something like a fashion statement. Aporia only makes sense if the image we have of thinking is of an actor in telic motion free to reach the end but not to deviate.

If some of the "aporias of *nous*" are in fact not aporetic, but fall under some other sort of negation, the negation in the phrase "not-always-thinking" is even farther from the straight path of the aporetic. "Not-always-thinking" affects the autonomous, autarchic, most intelligible, and incorruptible aspect of *noēsis*, what has often been called "active intellect." It could not be said to affect the passive, receptive aspect of the intellect, since according to Aristotle, passivity's normal modality is "not-always." Passive thought is nothing until it is activated by an object; it is pure potentiality. It becomes its objects over and over again, as they present themselves, and thus it is intermittent by nature. Passive *nous* can think everything, and the same characteristic that makes it capable of thinking everything renders it functionally analogous to perception.[13]

The first aporia of *nous* for Aristotle is therefore this: if it has the power "to rule" over everything, as Aristotle writes quoting Anaxagoras's political metaphor (*De anima* 429a18–20), thinking is nothing before it thinks. In *Metaphysics* Λ, Aristotle remarks on this problem: "For if it thinks nothing, why would it be holy? But it behaves just as if it were a sleeping man" (*Metaphysics* 1074b17–18).[14] The very power to rule over everything-that-is makes *nous* perfectly subservient to all that is not it. Anarchy reigns while the monarch sleeps. Whatever presses itself on receptive *nous* it has to accept. For this reason the analogy with perception, which sleeps until it is acted upon by perceptibles, does not go far enough in explaining the nature of *nous*. Akin to perception insofar as it is receptive, intellection is also substantially different (*De anima* 429a10ff.).[15] It cannot be identified solely with the determinate nothing of *dunamis* for fear of turning into the lowest thing, becoming pure receptivity, a plaything of the cosmos. For this reason the theory of *noēsis* must subordinate passive *nous* to something higher. Many of the obscurities of *De anima* 3.4–8 derive from Aristotle's attempt to demonstrate the existence of a higher thing within *nous*. The nothing of passive thinking does not in fact threaten thought, Aristotle claims, since thinking means two distinct things: an ability to receive the intellectual part of the sensible and the actual production of thought. From the earliest treatments of his student, Theophrastus, to the great Islamic commentaries of the Middle Ages, to Brentano's study in the nineteenth century and into the revival of Aristotle's theory of *nous* as one touchstone of twentieth-century Anglo-American philosophy of mind,[16] readers have struggled to untangle the meaning and interrelation of these two aspects of the Aristotelian intellect.

Through the total receptivity of *nous,* intelligibles impose their law on *anthrōpos. De anima* 3.4 makes this point at the outset. "Not-always-thinking"—wherever its cause, whatever its origin—cannot refer to this hegemony of the cosmos over the intellect. Rather, to become a threat, it must afflict productive thought, interrupting the intelligibility of thought to itself and thus its intelligibility per se. In acting "like light" as Aristotle describes it in 3.5, productive thinking produces actual intelligibles out of potential intelligibles (*De anima* 430a15). During the not-always of its intermittent inoperation this production would cease. The illumination would go dark, refusing to activate potential thought. Even if, as Hamlyn argues, "there is no indication in his [Aristotle's] words that the active intellect plays any role other than that of a metaphysical ground for the actualization of potentialities that make up the soul," even if, in other words, the productive aspect of the intellect is only the transcendental principle that thought activates itself, the danger is still great (Hamlyn 140). Only by being continually actualized and actualizing does productive thinking release *nous* from the other intermittency, receptivity. Only by being actualized and actualizing at any and all times—always—can *nous* retain its claim to sovereignty, immutability, and intelligibility.

As soon as Aristotle describes that part of intellect that "produces" all things always, ancient commentators find it necessary to interpolate the following line. As Hamlyn translates it: "and it is not the case that it sometimes thinks and at other times not" (*De anima* 430a22). This line is not in any of the manuscripts and Ross brackets this part of the line as corrupt, but Hamlyn tellingly takes it out of brackets. He argues that these words "are needed here; they are clearly about the active intellect. . . . The active intellect must always think because it is actual, not merely potential like the intellect discussed in Chapter 4" (141). What ancient commentators wanted and Hamlyn would like to return to the text looks very much like a response to or even a cancellation of Aristotle's earlier demand. *Nous* is simply not intermittent, it claims. And yet the line, which so many felt compelled to include, should amplify our worry about "not-always-thinking" rather than diminish it, since it fails to fulfill the most important part of Aristotle's demand. The *aition* of not-always-thinking is not provided.[17] Quite the contrary—with no further ado, the question of cause is discarded in favor of a dogmatic statement.

Though perhaps an understatement, let us call the results of Aristotle's demand curious: there are none. Providing an etiology for distraction may be more difficult than resolving the aporias of *nous*. In the tradition of commentary on this passage, the demand and its handling by Aristotle are considered either puzzling or trivial. Modern commentators usually admit that Aristotle does not fulfill it, but consider this unimportant, whereas ancient commentators tend to find indirect resolutions of the demand in other passages or doctrines, including the interpolation quoted above.[18] Both sets of commentators agree that the demand is abandoned, but neither speculates about the meaning of the sentence, or, what is more critical, the meaning of its abandonment. For, what could an investigator hope to gain from a theoretical investigation—*episkepsis*—of not-always-thinking? If one observed *nous poiētikos* and found it intermittent, occasionally out of operation, fickle or otherwise undependable, where would it leave *theōretikē* and the sciences that depend on its unobstructed and continual view of being qua being? A successful investigation might in fact prove that the power to investigate was intermittent, whereupon thinking would be thrown into a vortex from which no theory could rescue it. If *nous poiētikos* gained sight of the origin of its intermittency—assuming, that is, that its distraction had an origin—its own activity would prove untrustworthy, liable to disappear, at the beck and call of a will not its own. Such an abdication might also result in *noēsis* being unable, in the end, to trust the auto-diagnosis of its own limitations. Know yourself would change from an empowering possession of the limit of intellectual powers into an injunction that, like Aristotle's demand, could not be carried out.

"Not-always-thinking" thus has its own difficulties. The philosopher should distrust the investigation into *to mē aei noein* to the very extent that it was performed by an act of thought. If it did come to be thought, if it were found to be the case—to have, in Aristotelian terminology, an *aition*—the thought of it would be as intermittent as the faculty or activity affected by it. In response, it becomes imperative to deny not-always-thinking a cause or source. And so the demand is easier to abandon than to address. What could occur while *nous poiētikos* was "not-always-noetizing"? The good life and the life of the mind, being susceptible to sudden, unpredictable, and sourceless halts, might give way to malice, stupidity, and profanity; the polis might open its walls to barbarians; philosophers might teach false knowledge to the highest bidder; beings could occasionally forget being qua being—this is what it might mean for *anthrōpos* to not-always-think.

Is it a myth then that *nous* sometimes dies a death in life? It must be—everything in thinking is of life, for Aristotle (and life is motion, and motion being, so thinking moves, lives, is, always). Given that not-always-thinking does not coincide with potentiality or aporia, it seems not to belong to Aristotle's understanding of human being at all. What is a nothing that prepares for nothing in particular, a sleep from which one does not awaken, where awakening is sleep's secret purpose? What, in a cosmos where everything is in motion—where even rest is a kind of motion, where every stop is but a pause—what is a stop that disconnects the clockwork and bulwark of Aristotle's cosmic machine? What can be made of its peculiar intractability? A restless pause, a stop that will not pause, more than an interruption since its "halt" does not belong to the continuity with which it collides, a detention that occurs frequently though without attaining the necessity or continuity of "always" and so remains to the side of intelligible, a halt that breaks the link between infinitesimal limit points until the "now" no longer defines time, an unattractive repulsion that draws thought again and again out of its cycles, a move that is not a movement, a demonic stutter perhaps, bent against the immobile mover, a stutter that, by canceling thought's activity for an unspecifiable time simultaneously turns away from and advances on the divine, rebel and usurper, distraction would be—if it were given credibility by Aristotle—a moving unmover that disavowed the hierarchy of his system. Since *anthrōpos* has to think continually in order to look like a god, when we follow Aristotle's demand to its logical though perhaps unreasonable end, we find something much less and much more than *theos*; a hypergod—distraction—splits the heavens. Accepting the hypothesis that Aristotle's theory of *nous poiētikos* is the bastion of a god of cosmic order, we would be forced to say—from the perspective of not-always-thinking—that the reason it is imperative that *anthrōpos* think continually is that if it did not, it would become a *paratheos*—a mortal sprung out beyond or to the side of the chiasm that binds mortals to immortals in a fateful likeness—responsible for its own intelligibles and for deciding their order, or lack thereof.

A Moving Unmover

What "always" means in the Aristotelian corpus is debated by ancient and modern commentators.[19] Given Aristotle's definitions of time and infinity, *aei* can be understood in two or three different ways, depending on what being you look at. *Phusis*, for instance, is that which has its cause of motion within it. Its "always" is aggregative; it is the sum total of the relative motions of its parts: becoming, decay, locomotion, alteration, and so on—of potential as well as actual motion. The "always" of the heavens, in contrast, is continuous and one. Circular motion is primary in the heavens because, although spatially finite, it is temporally infinite, even if its temporal infinity is not expressed in any single turn of the heavenly orbit (*De caelo* 270a13ff.). The "always" of its motion also depends on its impassivity; like *nous*, the circling cannot be dislodged from its motion, neither deviating from itself nor subject to generation or destruction (270b13–16). Cosmos is a combination of these alwayses. Nature, as the totality of the repeated generation and degeneration, alteration, growth, and locomotion of its elements, is continually discontinuous, mortal in any instance, immortal as a whole. Heaven orbits in an unbroken circle, never deviating from its perpetual progress toward its end. *Theos* is also "always," but here the difficulties begin. According to Aristotle's late accounts, all motion originates in god, who moves (transitively) but does not move (intransitively); despite its immobility with respect to itself, god never rests. An unmoved mover can be deduced from the transcendental necessities of the system, but only negatively. The notion avoids an infinite regress of first principles, which would render the cosmos ultimately unintelligible. Our thought naturally comes to a stop upon reaching god. Second, the cause of causes, principle of principles, and actuality of all actualities cannot be sheer potentiality—that is, purely future motion—lest beings never become actual. So goes the transcendental deduction of the first mover in *Physics* 8.4 and 8.5. An intransitive cosmic attraction, which will become in *Metaphysics* Λ *nous noetizing nous*, the first mover persists, Aristotle writes, as the ultimate toward-which of all motion, but especially of intellectual motion, the love-object of thought (1072a26ff.).

"Not-always" poses a great challenge to the divine "always," precisely because it does not contradict it. This may seem counterintuitive, since they seem parallel and convertible: always, not always; *aei, mē aei*. According to the law of non-contradiction (one of the highest intelligibles, according to Aristotle), a being cannot be always and always not in some way in the same aspect. A being cannot be always a fish and always not a fish, a fish cannot be always white and always not white. To be what it is, a being must either always be itself or never be itself (it would be something else), or always have this property or never have this property. It may of course be on the way to being itself or in the process of falling away from itself, but in Aristotle's schema these *dunameis* do not affect what it means to be that being. Insofar as it states, always either "always" or "not always," the logical form of contradiction has a higher "always" internal to it. Formally speaking, the law of contradiction says nothing other than this ultimate always, and certainly allows no intermediary position between always and not-always, being and not-being. The law keeps eternal vigil over the line between the two.[20] Eternity, thus, is the temporal structure of contradiction (contrariness, *enantia*, is another story; it admits of degrees). Thus, to understand being as Aristotle describes it, the either-or of always and always-not can never give way. If the law of contradiction were in force at times and not at others, if the principle were challenged by a fluctuation within it, a higher principle would have to be found to regulate the alternation between always and not-always, between "at all times/at no time" and "at times," between a principle of contradiction and a principle of difference. This kind of distraction, intermittent thought, poses an enormous challenge to the hegemony of "always." "Not-always" opens out toward a principle higher than the principle of contradiction. A principle called upon to regulate the alternation between the principled and the unprincipled could not itself be a principle, however. The unprincipled principle is the logical form that would correspond to an ontological "moving unmover," a freely moving stop to thinking, a break in its bond with being; such a break glances out at us in Aristotle's worry over not-always-thinking. It points to a place beyond or beside the fates, where fate and indeterminacy are doled out in unequal portions, in a fluid staccato, without what could comfortably be called either chance or necessity.

At this juncture a brief excursus on the relation of a moving un-mover to time seems warranted. In *Physics* 4, *chronos* is called "the number of motion with respect to before and after" (219b1–2), but once Aristotle defines time in this way, a difficulty arises. Number, in the sense in which Aristotle means it here, is not the abstract thing with which one counts, and certainly not the arbitrary mark that commemorates it, but rather the combined noetic and ontological aspects of counting, in a unit that is at the same time an agent actually cognizing this "one" (219b2ff.). *Noēsis*, it is made clear, is the source for time-keeping, not nature. Motion is possible without cognition—indeed the cosmos is, by nature, the total order of motion, regardless of time. Furthermore, noetic continuity determines the continuity of time. For the sake of time's intelligibility at least, a part of *nous* must always be actually in *noēsis*. This is the point of confluence between his concept of time and "always-thinking." Thus Aristotle suggests—and this is the surprising part of the argument—that when "the *psuchē* appears to remain in a unified and undifferentiated [state]" there seems to be no time (*Physics* 218b32).

Just prior to this Aristotle notes: "When we do not change with respect to cognition [*tēn dianoian*], or if we fail to notice [*lathōmen*] that we are changing, there does not seem to us to have been time" (218b21). It would be wrong to say time stops, for this would reify time, make it into a natural motion, which it is not. In this sort of distraction, when thought's internal and essential motion freezes up, time disappears as an element of the cosmos. Insofar as constant change is the essence of nature, as the sum total of all irregular and inconstant motions, what would be lacking in distraction is not the substrate of time (motion, change), but the form of time (producing units and sequencing, counting). At stake is the a prioricity of time for the thinking being. Indeed, if thought is the condition for time, and not the other way around, whoever fails to notice change does not produce time.

Toward the end of *Physics* 4, Aristotle feels the need to illustrate this strange eventuality with a *muthos*. The not-thinking that corresponds to untime is like, he says, certain Sardinians who, in mythological accounts (*muthologoumenois*), ceased to mentally count time while they "slept with the heroes" (218b24).[21] Upon waking, these Sardinians, who incidentally have gotten as close to the autochtonos gods as anyone can, being in effect temporarily dead, register a lapse in the temporal continuum—the advent of untime—by fitting "the former now onto the latter," effectively "taking out the middle through anesthesia" (218b26). In this anaesthetic state, it is as if no time has passed, since nothing has changed. The first impulse upon waking, in Aristotle's myth, is similar to the sleeper's in Proust's *À la recherche*. Upon waking, the sleeper forges a false continuum between past and present, but the jarring effect of the syncope is also unavoidable.

Aristotle's text passes this scene quickly by, but Simplicius gives it more space in his commentary, affirming Aristotle's account of untime and adding a provenance for the *muthos*. Time, Simplicius announces, can indeed escape our notice (115). His extreme stoicism allows him to admit that even thinking may be susceptible to corruption. Where time is a dianoetic "mental tracking" (*parakolouthesis*, a "following alongside") of change, if "the unchanging thought of change carries with it the perception [*sunaisthēsis*] of time," as J. O. Urmson's translation of Simplicius's commentary presents it, then a faltering, a failure, slumber, or death—however it may be described—of the thought of change, would entail time's disappearance. Time, the number of motion with respect to before and after, vanishes in an unmeasurable interlude that corresponds to neither becoming nor decay. In the atemporal interval corresponding to not-thinking, the cosmos, the vast mechanical linkage between changes and classes of change, uncouples itself. In Sardinia *anthrōpoi* sleep "long sleeps beside [the heroes] for the sake of dreams or through some other need" (Simplicius 116). What is this other need? Neither Simplicius nor

Aristotle say. Yet both admit it needs to happen. Can anyone say this who has not experienced it? And conversely, can anyone who has experienced this attest to its having occurred? Can one testify to it without a standard by which the non-experience can be measured? There is no such standard, certainly not a universal one, if time is no longer ticking, turning distraction into experience. No experience of the nontemporal, no passing through or passing by it, because the break that unchains the continuum for the course of its lack of duration is stitched directly back onto itself. Continuity may in fact be sewn together out of these unaccountable lapses.

From the perspective of time, *to mē aei noein*, the uninvited guest in the house of being, is ungeneratable and indestructible. It will never decay, perhaps because it is dead already, or because within the Aristotelian schema it is neither actual nor potential. It enters and exits without so much as a nod to the now traditional, then revolutionary, circuit between being and not-being that transits through thought.

In trying to ground thinking in itself, Aristotle discovers a version of distraction whose cause has to be investigated. He includes it in his study of intellect, and, if only for a moment, considers it integral to the speculative construction of *nous*. And yet when elaborating "the problem of the moving principle of our thought," the motivating problem for the history of philosophy according to Brentano, Aristotle finds that primal distraction both has to be investigated and has to be abandoned—and how could it be otherwise? What theory of thought could originate without "problems" or "aporiai" and thus without the promise of clearing and passage? Where thinking means an essential, transcendent activity, producing itself eternally in isolation from all other forces, capacities, beings, and accidents, where it becomes, for itself and for human being, the untouchable ground for the other habits of *psuchē*, and thus the meaning of *anthrōpos*, whose only superior is a god who is really a reflex of it, an intellectual god, even the hint of an equally essential impotence, inactivity, or dependence on lower things has to be abandoned and forgotten. To abandon it, however, Aristotle has to address it. And this is an infrequent event.[22] And still Aristotle does not shrink from the fact that a capacious and threatening distraction could be as natural a part of the system as a capacious and godlike intellect. Aristotle's version, although hastily sketched out and then just as hastily dropped, goes beyond the weakened, narrow distraction-diversion of today. One might make this a general rule: the meaning of thinking correlates in scope and intensity with the meaning of not-thinking. To say this is to say that a thought that exceeds what-is might flirt with the limits of its own meaning, might allow itself to surpass—even itself.

Where thinking has been judged in advance and without a public hearing to mean attending at the proper time for the proper amount of time to the proper objects, grasping and holding on to whatever count as the current social goods, not-always-thinking disappears into double obscurity. Where thinking no longer dares move toward its meaning, where it no longer wagers itself to discover that it is precisely nothing that thinks when thought thinks its own meaning, distraction does not seem even worthy of abandonment. Aristotle, however, uncovers in it, if darkly and fleetingly, a potent threat to the "always" that clings anxiously to the meaning of thought.

CHAPTER 2

A Face for Distraction / La Bruyère

La Bruyère's *Distrait*

He goes downstairs, opens the door to go out and then shuts it again. On the street he stops a passerby to ask where he is and is not surprised to find he is on his own block in front of his own door. This is the way *le distrait* stumbles into literary history:

He realizes he has his nightcap on, and on looking at himself with a little more attention, he finds that he is but half shaved, he sees that he has fastened his sword on the wrong side, that his stockings are hanging on his heels, and that his shirt is bulging out above his breeches. (*Characters* E 183–84, F 399)

A clown, though an unintentional one, an unfinished version of how others ought to see him, home when he is out and lost in the most familiar surroundings, Jean de La Bruyère's *le distrait* inadvertently—how else?—reflects the conditions under which the concept of distraction might become thinkable. It may not have a concept, but with La Bruyère it receives an influential image. A man—in this century there would be no need to remark on the distraction of women; the two were thought to go hand in hand[1]—a man of means and character, yet unable to take advantage of either for his own advancement—this is how not-thinking returns, as an aggregate of unthinking acts.

Distorted from its Greek shape and well outside the bounds of first philosophy with its fixation on causes, not-always-thinking returns as an aristocratic nuisance, *la distraction*, reflecting and crystallizing the social and theological changes that had gripped the *Grand Siècle*. La Bruyère's book is the occasion, city life in Paris and court culture at Versailles the setting, and the waning of a great epoch the moment for not-always-thinking to reappear, or to appear for the first time, but no longer as an unfulfillable metaphysical demand. Now it is described without regard for cause as a phenomenon in its own right. The differences in intention are decisive, although in an important way La Bruyère develops a tendency already explicit, if not exploited, in Aristotle—the tendency toward typology. Aristotle's moral works in fact provided a theoretical basis for typology. Where Aristotle at times itemized potential deviations from an ideal moral type, his student and successor as director of the Lyceum, Theophrastus, perfected this tendency. Late in life Theophrastus produced a catalogue of moral types meant to serve as cautionary or exemplary cases by generations to come. La Bruyère takes Theophrastus's book as the chief model for his own, claiming thereby an Aristotelian lineage. Yet the differences between the two distractions are more striking. Aristotle's not-always-thinking is less a moral than a metaphysical or theological matter (even if morality is in the last instance also metaphysical and theological). It imperils the soul's divine core, which is to say that distraction is envisaged as transcendent, facultative, universal, and necessary, like thought itself. La Bruyère's distracted one—even though the figure, as he describes it, breaks in critical ways with typology (it is the only one of the "characters" that is in itself more than one type)—almost exclusively dwells in the sphere of social phenomena. He doesn't want to account for it, only to describe it. Moreover, the register of the description is resolutely empirical. Where soul and mind are discussed, they are but stand-ins for their effects. This comports with the basic idea of a type. Types offer a maximum of details and a minimum of explanation. They are amalgams of experience for the purposes of comparison and judgment. Whereas Aristotle concerns himself with the being of *anthrōpos*, it is always the empirical actor who attracts the growl of La Bruyère's pen. Like earlier moralists, La Bruyère is less concerned with defining the soul than with holding up a mirror to quotidian foibles, faults, and excesses, and so throughout the book he pursues effects rather than causes. It may well be his emphasis on manner, gesture, and routine that allows distraction to appear once again, now for the first time, no longer the child of necessity and universality, but rather a common and occasional phenomenon.

Although with its critique of court manners La Bruyère's popular compendium, *Les Caractères*, was very much a product of the late seventeenth century—the first edition appeared in 1688—the character called in retrospect "*le distrait*" is untimely in a heretofore unheard of manner. He belongs no more to his own time than to any other.[2] Perceval, another, more profound figure in French literature, arrives late to his own time and must hurry to learn its rules; *le distrait*, in contrast, is estranged from rules per se. He appears among La Bruyère's unauthorized sketches, *remarques*, portraits, and illicit caricatures of living persons, the seventh numbered passage in the section "De l'homme." Like Perceval, *le distrait* enters a world to which he does not belong; and yet, whereas Perceval learns from his experiences, *le distrait* does not—given that he cannot be said to have them. He is innocent of the requirement to experience. No matter how much he tries, he will never catch up to his contemporaries. That *le distrait* comes late to the seventeenth century and comes to be seen as a quintessentially modern figure is complicated by the name La Bruyère gives him. "Ménalque" names a figure from an idyllic past, a fixture of the dramatis personae in Virgil's *Eclogues*, and so he plays pariah in early-modern Paris.

In the famous quarrel between the ancients and moderns La Bruyère was known for his enthusiastic support of the ancients. He translated Theophrastus's *Characters* and placed his translation of the classical master's text at the beginning of the first edition of his own book, which he writes under the same title. This loyalty to classical models led La Bruyère, in the first edition of his book, to revive and continue Theophrastus's model. And yet the continuation of the classical in the modern becomes highly suspicious in the antics of Ménalque, who, as distracted, does not represent any ancient type that we know of, but is also not yet modern. As a classical ideal—protagonist of the Virgilian idyll—Ménalque should represent a glorious utopian past come to the present. And yet he arrives only to be ridiculed for his inability to make a home in modernity—a strange way to honor the ancients!

For his own part, although he traces a lineage for himself back through neo-classicism to the ethical scourges of antiquity, to Terence,

Menander, Theophrastus, and by association also to Theophrastus's teacher Aristotle, La Bruyère nonetheless shows some ambivalence about the project of classicism. He resists it in subtler ways than he claims to resist the project of the "moderns." His ambivalence toward both attitudes is already apparent in the preface to the book. "Some of the learned," he complains in the *Discours sur Theopraste*, "like nothing but the apothegms of the ancients" and "the history of the present is insipid to them." La Bruyère goes on to criticize the moderns as well: "ladies and courtiers, on the contrary, and all who have a lot of wit [*esprit*] without erudition, indifferent to everything that preceded them, are greedy for what passes before their eyes . . . [and] are fond of those who resemble themselves, but with whom they think they share no resemblance" (F 84, my translation). On one side of the stage sit the learned with their dreams of a golden past, on the other side the ladies with their modish wit, watching the present pass before them while remaining aloof from it. And "the distracted one"? Like the author, he is ambivalent about paradigms—as unable to take refuge in a golden past as he is to make a home in the present.[3] For the distracted one's untimeliness there is an ancient model, Chapter XII of Theophrastus's *Characters*. La Bruyère titles it "Du contre-temps" (rendering the Greek *akairias*). In his very loose version, more a paraphrase than a translation, the definition that opens the section on this character reads: "This ignorance of time and occasion is a way to approach people or to behave with them, always inconvenient and embarrassing" (F 123, my translation). In this way the distracted one passes before the eyes of the curious, but they do not think he resembles them: he is too embarrassing. It makes little difference, since he doesn't think so either; indeed, he doesn't resemble himself. When he dresses, he becomes a disheveled parody of what the present expects of him, sword hanging loose, an ape of the aristocracy, *les gens d'épée*, or a true image of the bourgeois who strives futilely to imitate the ways of another social class. When he remembers to look, he does not see himself in the mirror, just as his contemporaries do not see themselves reflected in him.

He has a strained relationship to time. In contrast to the champions of the moderns or ancients, the distracted one finds nothing less amusing than counting the hours. "While out in a boat, he asks the time; he is offered a watch; no sooner has he taken it than, forgetting all about the time and the watch, he throws it into the river as though it were something to be got rid of" (*Characters* E 185, F 402). He wants to ask not what o'clock it is, but what a clock is. The French reads: "Il se promène sur l'eau," an activity of noble leisure. On promenade along the classical emblem of time, the river, Ménalque resists the imperative to constant and reassuring change; he sacrifices its modern counterpart, the clock, to its currents, preferring—though we don't know this for sure—a time that, at least for him, does not confuse itself with flow. A stranger to present and past, he rejects the image of time that seems to connect them.

What at this moment would permit a figure to throw away time, to send time off on its own currents? How does a figure who does not experience time fit into history at all?[4] The streams of the *Grand Siècle* hardly flow in one direction. Paul Bénichou famously saw the intellectual, moral, and political currents of the century split between the aristocratic, heroic ideals of the preceding century, replayed in the works of Corneille, and an anti-heroic emphasis on human failings. La Bruyère gave the same critical assessment when he wrote approvingly of Corneille that the dramatist "depicts men as they ought to be," while his rival, Racine, "depicts them as they are" (*Characters* E 38, F 182). Between ought and is, however, there was little difference. The ought shows the longing with which the hero was wished for in a time that was no longer his. Following this logic, in the broadest outline, Corneille and Racine would represent the split in letters; historically the monarchists would be divided from the *frondeurs*, theologically the Jansenists from the Jesuits. A contest between two natures of man, between a fundamental capacity for glory on earth and a fundamental human wretchedness[5] were brought to an extreme of acrimony in the controversies over Port-Royal, the radical reformist abbey. Whether the division can be attributed to the religious wars of the century before or to the changing social and economic structures of the times, it does not find a solution in the seventeenth century, and La Bruyère, in this regard very much a writer of his time, falls into the tension between these extremes. On one hand, he holds himself to the strictest heroic standard for his own writing. "Among all the different ways of expressing a single one of our thoughts, there is only one which is the right one," a maxim from *Les Caractères* informs us (E 27, F 163). And the heroism of *le mot juste* has repercussions for the heroic potential of his readers as well. "When a book exalts your mind and inspires it with lofty and courageous feelings, seek no other rule to judge it by: it is good, and made by the hand of a master" (E 31, F 169). And yet reading La Bruyère is, in point of fact, not like reading Corneille. *Les Caractères* presents a dubious mixture of the morally uplifting and the utterly degrading. Which of the two characterizes *le distrait*?[6]

The context for his appearance is not philosophical; distraction does reappear in the work of a great thinker attempting to understand the workings of the intellect, the existence of God, the structure of the world. For Descartes, sensation and its confused ideas threaten to debase the glory of *cogitare*, but the dangers of confusion are finally overcome by the activity of the thinking thing. Doubt toward the senses banishes distraction. La Bruyère agrees with this in principle: " . . . but at least you must grant me, " he writes, "that what I call my spirit, whatever it may be, is something that thinks" (E 307, F 586). And yet, in his book such virtues are always mingled with baseness. "There exist generally, in every man, infinite combinations of power, favour, natural aptitudes, wealth, dignity, nobility, strength, industry, ability, virtue, vice, weakness, stupidity, poverty, impotence, vulgarity and baseness" (E 210–11, F 441). And so distraction appears in a discourse that touches on the spirit, but only insofar as it is overwhelmed by a host of infringements on its dominance. Where the aim of seventeenth-century moral handbooks—with which the project of *Les Caractères* differs in significant ways—not to mention the massive casebooks compiled for consultation by casuists, was to direct individuals' practice, the intellect continued to play an important role in morality. One look at Pascal is enough to show that intellectual activity holds a privileged, if tenuous, place in the moral education of humanity. Its preeminence in moral life is still, even for the thinker who most vigorously downgraded the human capacity to know, self-evident. "Man is obviously made for thinking. Therein lies all his dignity and his merit; and his whole duty is to think as he ought" (*Pensées* E #620, F #513). The Pascalian picture of *l'homme* and this demand for his thinking is—just as obviously—in conflict with humanity's base nature. Indeed, *misère* also afflicts thinking, and contributes to reason's deterioration. Without pretending that this one *pensée* is the key to all the others, one can nevertheless see in it a tendency, also reflected in the title of Pas-

cal's work, to locate the possibility for morality, here indicated by two of
its most magisterial markers, "dignity" and "merit," in the intellectual
sphere. Intellect leads human beings to the good, in part because it is
the essence of *l'homme* itself. "I can certainly conceive of a man without
hands, feet, or head, for it is only experience that teaches us that the head
is more necessary than the feet. But I cannot conceive of a man without
thought [*pensée*]; he would be a stone or an animal (*une brute*)" (E #111,
F #143). Human being is the thinking brute, yet Pascal also indicates
that it is not simply by nature that he thinks, but by exertion and as an
ideal—thinking is a duty. Within the discourse of decrepitude, misery,
falseness, and deception there is at least one aristocratic virtue left, thinking, when it does its duty. In Pascal's world, however, this is singularly
difficult for thought to do, since, as Descartes taught, *res cogitans* must
never be confused with *res extensa*. Experience teaches us that thinking
is analogous to the head, but thought teaches otherwise. The wish is that
one could remove the head, remove the experience of thought, and the
essence of thinking would not be affected.

These two sources for thinking follow Bénichou's split between
earthly glory and earthly abjection. In the *Pensées* the split runs through
thought itself, severing thinking from "thought," thought from "a"
thought, this head attached to this hand and the *pensées* that they together produce from a transcendent *pensée* that they approximate and
to which they refer, but only abjectly, and with some doubt as to their
ability to do even this. Pascal could not exempt human thought from the
vanity, self-deception, pride, and confusions of other human actions.[7]
Indeed, we find scattered throughout the fragments descriptions of the
asymmetrical and often disappointing experience of thought. When they
come, thoughts are in a confused order, and arrive by chance—"Hasard
donne les pensées" (F #459). This should not be confused with a phenomenology of thought, which reduces the experience of thinking to arrive
at a true thought of the structure of consciousness. Here, in contrast,
what is at issue is an empirical thinker and the largely inexplicable and
inconstant affair of having thoughts.[8] Empirical thinking is not rational;
Pascal's aim is to demonstrate this. In one plan he articulates for the
organization of his book, the book itself would correspond to such a
demonstration. "I will write down my thoughts here as they come [*sans*

ordre] and in a perhaps not aimless confusion. This is the true order [*le veritable ordre*] and it will always show my aim by its very disorder. I should be honoring my subject too much if I treated it in order, since I am trying to show that it is incapable of it" (E #532, F #457). Not completely aimless but still confused, the accumulation of thoughts does have one identifiable aim: to depict the lack of order. The depiction of the disorderly accumulation of thoughts leads us out of the mire of experience, away from the conflation of reason with the head. The movement away is the true order of abject things and is also where Pascal steps beyond Plato, by demonstrating the corruption even of human reason. Yet this also marks an extreme Platonism, insofar as thinking is itself nevertheless able to demonstrate its own inconstancy. "A thought has escaped [*Pensée échappée*]: I was trying to write it down: instead I write that it has escaped me" (E #542, F #459). Here it may be writing that can capture both the captured and the escaped. But it is also clear that reason has a substitute in times like these: the thought of its absence. This is the most reasonable thing in a world in which reason has become suspect, and these are the epistemological terms of the Pascalian exchange. *Pensées au lieu de pensée*, thoughts in place of thought, a structure which, apparently *par hasard*, reiterates, in a not-quite-aimless fashion, a clear and distinct intuition of thinking's failings.

No One Is Distracted

The few pages in La Bruyère's compendium that recount the adventures of the distracted one were added to the sixth edition of *Les Caractères* in 1691.[9] The portrait makes up a prolegomenon to a phenomenological description of distraction, though a strange and unsettling one. For one thing, Ménalque never utters a word about himself. No self-reflection interrupts his coming and going.[10] This unreflective quality afflicts most of La Bruyère's characters, insofar as it is their behavior that matters. Yet, whereas a fool at the very least has to be aware of his talents in order not to displease the king,[11] and a drunkard will undoubtedly repent of his excesses the next day—despite baroque depictions of a *menalcas ebrius*, in La Bruyère's version Ménalque often "forgets to drink throughout dinner" (*Characters* E 186, F 403)—the distracted one never identifies the elements of his condition. His distraction is never reflected back to him, no matter how many mirrors he looks into.[12] And there is little of the philosopher in him to lead him toward self-consciousness. Nothing in the world directs him less than the imperative "know yourself," which is certainly one of the earliest moral maxims and is implied as a paradigm in the maxim-ethos of the seventeenth century. Know yourself, know your character and others', and you will become capable of good. This is the rationalist imperative underlying the moralists' work. And indeed, readers are supposed to draw this conclusion from the negative example of *le distrait*. La Bruyère—whom acquaintances Racine and Boileau called "Maximilien," after his passion for maxims—seeks to provide the occasion for this kind of knowledge through his *remarques* and typological *portraits*. The book is a mirror in which the present can see its collective face, whereupon it is expected to transform itself. Yet, can we be so sure Ménalque is only a negative example?

Who can say: "I am distracted"?

This proposition, were it said by someone (but who has ever actually said it?—perhaps no one in history), would be inadmissible insofar as the source of such a saying could only speak truthfully once it had vanished. Ménalque teaches that whoever says "I am distracted" is not. The statement is a lie or a joke or an error, or else it is ironic. Worth noting in this regard is that distraction shares a linguistic peculiarity with irony. The distracted one also cannot speak of himself in his own words. He must be spoken of by someone else, or else he has to negate himself or overcome himself if he wishes to point himself out in words: " . . . he thinks and speaks, both at once, but the thing about which he is speaking is seldom that which is in his mind, so his remarks are rarely consistent or logical; when he says No, you must understand Yes, and when he says Yes, assume he means No" (*Characters* E 187–88, F 406). A corollary to this linguistic rule is: distraction has no present tense. Like most sentences that make a claim to truth, "I am distracted" wants to be said with the sanction of experience. Although words point to a state or condition someone could be "in"—the nouns "Zerstreutheit" and "distraction" attest to this—it is nothing as stable as a state, nothing as locatable as a place. No doubt we can experience its effects, and they may be drastic—by far the largest body of distraction literature is written about automobile accidents. A phenomenological description of this atopic non-state would start from the way its effects are encountered every day—

. . . I go away, and return, yet nothing seems to have come between these moments—in which I was not—and, perhaps more astonishingly, little seems to have changed. Where I was I now am again or still. Such thoughts—vague and after the fact—often have the character of a law applied retroactively. Oftentimes punishment is meted out ex post facto for an infraction the law did not think to condemn until after it was committed. Although it happens repeatedly, the recognition of distraction has this retroactive quality every time. The breach of the law of continuous thinking cannot be forecast, and so it cannot rightfully be prohibited. This is so because it is a crime for which the category of intent is irrelevant. One does not commit inattention, and yet still somehow it must be criminalizable. Who would want to sanction, implicitly or explicitly, its deleterious effects? In this way distraction poses a problem for the spheres of law and morals, whether it be the autonomous application of a moral law to oneself, the pronouncement of a maxim for the moral correction of society, or the execution of a penal code. The law commits what by its own code must be a criminal act when it condemns the distracted one for neglect. In the English journal *The Spectator*, which was deeply influenced by La Bruyère's *Caractères*,[13] Eustace Budgell wrote, with reference to his own version of a distracted figure: "My Reader does, I hope, perceive that I distinguish a Man who is *Absent*, because he thinks of something else, from one who is *Absent*, because he thinks of nothing at all. The latter is too innocent a Creature to be taken notice of" (May 29, 1711). One wonders, in a book like *Les Caractères*, whose portraits are meant to elicit a reaction, to be acted on, repudiated to the letter, what the proper reaction could be to the description of an innocent who nevertheless breaks all the rules.

I experience my own distraction belatedly, and because of the inability to have forethought with regard to it, I am technically innocent of it. That I will be distracted is a general fact but it is never true in any particular prediction. Vagueness penetrates its concept and anxiety surrounds its study. This much can be admitted: there is no experience of distraction insofar as distraction suspends experience. And yet it does not suspend experience, judgment, or knowledge either in the stoic or the phenomenological sense, for the purposes of self-preservation or self-observation. Suspending thought, I never catch distraction in the act. "I *was* distracted" is a meaningful utterance, but only after I have dispensed with the referent, or rather after it has dispensed with me. In this way it never goes beyond hearsay. I may confess to you guiltily that I was absent, that I lost focus and did not catch the meaning of what you were saying, yet such a confession has the same authority as telling what occurred while sleeping.

"Where did I go?" I did not leave my desk, my house, my street; familiar things surround me. This is surely not the right question: it is not a "where" to which I disappeared, the bounded space of another place, another world or a dreamscape to which I momentarily escaped. Other essences—including the essence or structure of thought or consciousness—make themselves available to phenomenology, at least ideally, and yet this one disposition or occurrence remains inaccessible to the *epochē*. This is in part because traditional phenomenology makes use of a concept of distraction in the foundation of its method. The reduction's basic gesture is to bracket out the natural attitude, pictured as a "distraction" to the progress of exact science. Formally, then, whereas phenomenological thought produces the *Einklammerung* of daily distractions, distraction of thought produces the *Aussetzung* or *Suspendierung* of phenomenology as a possible leading back, *reducere*, to the structure of thought. In such a non-teleological suspension, distractions would be released like furies into mind. Instead of leading backward in reduction, thought flies outward and radiates away. The "subjective side of Zerstörung," Walter Benjamin called it (*GS* VII.2 678).

Return from nowhere. What small measure of absence can be taken from the clock is inexplicable. This is the moment—when time and space are returned to me—in which the truly phenomenological aspect of distraction shows itself. Upon returning to writing, to the classroom, to the freeway, what was once familiar and part of the stream of experience suddenly appears contingent—on the nothing that put it there once again. The road I travel back from distraction to the world of beings is a freeway in another sense, free of necessity. After the disappearance, chance becomes the inexplicable source of the world's appearance. Its being in such and such a way seems uncaused, and it is this sense of causelessness that constitutes the genuine phenomenological result. However briefly, the United States Constitution, the history of philosophy, this stapler, the desk, their relationship—time—become unstapled from the continuum of experience. We greet each other cautiously, space, time, and I. If one could maintain this uncanny atmosphere one could make a theory out of it. Alas, the experience is more than fleeting. Yet in the instant in which time is regained, being, world, and experience appear—in coming to appear once again as if for the first time—as accidents, contingent on nothing.

In the old formula, being is bound to thought as its fate. Distraction can be considered a passing release from this fate. We find evidence of this release in Ménalque's face: "while answering your question so wisely, he has his eyes wide open, yet he does not use them: he looks neither at you nor at anyone else, nor at anything in the world" (*Characters* E 188, F 406). Whatever the distracted one lays eyes on, he colors with non-being; this is his unique privilege as well as the threat he poses. Like many other threatening figures, he has been relegated to the nursery as a harmless children's character, perhaps because of the terror he provokes in adults. A glance into his unseeing face chills you with the thought of your inexistence.

Distraction and Madness

Distraction—as it comes to the fore in the seventeenth century, largely through La Bruyère's book—is not a phenomenon that can be reduced to reveal a transcendental structure, nor does it correspond to an essentiality that the phenomenological method could capture. Nothing is more crucial to that method than the continuity of the scientist's own thinking, nothing more anathema than her distraction. La Bruyère makes this much clear. One cannot research one's own distraction.[14] In La Bruyère, the description of this figure arises less out of a concern for its transcendent nature than for the fading social conventions of the aristocracy and the aping of those conventions by the bourgeoisie. This is the context in which distraction gets a face. Class breaks down and political power undergoes a radical shift. Religious truths are no longer seen as unassailable. French moralists emphasize that life is lived by principles, and principles are instilled by representing the social situations in which they always apply. A "character" becomes worthy of a *portrait* or a *sentence* when it habitually transgresses a principle.

From the attempt to teach a lesson or instill a principle, another difficulty arises. A seventeenth-century observer has to distinguish the distracted one from several other types. Who is to say, for instance, when Ménalque turns his glanceless glance on you, that he is not lost in the deepest and most penetrating—even philosophical—thought? On this point La Bruyère concurs: "You would often take Ménalque for what he is not [or, more precisely: "for everything he is not"—"pour tout ce qu'il n'est pas"]: for a stupid man [*un stupide*] since he does not listen, and speaks even less; for a madman [*un fou*], since besides talking to himself he is liable to pull faces and shake his head unconsciously; for a proud uncivil man, since when you greet him he passes by without looking at you, or looks at you without returning your bow; for a tactless one [*un inconsidéré*], since he refers . . . to executions in front of a man whose father went to the scaffold . . . " (*Characters* E 187, F 405). Beheading on the scaffold emblematizes not only his own mindlessness but also the effect the distracted one has on observers: he is a mobile *acephále* and a walking guillotine. Take it as stupidity, boredom, discourtesy, pride, weakness of will, wickedness, hedonism, vanity, madness, fever—or genius—with these assumptions you will only come to know your error, but not even this much. None of these moral faults is precisely his.

Of these, his shills or doubles, there is one whose episteme has been exhaustively described. *Le fou* in Foucault's study of madness in Western history is knowable in four modes, one of which Foucault calls "enunciatory consciousness." Here the difference from *le distrait* becomes apparent. In place of uncertainty and doubt, a reasonable person knows *le fou* immediately and with assurance, sealing his knowledge with the assertion "this man is mad" (166). Appellation may be a minor mode of the consciousness of madness, yet it is an obvious example of the certainty with which *le fou* can be pointed out, and the stark difference from *le distrait*, who is habitually misnamed. Thinking "mad" (critical consciousness), saying "mad" (enunciatory consciousness), practicing the social exclusion of the mad (practical consciousness), and decomposing and organizing madness into a myriad of genres and sub-genres with their telltale signs and symptoms (analytic consciousness) all demonstrate the certainty that surrounds this figure. As surprising as it seems, the encounter with madness seems to produce this certainty. In turn the confidence with which madness has historically been identified, both in the classical age and afterward, also lends certainty to Foucault's undertaking. Genealogy can only be practiced on an episteme whose *Entstehung*, to use Nietzsche's term, cannot be mistaken for another, whose formula itself shares the benefits of the forms of consciousness that institute and reify it. With high hopes for enunciatory consciousness, Foucault intends that the assertion of a history of madness will allow us to know its object, and his book constitutes such an enunciation. Foucault confesses that, in writing the book, his enunciatory act, his theory of speech impelled him to look for "a language that remained sufficiently open for the decisive words through which the truth of madness and reason are constituted to find their place without being betrayed" (xxxv). Whether or not these words, which he included in the preface to the 1961 edition, sufficiently characterize those words, the words that make up the history Foucault wrote, they do enunciate a desire that seems to drive the writing. Presenting the truth of truths, the method might be called. He has, Foucault explains, allowed *la folie* and *le fou* as well as *la raison* and *l'homme de la raison* to speak in the very same words by which their being was once decided, and these words, insofar as they were decisive, that is, as original words in which a truth came to *Entstehung*, at the moment or moments when the true was forcibly separated from the untrue—these decisive words are, in Foucault's writing, subject to a very different mode of truth. Foucault's words are not decisive in this Nietzschean sense, but are truths of a different order. Insofar as they faithfully recall the decision they do not bring about a truth but merely record it.

For this reason, Foucault's book should be read as a different kind of true speech. We accept as truth his account, that madness maintains the limits of a history whose activity is to set limits. History is articulated by madness; madness is its edge, an abyss that history keeps always at hand as insurance that history itself never goes mad. How could it, if it is obliged to present the decisive words that made history? Foucault's theory of representation makes its entrance in this line of thinking. Nietzschean history, it could be called, except that it lacks the irony that puts genealogical assertions under the cloud of the big and little "perhapses"—a sincere genealogy of madness this seems to be, and yet—Nietzsche would admit, and Foucault does too, although his admission clashes with the tone of remarks like these—it is and has to be written irremediably from within reason's narrow perspective. A very reasonable proposition, the history of madness. This is why Foucault can predict in the preface to the 1961 edition that a dialectical history of madness is the West's fate and assert that its internal structure is like a tragedy.

Foucault writes a tragedy in which the madman, defined by forces he neither creates nor controls, forces that look for all the world like fate, threatens the norms of the polis. Over the course of this century, however, society changes its mind. Where it at first accepts the madman—Foucault's tragic hero—as but a more extreme version of its own tendencies, it soon rejects him completely and forces him into silence. Let us note that the confinement of the mad with the poor, sexual deviants and the venereal, alchemists, and libertines leaves out the distracted one altogether. The classificatory tables that Foucault includes do not list distraction as a symptom (191–94). More significantly, Foucault is generally uninterested in distraction as a variety of *déraison*, and this undoubtedly stems from the version of negativity that marks his history, much as he tries to distance himself from it occasionally in metacritical remarks. It is a matter, as it usually is, of comparing nothings. The nothing at work in the history of *déraison* cannot be so negative that it negates "the very possibility of history" (a phrase Foucault uses more than once) when it negates reason. A bit of reason remains in the course of history, and by association in the historian. The negativity of madness is thus defined in relation to history, as something less than history. Madness in particular and unreason in general function as weak historical forces, different not in kind but in degree. This is evident in the way he proposes to handle this lessness. "It is this 'less than' that we must investigate," he argues in the preface, "immediately freeing it from its association with the pejorative" (xxxi). The fear that the less-than-historical might not be deemed worthy of history because it seems vile or trivial is a pretext for putting the true relation on display. "Less than" is a stand-in here for the determinate negation that is the basis of history for Foucault. These are the licit nothings: from the perspective of reason non-reason, from the reader's perspective the unworthy, from the genealogist's perspective non-history—each the low-est degree of the effect that is desired. By suspending madness, reason becomes history; this is the tragic shape the genealogist must depict and reverse. The Hegelian provenance of this pattern is not hard to see in phrases like: "history is only possible against the backdrop of the absence of history" (xxxi).[15] In contrast to this, genealogy becomes another history by which the abnormal gains its rightful place as the excluded of history. Where history speaks by silencing its shadow, genealogy gives the silence, which was never very far from speaking the same tongue as reason, its true voice. Indeed—Foucault admits that the "wild state" of madness before its subjugation and definition by reason "can never be reconstituted." This is because madness is subject to a "primary dispersion" of the concept, because its presence is "torn" (164). But is this not in fact an admission that the other, more stable, reasonable madness is a projection of the method? Such an undertaking—to liberate madness from oppression—perpetuates and perhaps even strengthens the oppression—not least by envisioning a paradisal madness from which madness fell . . . into the hands of rea-son. In short, Foucault argues that the "critical confidence" with which madness has been negated can be reversed (164). Is his not the very same critical confidence? In Foucault's tragic history, *le fou*, silenced by the gods who exercise sovereign power over the social space that defines him, tests the limits of this silence and is crushed, but in being crushed reveals not only the position of the limit but its artificiality, insofar as force is needed to maintain it.

Despite the exclusive focus on madness, Foucault's treatise helps explain why something like a quotidian not-always-thinking would also become available for discussion in the seventeenth century. What Fou-cault liberates for us is a sense of the almost hopeless mixture of disposi-tions, mutations, degenerations, types and half-types against which the eighteenth century would mobilize its army of analytic classifications. The seventeenth century produces the crisis on which the eighteenth will pronounce its decision. As a kind of regression from the medieval clarity with which madness was assessed as sin, in the *Grand Siècle* the madman "faded into a general apprehension of unreason" that Foucault sums up with the term "involution" (188).

Distraction sidesteps these attempts to discipline unreason. Madmen in seventeenth-century accounts often think they are what they are not, a king, a messenger of God, and so forth. This megalomaniacal tendency may raise society's guard. *Le distrait*, in contrast, does not think he is what he is. As we found out, distraction cannot be experienced from the inside, by self-observers; they never collect themselves in time to report back on the facts. Moreover, it cannot be identified from the outside, since the distracted one retreats behind too many masks. We have been told that there is such a thing and so we talk about it, make images of it, laugh when we see it, but the laughter may be due to the fact that we never really know if it is present, or for that matter absent. In his theory of comedy Bergson places absentmindedness close to the source of all comic effects.[16] But even this response is ambiguous. One laughs because one knows a norm has been broken; laughter is the first step of discipline. One also laughs because one is not sure of the cause or the meaning of the effect. Ménalque "goes into the royal apartments and walks under a chandelier, where his wig gets caught and is left hanging; all the courtiers stare and laugh; Ménalque stares too, and laughs louder than the rest, and examines all the company to see who is showing his ears and is without a wig" (*Characters* E 183, F 400). At this exposure, his bare head, mistaken for a sign of an empty head, is greeted with laughter, a mixed passion of the soul. Here, in this scene of laughter, the moralist's use of laughter is turned on its head. Those who laugh are laughed at in return. The distracted one is, in fact, laughing at us, and with better reason. How can we trust that when we see him it is not we ourselves who have stopped thinking, misconstruing the scene entirely? And how can we make a study of it before we confirm these basic facts? *Le distrait* flouts social conventions, but because he is not a libertine, because he does not have the flouting of conventions in mind, he cannot be condemned or confined for it, and the motor of dialectical history remains idle. Many readers of La Bruyère see him reinforcing social conventions by provoking laughter by their infringement, but *le distrait* suspends conventions without breaking them. Cutting across the social scene, he lays waste to the very idea of convention, provoking guffaws that do not correct.

Against Diversion

Distraction can be said in many ways. This is the formula by which Aristotle presents a word's ambiguity so that it becomes a starting point for philosophizing. Although much of the time he is happy to let a multiplicity of meanings stand, he nevertheless always also intends to isolate the senses of a word into well-defined *logoi* with fixed horizons. It is important to note when saying this, however, that the multiplicity of a word is not, for Aristotle, a deceptive homonymy, as it had been for Plato; polysemy guides true thought by calling into action the power to distinguish—the source of the greatest human pleasure, according to the first line of the *Metaphysics*.

Through polysemy "distraction" gains a stability it does not deserve. More than many other words, this one has trouble being called a word. Every use seems a misuse. Over the course of our particular misuse of it, it should be heard as more than a symbol evoking multiple meanings.

Here is what a historically minded philologist might say about "distraction": in an ignominious beginning in fifth and fourth century Greece, when *nous* was first given a rigorous determination, questions about lapses in intellectual activity became unavoidable. Given the strict logic within which Aristotle was working—the Eleatic ban on not-being—a lapse appeared that threatened the stability and coherence of the system. So he leapt over the lapse, buried its traces under the theological image of the productive soul. Early Christian writing recalls these lapses out of oblivion, though under aspects less cognitive than moral and geographical. It is instructive to consider that in the Gospels distraction takes on a new shape. Its outline is legible in the choice put to Hellenistic and Palestinian Jews by Christ's early followers. "Whoever is not with me is against me, and whoever does not gather with me scatters [*skopizei*]" (Matthew 12:30).[17] Here the Torah scholar Matthew articulates the choice in terms a Greek-speaking Jew of the era would have understood. Jesus' threat of dispersal calls to mind a line from Genesis, "and the lord diasporized [*diespeiren*] them from there onto the face of the whole earth" (*Septuaginta* Genesis 11:8). For Greek-speaking Jews of the first century CE the threat that dispersal posed to religious and political unity, family livelihood, and physical life was all too familiar. In the Christian sect, geographic diaspora turns into the threat of affective dispersal, the potential to lose the love of Christ and the neighbor on which the community had begun to base itself. Worldliness, the diaspora every Christian carries in the heart, is an offshoot of the original doctrinal choice—"collect with me or disperse," which recalls and recasts the scattering depicted in Genesis. Any secular notion of distraction—including a psychologized one—would have to take these Hellenistic-Jewish, theological, affective, and political origins into account, in all their complex historicality. What's more, and more unsettling, to a clear division between religious and nonreligious spheres, a secular notion of distraction-dispersal cannot remain deaf to the Christian spirit in which *saeculum* itself is said. A diversion from the way and the truth is already at work in the concept of secularity. "Secular distraction" is, in other words, a pleonasm. *Animi remissio, otiositas, sensualitas, saecularitas* are the medieval theological coordinates by which worldly—and therefore still Christian—distraction, at least insofar as it denotes diversion from the one way and dispersal into the world, sets its course (Vernay 1346). When distraction is understood as dispersal, and dispersal as diversion from the one way, there cannot be worldly distraction because world is a totality of distractedness.

The seventeenth century seems to represent both an intensification of and a break in this genealogy. Between Pascal—who expands and codifies the notion of "diversion" in sympathy with the extreme theological stance of Port-Royal, in so doing establishing a negative role for amusement in the life of the mind—and La Bruyère—who invents or codifies the elements of the modern notion of distraction as absentmindedness—the deviation from the Hellenistic-Jewish past occurs. One is tempted to say that Pascal reminded the seventeenth century that diversion was the theological condition of humanity, while La Bruyère showed the eighteenth century how a secular man of manners could give himself over to not-thinking. One century's tragedy is the comedy of the next, but this is not quite correct. The conceptual differences between the two types of not-thinking are stark. One is a (negative) image of grace, degenerate humanity glimpsed from a divine perspective; the other removes the hope of making such an image.

They are two responses to a single problem. Following his friends at Port-Royal, as well as their precursors, Augustine, Jansenius, Saint-Cyran, in addition to—though somewhat reluctantly—his precursor, Montaigne, Pascal believes the most lucid proof of human misery is the tendency toward diversion.[18] Contrary to what we imagine today, however, diversion manifests as the most intense concentration, complete absorption in a single object, for as long as possible. La Bruyère brings to light a trait that afflicts all rational beings at some time, a break in absorption in objects, without, in turn, substituting for it absorption in God.

Different in education, experience, and religious outlook, Pascal and La Bruyère stood at two poles of the French intelligentsia, poles that could be called the intensive theological and the extensive social. A generation older, Pascal, having grown up immersed in his father's mathematical and scientific projects and surrounded by his accomplished associates, first as a prodigy and later as an adult, was directly involved in some of the most radical intellectual advances of the first half of the century. His turn to theology and to moral questions through a critique of religion occurred toward the end of his short life. La Bruyère followed the more usual path of a socially mobile bourgeois, entering public service and, presumably because of his education and character—very little is known about his life or personality—ending up as a tutor to the son of the then prince of Condé, Louis II, who was a member of the ruling Bourbon family, *frondeur*, and patron of letters. Where Pascal was intellectually ferocious, delighting in disputes with his contemporaries, La Bruyère must have been a clandestine observer who saved and savored the most candid reflections from a life at court to publish them late in his career, often to vituperative criticism by those he impugned.

The important difference between the two lies less in their biographies or types of intelligence than in their reception of the intellectualist trends of the age. Reason was pit against the passions and the senses in many spheres, in philosophy—Descartes' treatise on the passions takes this view—religion—a resistance to the threat, raised by Protestantism, of a new involvement in the world—and the general revival of stoic ethical ideals. Despite Pascal's frequent dismissal of neo-stoicism in the *Pensées* and elsewhere, a similar desire for an intensified mental experience marks his doctrines as well.[19]

Both Pascal and the Jansenist thinkers at Port-Royal who directed him spiritually and intellectually after his "conversions" were committed to religious practices that, compared to others of the time, seem highly intellectualized. In this respect, his conversions may not be such drastic departures from his scientific undertakings. Even if some Pascalian writings show a tendency toward mysticism, the intellectual emphasis carries over, especially in the *Pensées*, where, even when reason appears to become weak and despised, Pascal still shows great ambivalence. "Reason" may be ridiculed, its power to establish truths slighted, its ability to elevate man above beasts censured, the status of "proof" reduced to nil in matters of charity. Yet there are as many fragments that emphasize the strength of "thought" as there are fragments that emphasize reason's weakness and corruption. This is just the point: thought's strength and integrity lie in its ability to "former dans son esprit l'idée, l'image" of weakness and corruption.[20] In a word, thought thinks *divertissements*.

The meaning of *divertissement* remains unintelligible outside the specific meaning of *penser* in his late writings, where the prominence of these figures has both doctrinal and personal grounds. After his lifelong illness became grave in 1647, doctors advised Pascal to avoid intellectual strain and seek diversions. He moved to Paris and began to circulate in society for perhaps the first time, encountering many of the characters and vices with which he would later exemplify the miseries of *l'homme*. In the *Pensées*, misery becomes the condition, diversion the sign. Men are miserable, "the only good thing for men therefore is to be diverted from thinking of what they are" (*Pensées* E #136, F #168). *Penser*, to think of what you are, means making a private, interiorized image of your misery. That diversion is the sign of wretchedness is proven by an argument that is either tautological or nearly so. Man must be wretched because *divertissement* never fails to make him happy (*heureux*) (E #132, F #165). Phrased in this way, misery has a secret profit: a man's misery is his very constancy. In this picture, *l'homme* is constantly inconstant, ever looking away in order to conceal from himself his nature. This is the first positive element of Pascalian diversion, constancy. The second is the specific configuration of mindlessness: turning away by turning toward. We are now perhaps too familiar with this episteme to question it. For Pascal, the turn away from misery is accomplished by a turn toward what effectively conceals it. Somewhat similar to repression, operating by means of sublimation, *divertissement* produces happiness by subtracting strife; it subtracts strife through illusory attachments, which nonetheless produce only negative and temporary relief (E #132, #133; F #165, #166). To prove that this structure applies equally to all of humanity, in a famous *pensée* Pascal describes the most extreme situation, the case of the happiest person in the world. Far from carefree, however, a king in fact has to be the most diverted, since, being king, that is, having all his earthly desires fulfilled, he is more miserable than others when he discovers that he still needs to be diverted in order to find happiness (E #136, F #168). The existence of the court is evidence enough to support this assumption. The court is the playground of the king's diversions, and by extension, diversions in aggregate bind society as a whole. Each member of court and each social being depends for happiness on something exterior, and the sum total of this dependency, a cumulative exteriority and aggregative dependency, makes up the social arena per se (E #132, F #165). Even rank is a function of *divertissement*. Persons of high rank are proportionally happier than persons of low or no rank insofar as they have access to more things and people to divert them (E #136, F #168).

If diversion means dependence on the exterior for happiness, and if the phenomenon knows no social bounds, stretching to the highest rung (interestingly, the lowest are rarely mentioned), then social relations are indeed merely epiphenomena of diversion and diversion itself is of another order than the social. The contrary of diversion is introspection, and so we should not be tempted to confuse Pascalian diversion with dispersion, dissemination, dissolution, diaspora, or any other image of geographical or political scattering. Diversion is through and through intellectual, *de l'esprit*; it turns away, to be sure, yet it is still a version of thinking, a type of power, a quality of mind. Society then, for Pascal, at least from the perspective of a miserable humanity absolutely uncertain of grace, is a pale derivative of thought. Nevertheless and because of this, it takes the form of intense absorption in things. Pushing a billiard ball back and forth on a table, laying a wager on a roulette wheel, pursuing a rabbit—these activities fall under the rubric of thought, and they are called "unthinking" purely on the basis of the meanness of their objects.

The double figure of absorption and concealment to which Pascal commits in the *Pensées* has an analogue in Montaigne's essay "On Diversion," written between 1585 and 1588. Here the general economy of diversion is similar but its value is reversed. "Our thoughts are always elsewhere," Montaigne announces (E 633, F 87). The power to evade, side-step, move away from woe is no less ubiquitous than it is for Pascal, but Montaigne, in contrast to many of his seventeenth-century readers, celebrates it. Diversion is chiefly an antidote to the most painful experience, the experience of mourning, and on this model it also remedies lesser painful thoughts and toilsome occupations. In this way it is the height of realism about human experience. Perhaps nothing puts the truth-value of diversion more beautifully than this line from "On Diversion": "it is pricing our life exactly as it really is to abandon it for a dream" (E 638, F 96). The push toward realism and the dialectical relation that allows it to appear prefigure Pascal's *divertissement* structure. Likewise, the dialectics of large and small, worthy and unworthy pass through both writers. Montaigne's "it takes little to divert and distract us, for it takes little to hold us" (E 635, F 91) becomes Pascal's thought-annihilating concentration on trivial things (*Pensées* E #136, F #168).[21] Common to both is this formula: a different object becomes a substitute, the substitute allows escape from suffering, escape transforms and determines the self-relation: "changing place, occupation, and company, I escape into the throng of other entertainments and thoughts [*d'autres amusements et pensées*], where it loses my trace and loses me" (Montaigne E 635, F 90, translation modified). According to the logic of this trace however, the lost "me" becomes the mark of the new "me," which covets its loss as the most profound identifier.

What Montaigne praises and Pascal despises, Augustine holds in equivocal esteem. Absent is the realism with which they identify the human condition with misery and self-delusion. While Augustine certainly agrees that the senses corrupt and pleasure too easily substitutes for the more toilsome task of faith, thinking about it may not in fact improve the situation. True thinking, thinking that is not diverted, may not even be possible, since, although attention lifts one's heart to God, attention has its origin in sin. "It is one thing to rise rapidly, another thing not to fall" (*Confessions* X, 35, 57). The path to heaven is paved with sensual pleasures, one of which it goes without saying is the pleasure of attention. Augustine reflects on the fallen character of attention and the dilemma it produces with an anecdote from his own experience. "If by chance I am passing when coursing occurs in the countryside, it distracts me [*avertit me*] perhaps indeed from thinking out some weighty matter [*ab aliqua magna cogitatione*]. The hunt turns me [*ad se convertit*] to an interest in the sport, not enough to lead me to deviate [*deviare*] the direction of the beast I am riding, but shifting the inclination of my heart" (X, 35, 57). The terminological distinctions are sharper in the Latin text than in this translation. Augustine makes a distinction between corporeal *deviare* and affective or intellectual *inclinare*, both of which overlay moral values on the more general *avertere* and *convertere*, two cardinal points of the Augustinian compass—aversion and conversion. In this new scene of conversion, unlike the earlier more famous one, aversions abound. A decade or more after Augustine's conversion in the garden, where a child's voice urged him to read Paul's invective against concupiscence—"make no provision for the flesh, to gratify its desires" (Romans 13:14)—the fleshy drives, here given the flesh of a horse, have been trained not to deviate, but the heart, where weighty cogitations occur, still inclines toward sense experience, away from thought. His body was converted but his heart still averts, turning toward the senses. This is where the thorniest difficulty lies. From a theological perspective, the heart's potential for *conversio ad se* constitutes both its strength and its temptation. There is no higher instance within the heart to judge the *ad quem* of its conversion, and the sources for its inclinations are always first of all sensual things. In experience, conversion begins with inclination. He hears a voice, he reads, and only then does he undergo a spiritual conversion to the true God. Faith begins in the senses, or, to say this another way, you fall upward. Someone with strong inclinations of the heart can rise rapidly to reach the thought of God, but the rise is directly proportional to a fall. How can one leave corruption behind by means of a corrupt activity?

In the postclassical world, the question of distraction must be asked in the terms this passage sets out. First, we are burdened with a corrupt faculty; second, it is only through this faculty and specifically through its corrupted and corrupting acts that a motion away from corruption can begin; third, writing acts out a recognition of this fact—here as *confessio*—but insofar as it does so as an ambiguous plea to be saved at the same time from, through, and for *intentum*, which may be rendered "attention," the writing itself remains extremely polyvalent and perplexing. The economy of conversion and aversion, as well as *intentum* and *deviare*, are shown to operate in this manner: the supplement, aversion, has already been taken up and cancelled from the outset by attention, as another form of conversion or adversion (of the soul, *animadversion*), the paradigmatic mode by which one is affected by the other in Augustine. The source for this paradigm in an intellect that replicates a body with senses is worth noting. All these terms for turning toward and away are infected with the very physical realm that Augustine claims to have overcome. Moreover, in the hierarchy depicted here—and it is the same in Pascal—the turn "toward" is transcendent. To the very extent that direction-to is the desideratum and considered primary, direction-from returns repeatedly and secretly to interrupt the relation. In Augustine's mature theory of piety, those attitudes the believer believes he left behind after his conversion come back to raise doubts about its success. They break into the life of piety with the thought that the conversion may never have overcome the impure inclination from which it began. In *Confessions* X, this doubt remains operative and open to the very end. It is operative first of all in the figure of the hunt, the archetype of diversion that Pascal later also adopts. In this scene hunting captivates Augustine. On one hand, it turns his thought from a cogitation of the spirit to an experience of the senses. At the same time, however, the hunt figure is active in another sense. It is also an ideal image of the path from diversion to a transcendent end. It leads the senses onward toward a non-sensuous goal that in the end will render the sensual experience of hunting inconsequential. Hunting is a model of the very attention that Augustine needs for his theory of piety, and yet by rights he should not be drawn to the hunt, since in an empirical hunt the end justifies the means, whereas in a hunt of the spirit these means are the very antithesis of the end (the abysmal dialectic of the hunt is perhaps best summed up in the first half of Plato's *Sophist*). In this startling passage, Augustine comes close to admonishing God for leaving him in this terrible dilemma, which grows more and more complex as the passage unfolds:

The hunt turns me to an interest in the sport, not enough to lead me to alter the direction of the beast I am riding, but shifting the inclination of my heart. Unless you had proved to me my infirmity and quickly admonished me either to take the sight as a start for some reflection enabling me to rise up to you or wholly scorn and pass the matter by, I would be watching like an empty-headed fool [*hebesco vanus*]. When I am sitting at home, a lizard catching flies or a spider entrapping them as they rush [*inruentes*] into its web often fascinates me. The problem is not made any different by the fact that the animals are small. The sight leads me to praise you, the marvelous Creator and orderer of all things; but that was not how my attention first began. It is one thing to rise rapidly, another thing not to fall. (213)

Many of the conflicts over the meaning of distraction after the seventeenth century are already legible in this fifth-century text. Overall, the passage is motivated by a worry that even attention to God is a diversion, a plea-sure of the senses that while leading toward him also obstructs and leads away. Augustine has the intuition, in other words, that the turn away is in fact primary, and all potential turning toward must be preceded by an actual turning away. As a corollary, one must practice and maintain the power of diversion in order to remain in conversion. Thus, unlike his well-trained beast, the Bishop of Hippo's heart cannot get used to being led. These three figures—the non-deviating horse, the still-inclining heart, and the empty-headed fool—recall in advance the three possible positions on distraction in modernity. Horse and heart keep to the path or else one of them strays. This choice is made within an already-understood context of the divine mandate: "he who is not with me is against me." Straying is one pole of this either-or, either attention's spin-off or its foundation. And yet what seems to worry Augustine as well in this passage is the inkling that attention and diversion are not the only starting points. The third possibil-ity, a mental turning that may not even fall into the theological field adum-brated by Jesus in Matthew, takes effect if God does not give his directive soon enough. The turn may then begin with *hebesco vanus*, "an empty one, I grow dull." No turning at all or a *vertere* without direction compromises the secret complicity between attention and diversion—an ambitionless spin. Each opportunity for concupiscence or piety is at the same time an opportunity for a dim-witted and vacant itinerancy, in which the context for sin has not yet been imposed.

Sitting at home, the theologian is once again captivated by a scene of capture. Does the pious one wait like a spider to catch God as he flies into the web? Or does God lie in wait for him? It is not decided. What is decided is that, in Augustine's anecdote, the flies are "rushing into" (*inruentes*) the web. They do not wander dimly by, oblivious to the

danger, or fall in with no ambition of their own. In this fantasy, there
are no unintentional actions. Caught in the web spun by the terms of
his argument, Augustine reveals his overweening attraction to attraction,
and then once again a third possibility interpolates itself. Both allegories
of faith, hunter and web, rabbit and fly, lead Augustine to praise God as
"creator and orderer of everything" (*creatorem . . . atque ordinatorem rerum omnium*). Nothing is truly small, and nature itself is a web spun between all small things to capture all our thoughts. And again he doubts,
admitting that it is "the sight" of this that leads him to God. We could
say that Augustine vacillates in this passage between an allegorical and
a symbolic understanding of experience. As symbol it annihilates itself,
leaving only its meaning. As allegory, it leaves a residue of sensibility by
which it continues to function, in order to be mistaken for a symbol,
and yet to the keen eye, the residue may become visible and raise doubts.
Unlike a horse, the heart must be taught again and again not to mistake
its visions for truth, up to and including its vision of truth. All routes to
truth—here the hunt or the web—become susceptible to this penetration
by sensation and the constantly doubling doubt of the process. Prayers
are interrupted by "frivolous thoughts rushing in" (*inruentibus nugatoriis
cogitationibus*)—a different sort of inrushing than that of the ambitious
flies. Thus the language of conversion is tainted by the language of inclination, and confession is a better genre than prayer only insofar as it
presents the whole amalgam as an ongoing problem. It is able to narrate
the hunt for God that leads back to the hunt.

In Pascal's adaptation, aversion from God is precisely equal to absorption in the world, and thus there is nothing left over to cause doubt,
as can be seen in the economical form of a *pensée*, which, as a pure thought
of this structure, repeats and redoubles the force of absorption. The turn
inward is still, formally speaking, diversion from diversion, but Pascal
fixes Augustine's model and makes it into a rule and a technique. The
methodological version of double diversion in the *Pensées* is inversion.
Blindness illuminates: the blindness of those who do not seek God proves
his existence (*Pensées* E #163, F #195). Wretchedness is good: knowledge
of wretchedness has greatness (though not grace) (E #114, F #146). Humanity's inconstancy is constant.[22] If diversion is the natural, continual,
and necessary state of human being, as many *pensées* claim (E #70, #198,

#298, #395, #408, etc.), through an inversion, diversion is shown to be humanity's substance. This is why only the vulgar laugh at those who are diverted (E #101, F #134)—they miss the point entirely; the diverted are right, for a special reason. Take, once again, the hunt. Augustine's hunt (*venatio*), which in the *Confessions* started and ended in emptiness (*vanitas*), Pascal abbreviates and condenses into *la chasse*, whose epistemic structure forgoes Augustine's ambivalence. "The hare itself would not save us from the sight of death and the miseries which are distracting us [*qui nous en détournent*], but hunting it does so" (E #136, F 168, translation modified). Pursuit is diverting and the goal of diversion is pursuit; the goal of the pursuit—catching the hare, winning a bet or game—is a secondary consideration, a necessary fantasy, to be sure, but not at all the objective. That is why, on the ladder of diversions, goalless ones are higher: billiards, dancing, a spectacle, and perhaps (although he doesn't say this here) love, certainly self-love. Rest leaves us to think of our distance from the goal, while the goalless agitates us and "turns our mind from thinking" about the end, "nous détourne d'y penser," and "this is why we prefer the hunt to the capture" (E #136, F #168). Here capturing the hunt, so to speak—the activity of *penser* for Pascal—does not fall prey to its prey, as it did for Augustine. Thought springs fully formed from diversion from diversion. "You would only have to take away all their cares, and then they would see themselves and think about what they are, where they come from, and where they are going" (E #139, F #171). What they think when they suspend not-thinking is "where they are going." The diversion-drive originates in death, in the thought of death, as an attempt to evade it. The reverse is also true: ceasing to think of worthless things, death fills my thoughts. But the latter is only for those inclined toward difficulty. "It is easier to bear death when one is not thinking about it than the idea of death when there is no danger" (E #138). "*Divertissement.*—La mort est plus aisée à supporter sans y penser que la pensée de la mort sans peril" (F #170). In the moment of dying, when it has become a present possibility, the thought of death is easier.

Up to this point everything, life, is evasion. For Pascal, the true death of thought, which occurs just after the only true thought, the thought of death in the throws of death, plays an obviously personal role in his desire to write down his *pensées*. The loss of thinking toward which the thinker is inevitably directed calls him to gather up the traces of his thoughtful activity. To once again quote this *pensée*, which comes to seem more and more the essential assumption underlying his method: "Man is obviously made for thinking. Therein lies all his dignity and his merit; and his whole duty is to think as he ought. Yet the order of thought is to begin with ourselves, and with our author and our end" (E #620, F #513). Beginning with the end, the thinking life never for a minute shakes the thought of death. In this way Pascal contributes to a long tradition of *mors contemplativa* that culminates in Hegel, then continues after him in Heidegger, in which death can be converted into a power for thinking. These *pensées* make an early attempt to delimit the clandestine relations between thought and death; the question is how it delimits them. One thing is clear: death's purported fixity offers itself to the act of *penser*. Thinking accepts the burden of finitude, but in exchange it draws enormous powers from it, one of which is the power to think being. To complete this thought about the order of thought—about its fixation on death—Pascal goes on: "Yet what does the world think about? Never about that [self, God, and death]! But about dancing, playing the lute, singing, writing verse, tilting at the ring, etc., and fighting, becoming king, without thinking [*sans penser*] what it means to be a king or to be a man" (E #620, F #513). It is not only the tone of this and other fragments that gives the impression of great certainty. Being, the steady companion of thought, makes its appearance here as well. Death is the *to ti ēn einai* of humanity, death is what it means to be *l'homme* (or the king insofar as he is the exemplary diverted one). And diversion, being "sans penser," means not thinking about death, man's essence. In the same gesture Pascal refuses all other grounds for thought. *Divertissements* become the grounds for thinking, uncertainty becomes a certainty about uncertainty—a critical structure that Pascal codifies.

"A Lapse of Fact"

Although his goal was to "surpass the ancients, by imitating them" (French classicism's paradoxical commonplace) (*Characters* E 26, F 161–62), La Bruyère, in the preface to the first edition of *Les Caractères*, "Discours sur Théophraste," credits two "modern" models along with his ancient master. The first of the two "ouvrages de morale qui sont dans les mains de tout le monde" is Pascal's *Pensées*, which La Bruyère read in the Port-Royal edition of 1670, where most of the fragments on *divertissement* had been reordered by the editors into Chapter 26, entitled "Misère de l'homme." La Rochefoucauld's *Refléxions* is the other modern model. An anxiety surfaces when La Bruyère mentions these works. In the same paragraph he reproaches in advance those readers who mistakenly think his *remarques* are direct imitations of Pascal's and La Rochefoucauld's works. Both thinkers are, from his perspective, moralists like he is, bent on leading men to virtue, the one by making "metaphysics" subservient to "religion" and thus arriving at the virtues and vices of the soul, the other by revealing all error to be based in self-love. Yet La Bruyère differs in method—his, he claims, is no method at all (F 97). Rather, he says he is an indifferent examiner whose objective is "to render man reasonable," that is, neither to save him or show the path to salvation, nor to make his actions moral by undercutting his arrogant *amour-propre* (F 98). "Raisonnable" can be used in any number of ways in the late seventeenth century; it might mean fair or logical. Yet La Bruyère makes it clear that it is the soul he means to correct. Where precisely does the author surpass the ancients by imitating them? La Bruyère says that he goes beyond Theophrastus by shifting the focus to the "vices of the spirit" (*vices de l'esprit*), of the heart, and of "the whole interior of man" (F 98). What kind of vice of the soul does *le distrait* exemplify? Or does he by chance correct one?

If we take him as a response to Pascal's theory of *divertissement, le distrait* is either not diverted enough to become absorbed in any trivial thing, or else he is so diverted by everything at once that diversion no longer has theological significance. He does not have the power to signify his opposite. Instead of absorbing himself in a worthless part of this world that allegorically raises the specter of the next, world—if it can still be called that—takes possession of *le distrait* so completely that it expresses its overwhelming riches through his mental poverty.

The diverted one is a figure—in Pascal's sense of the word, when he uses it to describe the continued relevance of "the Jews" for Christians—whose purpose is to be read and overcome. In this economy of reading, the figure does not have a full quotient of being, but makes itself available in its decrepitude for others as partial, lacking, as the cause for its own misery, to the extent that it is not what it could be and indicates its opposite. This semiological assumption, that suffering indicates its opposite, is truly eschatological, and without it the concept of diversion would not make sense. Suffering is always comparative, and with Pascal as with his great reader Kierkegaard, the way out of suffering is an authentic movement into suffering as the allegory of its alleviation. In effect, turning suffering into a sign both prolongs it to fill the whole of life (because it can never fully be understood until it ends) and cancels it (since one must go through it instead of merely undergoing it). Happiness means rest, and rest and agitation, the two poles of desire, correspond to the structure of morality, a comparative dance that seeks to make use of evil, at least intellectually, to arrive at the good. It would be hard to conceive of an intellectual activity that does not participate in such a Gnosticism. As may be apparent, the conceptual structure of attention-deficit disorder is also eschatological in this way.

And so in Pascal, *l'homme* turns away from the proper work of suffering meaningfully, toward pleasure, and the theorists' task is to quickly and thoroughly reassimilate that turn to the structure of significance. Diversion must become part of suffering. The epistemology of pleasure holds that evading being and death through artifice is pleasurable because truth is suffering. As one can imagine, *le distrait* one does not operate according to this pattern, and his theorist does not try to reabsorb him into a larger eschatological narrative. From this basic difference, a series of ancillary distinctions follow. Diversion is the prototypical solitary activity. As a vice and as the basis for all vices it begins by negating the individual, who otherwise would be alone and "quietly in his room"; then it injects him into society, which is little more than a loose aggregate of self-alienated *solitaires*. The other, distraction, takes its departure from the social realm, which, consequently, is seen less as an escape from his essence than as an essenceless agglomerate of habits and decisions, which the distracted one temporarily abandons.[23] He becomes isolated at court, in the salon, the family, the army, but only by falling out of the set of highly stratified habits, reflecting, as a single individual, their ultimate groundlessness in the nature of man. Alienation from grace through illusory happiness becomes, in *le distrait*, a break from habit through

buffoonery. Here we can see how the same fundamental ontological assumption can lead to various conclusions; or perhaps it is more accurate
to say that the assumption that humanity is naturally corrupt can take
several forms and lead to varying prognoses and plans of action. That the
French writers whom we still admire from the seventeenth century all
hold this pessimistic view should tell us something about our continuing
indebtedness to the idea. The disappearance of distraction outside an
eschatological framework belongs to this turn of events as well. For the
diverted one, grace is uncertain, but when he understands diversion as
a turn away, he is rewarded with sure knowledge of that which grace is
not. Grace does not enter the distracted one's thoughts. After distraction
he will return to his house, his rank, his costume and habitual thoughts.
For Pascal, the thought that reason and the senses deceive is the highest
truth available to man (*Pensées* E #45, F #78 p. 73). Thus "man transcends
man" (*l'homme passé l'homme*) (E #131 p. 34, F #164 p. 116) and although
he is as frail as a reed, he is nonetheless a "thinking reed" (E #200, F
#231). Stating this in no uncertain terms, *les pensées* themselves manifest
the power of thought; and although in the experience of thinking, these
thoughts "come at random and go at random," the thinker's own intellectual inconstancy can be recorded such that it too comes to mean its
opposite: "A thought has escaped: I was trying to write it down: instead I
write that it escaped me" (E #542, F 459). This is what it means to write
a *pensée*, to subtract randomness by marking it down, to fix inconstancy
by naming it, to write the one maxim that produces distrust in maxims,
the one written text that produces distrust in all other written texts, to
withdraw—by committing his experience to paper—the thinker from
the contingency of the thinking act, allowing him to take refuge in a
generalized finitude and contingency. Pascal's mechanics of composition
has a similar structure: thoughts are written as they come (or do not
come); later the very paper is cut up, re-gathered, put in the order of an
apologia for his method.

Pascal himself, with the help of Arnauld and Nicole, offers a way
to understand *le distrait*, in the fourth *Provincial Letter*. The Jesuit moral
principle he wants to attack states that there are no sins of omission, only
of commission. For an act to be a sin, his interlocutor the priest argues,
one has to know in advance that the act is not good. If one is ignorant of

the moral value of the act, one cannot be guilty. At issue are those who do not think of God at all when they act, and here there is a core difference between Jansenist theology and Jesuit theology. For the Jesuit these are not sinners. It goes without saying that the Jansenist disagrees vehemently. He argues that the lack of forethought, which we can call a first-order thoughtlessness based on the assumption of reason, cannot ever excuse sinful behavior. Here Pascal and his co-writers have recourse to the distinction between right and fact that had been used, quite controversially, by defenders of Port-Royal to shield the Jansenists from decisions at Rome. Not thinking of God when acting is a lapse of right or faith and cannot excuse the action from condemnation and the sinner from penance. This would mean excusing rational beings from moral behavior altogether. There is, however, another case. Some undergo what the Jansenist calls a lapse "of fact." These might know the principle and not plan to do evil, but an empirical lapse or accident prevents them from doing good. This second-order thoughtlessness does not make reference to a central rational faculty. The first is a libertine in love with his *divertissement*, the second *un distrait*.

Collective Distraction

La Bruyère's *distrait* forgets but his way is not equivalent to forgetting. It is like a mood but it inhabits no metaphorical mental locale where moods play out their changes. Neither an attitude, since it is not "ad"—toward—anything, nor a disposition, since it dispossesses bearers of their positions, it moreover resists the usual contrasts with intention, desire, and other images of internal means to external ends.[24] Flight from the world it cannot be since, as we have seen, it embraces the world when it ceases to recognize any single object in it. Not equivalent to mourning: the past that the melancholic clutches tightly runs through the distracted one's fingers. Sleep is alien to it, since it only occurs in one who is awake, although in some ways it reminds us of sleep. No character from the everyday looks more like Ménalque than the sleepwalker. Hannah Arendt, who often assumes the worst of not-thinking, makes this connection directly. "Unthinking men are like sleepwalkers" (191). Not all types of unthinking, however—that of Ménalque for example, but there are other cases; Chaplin's little tramp comes to mind—permit evil acts by the weakness of their thought. Sleepwalkers, one might argue, in an effort to draw out the implications of Arendt's simile, are not under the control of anything besides the incoherent dreamworld that misdirects their steps. Not-always-thinking—this is the most surprising detail—does not appear to belong to the life of the mind. It is after all an intra-mental demise of the mental, implying a lack of autonomy to be sure, but not every lack of autonomy becomes servitude to dogmatic ideologies. One could argue that the banality that gives way to evil is not distraction at all, but a very specific image of thinking—and a common one at that. When we say that men like Eichmann acted "without thinking" we mean of course that they did think, but according to principles that they did not subject to critical scrutiny. Thinking without thinking relies on unthought principles. Of course if one reconsidered the rules of thought before each act, one would never think at all. We cannot help but act and think unthinkingly most of the time. Perhaps one who is "unthinking" in Arendt's sense is merely unaware of this problem. The zombie and the maniac—these thoughtlessly follow hard and fast rules of thought and action. Maniacs receive inspiration from the gods, zombies commands from the devil, but the distracted one is under no one's spell. Not even an unconscious can answer for his errancy: in Ménalque's antics everything stored up for the future is discharged. Is he therefore a nihilist? To this one can only say, again, "no," with the proviso that saying no to nihilism is not itself nihilistic. A nihilist wills nothing, but will is nothing to the distracted one. Nihilism crashes through existence annihilating things of value; distraction disarms the will with an "I don't think so," and as a result bumps almost harmlessly into things. Ménalque, "if he walks in the public square, he suddenly feels a sharp blow in his stomach or in his face; he can't think what it may be" (*Characters* E 183, F 399). One provokes a *horror vacui*, the other laughter. One is solitary, the other ineluctably collective.

The peculiar if not also sacrilegious collectivity born out of distraction is prefigured in a footnote to the section on distraction. In it La Bruyère sets forth the peculiar terms of the character's tendency toward politicization. It should be noted first that many of the character's reflexes are already political. *Le distrait* "meets a prince face to face" in the street but does not step aside to let him pass. He sends a letter to a peer of the realm requesting a provision of hay while he sends a farmer an obsequious letter beginning, "Monseigneur . . . your Grace . . . " (E 185, F 402). "He addresses his lackey, in all seriousness, as Monsieur, and calls his friend by his lackey's name, La Verdure; he says Your Reverence to a prince of the blood, and Your Highness to a Jesuit" (E 188, F 406). This obtuse egalitarianism heralds a historical changeover.[25] It reflects the demise of the feudal aristocracy in the inattention to aristocratic norms; it also ridicules other modes of social distinction, bourgeois mobility, for example. With respect to his own wealth, his means of advancement, *le distrait* is yet more progressive. He gambles his money away without remorse and fails to react when his servants violently rob him. These gestures are certainly not trivial, but the deeper politics of *le distrait* are found elsewhere. La Bruyère uses the footnote as a warning: unlike other characters in the anthology, Ménalque "is less one particular character than a collection of examples of absent-mindedness (*un recueil de faits de distraction*). There cannot be too many of them, if they are amusing; for since tastes differ, everyone can choose" (E 216 note 1, F 399 note). La Bruyère finds it necessary to distinguish this type of collection of traits from all the other *caractères*, who themselves are not individuals, but rather types. Here we learn that Ménalque is not a type but a *recueil* of missteps, mistakes, and stupidities that have affected many, perhaps all, the other types. The distracted one is truly a democratic character, and as such he goes against the spirit of the book; as a set of free-floating, undiscriminating characteristics, his "power" belongs to all, accompanying every other vice and virtue, and complicating attempts to moralize about them. For this reason he cannot become a cautionary example (La Bruyère recognizes this amoral quality, insofar as he admits that the character is meant not to teach but to delight readers, to be *agréable*). As the footnote also indicates, when these acts are committed, no particular character is to blame, and so no particular character and no group made up of individuals can be held accountable for this lassitude.[26] It is, strictly speaking, nobody's fault and thus everybody's deliverance from virtue ethics. Distraction in general has this atypical characteristic: it is ubiquitous among characters but not specifically attributable to a subject or a self. How could it be considered a single, nameable, reproachable, and therefore correctable vice? Insofar as it pertains to no one in particular and at the same time to everyone,[27] at any moment a diaspora of *distraits* cuts indiscriminately across otherwise constituted groups—senates, armies, student bodies, congregations, families, nations, globes. More interestingly, perhaps, only counting all possible moments together does the inconsistent plurality constitute a *recueil*. In this way the drama of *le distrait* leaps out of the seventeenth century; the degree of his unrepresentability is infinite. There cannot, as La Bruyère warns readers, be too large a number of distractions.

A Refusal to Be

Roland Barthes contends that in its disintegrating language and fragmented rather than narrative mode *Les Caractères* is a forerunner to twentieth-century avant-garde literary forms (234). For different reasons the section on *le distrait* anticipates certain traits of Kafka's fiction. Note the tone of this passage, not to mention its structure. It is shaped like a joke, whose vehicle is a "miscarriage" of justice: "On leaving the *Palais de Justice* he notices, at the foot of the main staircase, a carriage which he takes for his own; he climbs into it; the coachman whips up his horse and, so he thinks, drives his master home; Ménalque jumps out of the carriage, crosses the courtyard, takes the stairs, goes through the waiting-room, the parlour, the study; it all seems familiar, nothing is strange to him; he sits down, takes a rest, feels at home. The master of the house appears; Ménalque gets up to receive him . . . " (*Characters* E 184, F 400). The rest is easy to imagine. Ménalque welcomes the master of the house into the man's own study with all the courtesy one would expect of a seventeenth-century bourgeois *gentilhomme*. If we were told that these scenes took place in *The Trial* or *The Castle* we would not be surprised. Here are Kafka's "ordinary rooms" made extraordinary by their unfamiliar familiarity. Here is a city in which all roads lead to the Palace of Justice, where masters are interchangeable, and nothing can be out of place enough to require explanation. Welcomed home by a stranger occupying his own chair, the master in question might well be named "K." More than these similarities, however, the question of justice haunts this section of *Les Caractères*. Justice, it is revealed, will not be dispensed in the *Palais de Justice*, but only in the general distribution of things: from coachman and masters to the privacy of private property and the supposedly protected inner space of the home, even to the structure of space itself—all these have their lack of justification remorselessly exposed. As it does to *le distrait*, the world's architecture often painfully strikes Kafkan characters as though they had not been born to inhabit it. To repeat: "if he walks in the public square, he suddenly feels a sharp blow in his stomach or in his face; he can't think what it may be" (E 183, F 399). Often the only public response left for Kafka's characters when the world hits them is *Zerstreuung*. This is because distraction suspends epochal processes such as world, consciousness, experience, and history by releasing their horizons and with them being as the sine qua non of existence. The distracted one exists but does not lend being to what he encounters, even if they are distractible beings like him. He does not even recognize them as similar to himself, and perhaps that is what La Bruyère means by this obscure remark: "he is never there with those he appears to be with" (E 188, F 406). An enabler of a politics without being-with: this is how *le distrait* appears.

CHAPTER 3

Labyrinth of Pure Reflection / Kafka

If the distracted one subtends a community without being-with, one might well worry: when thought yields its privileged place to distraction, who takes responsibility for ethical and political life? In a journal entry from January 1920, Kafka raises a similar question. With a barely concealed reference to debates on the meaning and value of Zionism (at that time, as now, more than one movement, more than one idea, so at least we should say: Zionisms), he inquires into the ethical status of a principle of distraction, suggesting that, if the principle were accepted, a reform of ethical concepts would have to follow.

He lives in distraction/ dispersal/ diaspora [*Zerstreuung*]. His elements, a freely living horde, ramble around the world. And only because his room also belongs to the world does he see them occasionally in the distance. How can he carry the responsibility for them? Is that still called responsibility? (*Tagebücher* 850)

One notes the vastly changed circumstances here, while at the same time there is more than a hint of a return to earlier dilemmas. The doubt that flashes across Aristotle's *De anima*, the clownish figure that trips through La Bruyère's compendium—the two here become something Kafka calls "living." Let us not assimilate this word immediately to our expectations. Living has little to do with biopolitics and less with *Lebensphilosophie*. The reference to *Zerstreuung* directs our gaze elsewhere. Without referring to Aristotle or La Bruyère at all of course, with little or no knowledge of their distractive episodes, Kafka's figure—named in German simply "er," "he"—

seizes a potential that was perhaps latent in both. The disruption in the most unified and universal human activity (Aristotle) and the *recueil* of misfires in the moral and ethical agent (La Bruyère) become a political phenomenon in Kafka's depiction of diasporic-dispersed-distracted "living."

Living in *Zerstreuung*: who will be responsible for them? When one lives, when "he" lives, "er" is in *it*—distraction-dispersal-diaspora. "Er"—Kafka's reflection belongs to the small group of aphoristic writings from 1920 that revolve around this pronoun. "He"—the reportedly objective pronoun, the pronoun that speaks from outside, reports on, gestures toward a non-intimate relation, toward a being or a position not crossed by the power struggle between an *ich* and a *du*. "He"—an outsider, free of the threat of direct address—can be described from a perspective that can, in theory, encompass him without loss. Perhaps this is the only way a description of diasporic life can be given: never from within. Then again, the pronoun reproduces a fantasy of which we are meant to grow suspicious. It implies: it is never *I* who lives this way; someone—who knows who, someone still to be specified, a figure unaffected by the relations described—is undergoing this "life," and this someone is thus specified by an *extra* someone, who points toward the "he," but also lives a safe distance away from "him." We must try to think of "he" as a name. The experience "he" has of others (whom he might in turn call "er") the passage tells us, has an intermittent character; it is mediated—and perhaps also vitiated—by the distance that engenders it. As we have been saying, "he" already marks a grammatical distanciation, as though the first-person fiction could not even be suggested under these conditions. Another must take its place and the displacement must be passed on to the narrator; in place of I-Thou, he-he. And so we do not find an ethical relation between individuals, even one mediated by God. Coming face to face is unlikely; so is summoning the other. "He" and his group, an internally estranged group of "third persons," are not on speaking terms. We receive a report that "he" is living abandoned by his "elements." Freedom means something like this in a Kafkan diaspora: to be abandoned by your constituent parts. A wild chemistry, the elements that make up the being relate through distance and secondhand report. From the perspective of ethics he is irresponsible, anarchic even, a bad neighbor.

This is not simply chaos, however, and it is certainly not relativism.

Kafka ends the inquiry here, with a question, in tone almost a cry for help—but he does not abandon it. Third persons mark social relations in much of Kafka's late fiction, from *The Castle* to the last story, "Josephine the Singer, or the Mouse People." More extreme than third persons, another elaboration of the problem of "life" can be found in another fragment from 1920; here "er" is replaced. There is no agent or subject of life at all. "Life is a continual diversion [*eine fortwährende Ablenkung*] that never once allows coming to reflection [*Besinnung*] on that from which it diverts" (*NS II* 340). The problem is sharper here, though no less intractable. Life means, enacts, and produces a lack of reflection on its continual reflectionlessness. No idealized intellectual faculty mars the perfection of life's non-thought here. Life, like "le distrait," is the most distracted from its own distractibility. Acts of reflective thought, as a consequence, are perversions of life. Reflection, one might say, when it happens, implies the pervasiveness of not reflecting. What remains to be shown—if it can be— is where this elemental, general, and primal distraction breaks through the crust of its continual self-denial to appear to us as what it is. It is articulated desperately and partially in Aristotle, and it appears quite unreflectively in La Bruyère, as an image, a figure. In these fragments Kafka gives it a high status, and a formula.

But it is the very late story fragment, "Der Bau," that offers a scenario in which a thinking creature can move from the most obstinate, intensive thinking to something like primal distraction. One of Kafka's most intricate arguments against thought, "Der Bau" at first sight represents the antipode to diaspora and the distraction that accompanies it. The creature who narrates the tale has no community and wants none; moreover, it has dedicated its life to reflection. At the same time the story repeats and develops the distance, falsity of reflection, and failure of ethical relations that Kafka began to explore in the 1920 fragments. Here, however, "he," or in this case, rather, "it," is a creature already in Zion, inhabiting its homeland.

From the start, the creature that builds and lives in the Bau, burrow or construction, acts out a mania for separating things: primarily dividing out there from in here. It is mad for dividing things in two. Not just any things—the most meaningful units of the narrator's existence are divided by walls and fall into a series of doublets, each one rolled up, doubled against itself in the manner of a cuff or a pocket. On one side of the seam lies the creature's narration, the stillness of its home, the orderliness, security, storage, but also emptiness, whose corresponding sense is hearing and whose mental form is forethought, whose sensual appearances are packing firm the dirt, deep peaceful sleep, and, occasionally, becoming intoxicated with life's pleasures. On the other side of the roll or pocket stands the enemy, freedom of movement, and "the foreign" (these three in secret alliance). The latter consists in chaos, exposure, and the strong probability of loss, but surprisingly also fullness, fantasy, and expansiveness of vision. There is little doubt in the creature's mind that some contiguity exists between these doubled and split terms and fields of activity, though how the two relate almost entirely escapes it. Despite its ceaseless reflections, it seems incapable of reflecting on the larger logic that determines its dwelling and thinking. Nevertheless the creature moves across the divide, through the pocket created by these opposing constellations, and in response to these rolls in its world or worlds, the creature constructs its thought. Moving back and forth across the crease imbues its mental activity with the urgency of decision. Should I choose freedom and exposure outside my burrow or restraint and shelter within it? Should I think or run, plan ahead or stumble blindly after the future? Which shall I call "life"? it seems to ask: disappearing into the heterogeneity of beings on the surface or distinguishing myself radically, ritually, and finally from all others by building my perfect burrow? Am I "he" or "we"? These are the two poles of its "life," and, combined, they drive it toward indecision and mania.

For this creature whose species we are not told, the name for its often frantic, dualistic activity is "thinking," denoted variously over the course of its monologue with the words thinking, understanding, planning, thinking over, and reckoning up.[1] It plans to cross out of its burrow to the upper world, considers the difficulties of returning, calculates the intentions of its enemies, thinks over rebuilding its home, over and over again. Walter Benjamin's experience of reading Kafka is especially apposite for this creature. "One can read Kafka's animal stories for a good stretch without perceiving in the least that they are not about human beings" (*GS* II.2 419). The story grows out of the gesture of thinking; it is a thought-story, a series of thoughts linked together like chambers in the Bau; but let us beware of analogy. Analogical thinking belongs to the ethical world of responsibility, and this text is a meditation on diaspora—albeit through its contrary: a lone creature, alone in its most solitudinous solitude. This, we know from Nietzsche, is the condition for thinking the weightiest thoughts.

But this logic is driven to an absurd point. Always alone, the creature thinks and rethinks everything it has already thought; the cul-de-sac of reflection gives the story its anxious quality. The first line already belongs to this tendency. "I have constructed the Bau and it seems to be a success" (*Ich habe den Bau eingerichtet und er scheint wohlgelungen*) (Kafka *NS II* 576). But it is not a success; there are innumerable problems and potential problems that it must, once again, think out. A pathos of persuasion infects the creature's tone. You must believe me, the creature seems to urge us, in order that I may believe myself. It is more than doubt; it is a lack or an equivocation built into the Bau, a call to rethinking that returns most strongly at moments of seeming success, a call for confirmation, which, in its self-built isolation, the creature can only ask us to provide, we who overhear its narrative. And yet, whom can the solo animal address but himself?

Like the creature's worlds, the story itself cuts in two, rolls back on itself. In years gone by, the creature built the Bau, and it begins its narration by describing the problems with the original construction. Thus from the outset there are two zones: the planning and the evaluation, the research and the development; in intellectual terms, these resolve into: dogma and critique, the usual poles of thought. But the creature goes further. After it builds and after it critiques what it has built, it encounters an insurmountable problem: the onset of *Zerstreuung* and the very difficult thought of distraction. When it falls between these doublets, into the crease, the text in fact moves toward the most extreme repudiation of thought: toward one impossibility of thinking. Let us begin by briefly describing the story's first movement, which goes from construction to rethinking, from planning to critique.

Thinking and Building

Kafka most likely wrote the text in the winter of 1923 in an apartment in Berlin, shortly before his tuberculosis took its last turn. Published posthumously by Max Brod under the title "Der Bau," his second-to-last story remains, though quite long, what you could call a fragment: it breaks off in a perplexing manner at the most intense point of the narrator's crisis, in the second part of the story.[2] The first part begins with a description by an unnamed creature of the house it has built for itself in the earth.

A note: it is best not to think of the Bau as a symbol for thinking or as an analog of consciousness. The construction is a real product of a creature who thinks. This should leave the story beyond the reach of metaphoric readings that seek in every detail something other than what is spelled out there.[3] Nonetheless, the proximity of building and thinking in the logic of Kafka's story is as unmistakable as it is non-metaphoric. Building metaphors have been, of course, popular vehicles for approaching thought, at least in philosophical texts. For Aristotle the builder is analogous to a first cause, Descartes seeks the *fundamentum*, later thinkers build houses of being and language. This is not what happens here. One could say that this story reveals the root of the metaphoric relation in a real relation, the relation between planning and construction. Thinking and building are reciprocally determined, and they result in one type of thinking and, equally, one type of building. The thinking animal builds what it has thought out, and in turn, its Bau or construction sets out the limits of its thinking. The building is limited a priori by thought and thought is limited a posteriori by the building—this is the real relation at stake. At first they seem at least temporally and logically distinct yet one does not want to determine the order of these limitations too hastily. The creature banks on this: that thinking precedes building. After the last meter of wall has been packed firm and the enemy banished, there will be no further need for thought. This is its primal fantasy, and one that drives the project's first phase and the story's first section. In fact, however, building precedes thinking just as much as thinking precedes building. According to its self-narration, when the creature began to think, it was already thinking of a building, a burrow, a Bau. That is to say, its thinking, the way it thought, what thought meant was already conditioned by the project of construction. Project/construction, these are virtually the same. And so, in the story there is no other kind of thinking than thinking about building,[4] although the procedure has at least two phases. The goal had been to build and thinking meant projecting the goal and constructing the steps by which to produce it. Projecting, however, means walling out what does not belong to the plan and defending the plan with teeth and claws from attack, derailment, or decay. Before the first cornerstone was laid, then, the creature's thoughts ran along corridors, shored up walls, closed the entrance behind it. The reciprocity of building and thinking is born, for the creature, in one imaginary fact: that all the while a great enemy is coming to attack it. Building is not an analogy for thought: it is the same thing. Thought and Bau strive for completeness, resist penetration by foreigners and enemies, wish to endure as they are, consolidate their elements, move their inventory around from chamber to chamber, striving ceaselessly to become perfectly impenetrable. Expectation would be the temporal form of both. And yet, it soon becomes clear, the whole complex of thought and building, the furious thought-activity meant to bring about only what has been expected, nothing more or less, also produces something unexpected: dispersal. Thought and building cannot be condensed or solid enough. The Bau extends, thought runs out with it: enemies multiply. In order to become compact, they overextend themselves. When the creature becomes distraught about this unintended dispersion, it laments "the monstrous extension of my Bau" (*NS II* 577). Instead of making it smaller, more thinking-building makes it bigger. In place of security, the creature's almost continual rumination and retrofitting make it more vulnerable. The creature sleeps badly.

You might say building is a stage in the thought of building. The creature plans and then builds according to plan; the act of construction adds but an appendix, albeit in another medium (dirt), to the blueprint. The converse may also be true: thought takes on the traits of the building. Building thinking projects, laying out onto fixed coordinates, carving out a territory from a seemingly impassive medium—non-thought, earth—fixing and firming up barriers against what is alien to it, and protecting the goods—its precepts, prejudices—that it hoards within its innermost rooms. Building thinking violates the heterogeneity of nature with an ordering based on consolidation and exclusion. Common to both extended and intended building (construction and thought) is a single component: the wall. The wall's connective potential Kafka already explores in the "er" fragment, and elsewhere. Here another wall enters the scene: a wall before walls. The most basic roll or pocket in thinking, before the Bau or building or burrow rolls itself up in defense against the surface world, is temporal. All thinking is either planning or retrospective rethinking of what was previously planned. All thought, in other words, is forethought, putting up walls against contingency. One makes a wall to prevent spillage or penetration, but thinking has already built a wall against other forms of thinking, as well as against not-thinking. Before even forethought, then, there is a primordial ante-thought in which the image of thought is decided upon, built up, such that everything after it appears to have been built in from the beginning.

Herein lies the story's major contribution to a theory of thinking. It is best seen in a joke. In the innermost part of the building, the secure room, a building within a building—the so-called *Burgplatz* or castle-keep—the walls have been made firm by a special procedure. "For such a job I have only my forehead," quips the creature (*NS II* 581). The construction of thought is the construction of walls; both heads—forehead and forethought—beat themselves bloody against it. Thought and building wound themselves to stave off the danger of an unwalled future. "So with my forehead thousands and thousands of times all day and night long I hurled myself against the earth, was happy when I beat it until I was bloody, since this was evidence that the wall was beginning to become consolidated [*Beweis der beginnenden Festigung der Wand*]" (*NS II* 581). Consolidation wounds, but the wound is of a higher rank than the injuries one might incur, defenseless, out in the open. There is the open, *das Freie*, above, but also the future to be defended against.

And so the creature dwells almost exclusively in the past, when the contingencies against which it would compress its walls were first imagined. Even contingencies become walls, solidified into expectations. At the time of narration, the present is so thick with the past, there is barely space among the creature's reminiscences for observation of the actual edifice. The Bau becomes a graveyard for a science so nostalgic for the heyday of its promise that it can only repeat old experiments, recall hypotheses, and lament what it failed to predict. Like the possessions the thinker most covets, the corpses of lesser beasts it has killed and on which it nourishes itself, the Bau, a storehouse for the macabre fruits of the past, radiates an unmistakable scent that, the creature fears, will make it vulnerable to a single, total attack (*NS II* 593). This is the scent of absolute forethought.

Thinking is building without materials, to adapt a phrase from Mallarmé. And so we can reduce the terms of the argument to three: the options available to the creature are pre-building, building, and rebuilding. There is little else. Even the realm of nature, the forest on the surface above the burrow, although it seems to be the contrary of the construction, has its meaning so thoroughly determined by the Bau that it seems to have been built itself by unseen claws. Nature is erected to be heterogeneous, free, open, visible, with an almost infinite spread of danger across all beings, places, and events. It is the purely unbuilt, *der Unbau*. What lies below, as well, is only conceivable in reference to building-thinking. Thus the earth outside the burrow is, according to the creature, clearly another burrow belonging to the enemies. "These are creatures of the inner earth, not even legend can describe them, even those who have become their victim have hardly seen them, they come, one hears the scratching of their claws right under one in the earth, which is their element, and one is already lost. Here it is not valid to say that one is in one's house, rather, one is in their house" (*NS II* 578). Everything is a house. And so the creature lives between the construction of the master builder, the perfect physiocrat dwelling beneath it from whom it robs a corner for its nook, and the inbuilt unbuilt above it to which it vainly longs, at times, to escape and throw off the burden of building-thinking. So thoroughly determined by building-thinking and thinking-building is the creature that, when it does finally go up to the surface—this should come as no surprise—it experiences nothing but a more intensified thought of the Bau it has just left.

Complications of Bau Life

Thinking and building are just as much walling out as walling in, against incursions as much as against dissipation. Walls accomplish the double goal of excluding foreign elements and consolidating possessions. The obsession with walls is justified by an image of a counter-builder. "I live in peace in the innermost part of my construction and in the mean-

time my opponent bores slowly and quietly from somewhere toward me"
(*NS II* 577). The ante-thought or image that paves the way for thinking-
building depicts an enemy that will disturb the peace and destroy the
building *from the outside*. Before it is even built, this is the motivating in-
stinct. The thought of building arises from the thought of an enemy who
will be a direct competitor and counterforce to the builder. Building thus
has its source in an image of total destruction by another exactly like me.
The wished-for sanctity of the individual originates in an enemy's attack,
and life begins from a projection of an image of violation of the proper
and the possessed. It should be stressed that this situation is the norm for
a creature that builds and thinks. It is not paranoia, but *noēsis* that anticipates an end, establishes a project, walls out annihilation, inhabits its
walls, owns it possessions, and circles twitchily around its wall, awaiting
violation.

There is a standard or measure for the success of building-thinking. The state of mind and the sensory condition that correspond to this
paranoid political construct are peace and quiet. Interpreting the foreigner (*der Fremde*) as the enemy (*der Feind*) contrasts peace and quiet
with their contraries, war and noise. Not all sounds are the sound of
an invasion of course. Certain heterogeneities can be absorbed into the
construction. The rustling (*Rascheln*) of the little harmless creatures (*das
Kleinzeug*) that move through its walls as if they were air, along with
the trickling (*Rieseln*) of water through the soil, confirm, rather than
disturb, the stillness and sanctity of the Bau. These pose no threat. The
main mark of the successful Bau (" . . . er scheint wohlgelungen") is the
particular stillness that indicates that the walls have not been breached
(*NS II* 579). "The quiet that rules here unchanged day and night" (*NS
II* 580) is the sensory evidence upon which the creature remarks again
and again. It is of course also true that enormous efforts are required to
maintain the silence as well as the belief in silence. Silence is the absence
of evidence, not proof that there is no enemy. And so, in the center of
the Bau, in the *Burgplatz*, the creature retires to become drunk on the
rotting flesh it has piled up, its drunkenness in fact an anaesthetiza-
tion (*Selbstbetäubung*) deriving from the experience of a full, successful
completion of the plan of building, the faultless transition from thought
to Bau, full possession of the possessions it protects, and the silence that

proves it all (*NS II* 585). Intoxicated by seclusion among its possessions, in this moment, however, the inverse relationship becomes all the more clear: this may be the moment before the big attack. In center of the center, let us say, right in the very unmediated possession of its things—life is the most precarious. In the most peaceful moments the creature is the most anxious; it repeatedly bolts awake "out of deep sleep": the thought of an intruder pursues it (*NS II* 580).

From the *Burgplatz* where it identifies completely with its possessions, it can proclaim that the entire Bau is "equally quiet and empty" and can abandon itself to homogeneous silence, believing, for a while, that this is the sign of the lack of a source (*NS II* 601). In this perfect union of Bau and creature, thinking becomes superfluous, or so it seems. It confirms: "it would not be at all necessary to make clear to myself through contemplations what the Bau means to me, I and the Bau belong together" (*NS II* 601–2). At the center of the Bau then the creature can dare to practice a kind of not-thinking. Insofar as the construction is totally successful there, which is to say that the building and the pre-building perfectly coincide, precluding rebuilding (rethinking), no thought is necessary, or indeed possible, by this model at least. This is what the word "castle" means. When it sits in its central stronghold, "then," it avers, "the thought of security lies far from me, then I know precisely that here is my castle . . . my castle that in no way can belong to anyone else and which is so very much mine that when all is said and done I can even calmly embrace here the fatal wound from my enemy, since here my blood [*Blut*] seeps into my own soil [*Boden*] and does not get lost" (*NS II* 601). The grim joke about the relation of death and nationalism, whether about Zionism or about German or Czech patriotic movements, or both, should not be missed here. Soon after this scene, the will to total peace, endless time (*NS II* 604), absence of change, pure sameness unmixed with foreign things, in short the whole dialectic of the Bau begins to buckle under its own weight. The thinker stands before a choice. Total protection in the central stronghold produces too much of a sense of security that thought becomes superfluous. This is in fact the most dangerous situation; the closed center of the Bau is the most radically susceptible to attack. The alternative, partial protection in the manifold of plazas that stretch outward from it, brings its own difficulties. "The multiplicity of the Bau gives me therefore more multiplicitous possibilities," it remarks (*NS II* 582). But multiplicity opens the Bau to small incursions in the outer extremities, even though a single attack could not demolish all the extremities at once. The Bau, though perhaps not as unruly as "the free" above it, is nevertheless itself double, rolled over on itself; it is centralized and dispersed at once. An internal battle rages within building-thinking. Gathering is dangerous because all your possessions may be decimated at once; yet it offers at least the possibility of total defense. Dispersal is dangerous because possessions may be picked off one by one, and no concerted defense is possible. "It is indeed dumb but true that self-assurance suffers when one does not see all the inventory together and so knows with one single glance what one possesses" (*NS II* 584) . There is almost no need to posit an exterior world of foreignness. The enemy, so to speak, is within, is *the* within.

Continually proofing the foundations of its edifice, the creature—most likely a mole[5]—becomes part of the tradition of self-critique that runs from Kant to Nietzsche (both of whom, it should be noted, use moles to represent this "Untersuchung").[6] The only answer to failed thinking is more, better thought, rebuilt from the foundation up. All extrinsic actions done to the Bau are in fact intrinsic to its system. This is the logic of self-critique; it is the logic of a trap. Conversely, however, all movements intrinsic to the Bau also have an extrinsic component that its logic cannot quite capture. In the creature's vocabulary: the *Ausgang* is also an *Eingang*. "I have constructed the Bau and it seems to be a success" (*NS II* 576). The "it seems" (*es scheint*) in the first utterance of the creature's report now appears to be an incredible self-deception. Where the creature attributes any difficulty to "an error in the Bau" that it can now, through better forethought, correct, we can now attribute the difficulties to its desire for total security arising from the fantasy of an exactly opposite and equal enemy, against whom it thinks/builds in total isolation and pure thought (*NS II* 584). Seeking to protect its purity, pure thought runs ahead, turns against and infects itself, invents a threat, and attacks itself in order to keep up the defensiveness that has become its nature. Then *noēsis* becomes paranoia. In short, the story is a farce. "Der Bau" seems to be a paean to pure reflection, the story of a creature with unrivaled powers of thought that thinks ceaselessly and "successfully." But this hyperbolic image of thinking soon appears obsessive, exaggerated, and dangerous to the creature itself.[7]

The Artist's Clear Eye

Written almost two decades before the Bau fragment, one of the few documents that survives from Kafka's early literary activity gives some clues about his interest in and understanding of a counterpoint to thinking, a suspension of the intellect, something that might be called *Zerstreuung*. The critique of "pure thought" that reaches a climax in the Bau fragment had one beginning sometime after February 1906, while he was in the last stages of completing his law degree, when he made a list of five points on the relationship of art to consciousness. According to Max Brod, who preserved them, the points were written in response to two articles Brod had published under the joint title "Zur Ästhetik."[8] While rejecting almost all of Brod's ideas—for instance, Brod's equation of aesthetic beauty with "newness" Kafka turns down unreservedly—over the course of the five points, Kafka develops a rigorous defense of something like not-thinking or distraction as the proper experience of art. Let us summarize his refutation of Brod, as it is printed in Kafka's *Nachlaß*. The text begins with the reproachful words: "One must not say" (*Man darf nicht sagen*):

> "*a* one must not say: only the new image awakens aesthetic pleasure" (*NS I* 9). Kafka proposes that this argument, made by Brod in his articles on aesthetics, is wrong. Aesthetic pleasure, he counters, is in fact awakened by a *Vorstellung*—an idea, image, representation—which does not come into contact with the sphere of the will: "our sphere of willing is not touched." New things are willed things, this implies. In a Schopenhaurian register, what the will wills is always something as of yet not attained, something new. Because it is not touched by the will, the aesthetic image, extra-voluntary, unwilled, or inadvertent, relates neither to plans for the future nor to the rejection of old possessions. Thus, we must not call it new.

> "*b* It would be necessary to explain more thoroughly, or actually to explain at all, 'aesthetic apperception,' an expression perhaps not introduced until this point." Kafka mentions the technical term

Brod used, "apperception," which, although it is probably Leibniz's invention, is most likely drawn here from Brentano's empirical psychology. This "aesthetic apperception" is questionable for Kafka if it is equated only with the lust for newness. How does it differ from other kinds of apperception? Its pleasure cannot be the same as the pleasure caused by new things that strike consciousness, such as scientific discoveries or news from a foreign land—things that might be objects of willing. Insofar as consciousness is identified with the will, art and the faculty that receives it, aesthetic apperception, are not part of conscious thought. But this does not mean that they belong to an unconscious, least of all to a Freudian version.

"*c* The chief evidence for the new perspective is a general physiological, not merely aesthetic, fact, and that is exhaustion" (*NS I* 9). Brod shows that aesthetic apperception, the mode for receiving art, is aimed toward the new by nesting it within a general image of modernity as a quickly shifting milieu. By this logic, however, everything exhausts us in modernity, not just art. Art must exist differently than other apperceptual data. Art may exhaust us, exhaust our apperception, exhaust consciousness, but not for the reason that Brod suggests. This description of the velocity of modern life bores Kafka in 1906. It is not because, like other objects, it comes and goes quickly that art exhausts consciousness, but rather because it presents an object that is off balance (*der Gegenstand hat das Gleichgewicht verloren*) (*NS I* 10). The will to newness is a kind of enthusiasm for the most recent past (*Liebhaberei der knapp vorhergehenden Zeit*). An art object does not rush by, causing us to lust after it and to renew our will in it; rather, the object itself tips over, goes off-kilter, such that it cannot be apperceived as a regular object. Art exhausts apperception in this way: it presents a relation to objects that apperception, thought, cannot receive. Kafka adds: it loses its balance "in the bad sense" (*undzwar im üblen Sinn*) (*NS I* 10).

"*d* Is there a difference between aesthetic and scientific [*wissenschaftlichen*] people" (*NS I* 10). Given that objects are out of kilter and consciousness itself is what is exhausted, Kafka notes the need to ask whether aesthetic human beings therefore differ from scientific human beings. In the next point Kafka affirms that there is indeed a difference.

"*e* The concept 'apperception' is what remains uncertain" (*NS I* 10). Most surprising is the last of these somewhat cryptic points or notes, which reveal as much about Kafka's thinking about art at the time as they do about Brod's limitations. In the last point, Kafka claims that, perhaps because of an art object's tendency to exhaust thought by changing the nature of objects, there is in fact no such thing as "aesthetic apperception." In fact, apperception cannot be a concept in aesthetics at all. This cannot be proven, he claims, only illustrated. "Maybe it can be presented like this" he writes (*NS I* 10). There follows a parable. Say Kafka arrives in Prague as a foreigner. If he wants to write to Brod, he can ask for his address, receive it, and then he will never need to ask for it again. "Your address is something 'old' for me; this is how we apperceive science" (*NS I* 11). If he wants to actually visit Brod, however, he must ask the way again at every corner and crossing, "always always ask, never will I be able to dispense with passersby, an apperception is completely impossible here" (*NS I* 11). This is the way art is received. Possessing the address means never visiting and visiting means being dispossessed repeatedly of the assurance that the apperception of the address gives, or seems to give. Beyond the comfortable fulfillment of a desire for the new, art slips past the will, and thought as well, neither old nor new, non-consciously. This procedure, the repeated dispossession of consciousness when confronted with the strangeness of the empirical, as we shall see, reflects the non-conscious attitude that artworks are supposed to produce in the spectator. To lighten the mood, or to appease Brod's ego, he ends with a joke—of course, he might become tired or give up altogether, but still, in the face of an artwork, he would still not have apperceived.

The main technical terms of these theses on art and thought (here abbreviated and paraphrased by me) like the terms of Brod's articles to which they apparently respond—*Vorstellung, Appercepzion, das Ästhetische,* among others—are most likely taken from Brentano's descriptive psychology, as it was practiced and taught by his students and followers in Prague, from whom Kafka and Brod had ample opportunity to absorb the science's lexicon. They both attended Anton Marty's and Christian von Ehrenfels' lectures at the university, but perhaps more importantly, they both frequented talks and discussions at meetings of the Brentanist group at the Café Louvre.[9] That Brod is thinking of this set of terms and the force with which his teachers—the more orthodox of Brentano's followers—and this group disseminated them is likely. Whether Kafka was addressing the Brentanists directly or just his friend Brod, his conclusion nevertheless challenges Brentanist doctrine in at least one crucial respect. The new science of the psyche can do nothing for the theory of art, since unlike perhaps every other sphere of knowledge or life, art does not "touch" consciousness, at least insofar as consciousness remains tinged with will. When he says that apperception "as we know it, is not a concept of aesthetics," Kafka opens a discussion on the limitations of consciousness as he and Brod and others in their milieu knew it (*NS I* 10). Good students of Brentano knew consciousness, and its technical synonym, the word that had become popular in empirical psychology, "apperception," as the minimum awareness necessary to notice what one is thinking and that one is thinking that accompanies every thought-act. This minimum of mental activity founds the new science of descriptive psychology. Without it, the science cannot operate. If, according to Kafka, "apperception" plays not the slightest role in "aesthetics," two questions immediately arise. What human capacity, if any, does belong to aesthetics as Kafka sees it? It seems almost impossible to imagine a faculty, useful for art theory, that made no contact at all with consciousness. Art would be for the mad, the comatose, or the sleeping, but not for thinkers. And the second question: is there an activity of which Brentanists were perhaps unaware, another way to construe human capacities that might become a methodological touchstone for art theory?[10]

Descriptive psychology's view of art is not fully spelled out. Neither Brentano's early *Psychologie vom empirischen Standpunkt* nor the partial transcripts of Anton Marty's lectures go into detail about aesthetic matters. Both, however, include aesthetics among the disciplines that will be revolutionized once the science of consciousness is fully worked out. In an introductory session to Marty's lecture course from the year after Kafka took it—the year for which a full transcript has survived—Marty insists that descriptive psychology will serve as the groundwork (*Grundlage*) for many disciplines, among them: "aesthetics, pedagogy, ethics, logic, philosophical political science" (Marek and Smith "Elemente" 54).[11] Brentano had gone further, though also without elaborating. "I indicate only fleetingly how the roots of the aesthetic lie in psychology, roots which, with a fuller development, will unerringly clear the artist's eye and secure his progress" (*Psychologie vom empirischen Standpunkt* 30). How both the production and theory of art will be more securely grounded once its rootedness in the science of consciousness is fully demonstrated is not explained. We can infer the nature of the wished-for psychological grounds for aesthetics, however, from the goals of descriptive psychology and the foundation it is supposed to offer other spheres. It clears, as Brentano puts it, the artist's eye, and what's more, it does so unerringly. The clear, unerring eye corresponds to an insight into the structure of consciousness and a new kind of truth that descriptive psychology claims to provide.

The truth descriptive psychology's "clear eye" wants to extend also to aesthetics is the self-evidence and certainty with which inner experience is perceived, or as Brentano calls it, apperceived. Apperception of inner experience is not prone to error, at least to the extent that now, with the new science, apperception does not differ at all from its object. This is where we can see Kafka take exception. An object that loses its balance jars loose from the apperception of it, differs from the thought of it. For Brentano, apperception is modeled on perception, and yet it solves the problems that beset perception from antiquity onward. At a distance a camel appears to be a horse, the tree on the horizon might be a mirage; the clear eye sees through these illusions, not because it sees the truth behind appearance, but because it dispenses with objective truth and replaces it with the truth of appearance. This inner vision, apperception, accepts the mistaken vision of a horse and the mirage as true images. Brentano makes a crucial distinction that allows perception to become truth. "Inner perception," the doctrine goes, is always true (*wahr*), whereas outer perception (*äußere Wahrnehmung*) is subject to error, illusion, distortion, and so forth. Inner perception is true because it recognizes the error, illusion, and so forth, the varying qualities of psychic acts, as the truth of experience. Anton Marty, whose introductory course Kafka attended, calls it "inner experience" (*in-*

nere Erfahrung), the new science's highest truth (Marek and Smith "Elemente" passim). One can only imagine Kafka's reaction to a statement like the following: "The laws of descriptive psychology can come to have a completely exact organization, they are valid without exception" (Marek and Smith "Elemente" 53). Here is a much more far-reaching law than the Bohemian legal code that Kafka would later study. If he had wanted to become a philosopher he would have had to serve this other, more imperious law code, that was furthermore, unlike the Law, not susceptible to critique, or for that matter crimes. And although he did not continue in philosophy, the suggestion of a "psychology without soul," as Brentano put it, quoting Albert Lange (*Psychologie vom empirischen Standpunkt* 16), must have interested Kafka, since, if there is a psychological aspect to Kafka's fiction, it makes no reference to a soul. Brentano and his students taught the soulless science as a series of axioms. The first axiom states that inner perception is always true, since what it perceives it perceives as being a perception, that is, it apperceives the perception in exactly the way that such and such appears to consciousness. What appears is true in whatever way it appears, partial, fictive, hazy, as fantasy, et cetera. Internal clarity and certainty are possible for what is externally neither clear nor certain. Another axiom states that thought is a set of thought-acts directed toward objects, thinking is always thinking something, and intentional objects are true because nothing more is required of them than that they be those things which thought intends, and this, by definition, they are. There is still of course a discrepancy between external and internal perception, but the difference only serves to confirm the mastery of the inner sense and the primacy of this mentalized experience.

"Inner perception" or "inner experience" raised to universality is "apperception." As Marty defines it in the lectures, apperception is "an explicit conceiving [*explizites Erfassen*] or a recognizing judgment [*anerkennendes Beurteilen*] of that which is already implicit in perception, what was already contained in mere perception [*in der bloßen Wahrnehmung*]" (Marek and Smith "Elemente" 58). This description Marty seems to have copied from a series of Brentano's notes, which were published posthumously under the title *Deskriptive Psychologie*. Brentano's notes contain a long section on apperception under another name "noticing" (*Bemerken*), where he claims to resolve a contradiction that beset his book on empirical psychology. In the earlier book he had to deny positivistic science a foot-hold in consciousness by denying the primacy of physical processes. At the same time, he had to allow the new science of apperception to develop a method that was different from the physical sciences, though equally dependable, for investigating psychic structures. In this spirit he tends to propose ironclad laws for the science. "It is a universally valid psychologi-cal law that we never are capable of paying attention [*Aufmerksamkeit*] to the object of inner perception" (*Psychologie vom empirischen Standpunkt* 41). This is a crucial but also a dangerous assertion, and also diametrically opposed to the assumptions of then budding cognitive science. What, if not "Aufmerksamkeit," will provide access to inner perception, such that its truth can be made available to the psyche's science? He is unable to pro-vide a satisfactory answer. If apperception cannot be directed and focused in the manner of "attention," there seems to be no way of confirming the science's justification and raison d'être. The difficulty of finding a solution to this problem is signaled in a subsequent statement. Here, Bren-tano seems to require the very "Aufmerksamkeit" that he earlier banned. "Turning attention toward psychic phenomena in the imagination" is the "epistemic source" (*Erkenntnisquelle*) for all psychic laws (*Psychologie vom empirischen Standpunkt* 41–42). "Aufmerksamkeit" must be banned since it is the single mode of perception recognized in positivistic science and as such it represses all the others, yet here it returns to become the one and only source for psychic laws. Brentano wants to banish it because of its relation to the "genetic" sciences and their monoptical view of sensation, and yet he cannot disentangle himself from the methodological exigencies of science per se. Coarsely put, the methodological requirement is that one be able to look at what one wants to see. Kafka's distinction between scientific people and aesthetic people intervenes here. Aesthetic people, for him, cannot and do not see what they want to look at, but rather, the object puts their looking askew. In order to guarantee access to psychic events, Brentano, in contrast, moves toward attention as a paradigm, even though attention reduces all psychic events to one kind of event.

This is the double-bind handed down by this first teacher of phe-nomenological method—you cannot pay attention, you must pay at-tention. It causes the short circuit in the science for which the idea of distraction appears as a remedy in those thinkers who are influenced by, yet depart from, the fundamental problems of phenomenology. Heidegger and Benjamin respond to the double-bind, but Kafka does as well. Husserl develops the eidetic and phenomenological epochēs in response as well, and yet his will be another attempt to develop a kind of attention in an arena in which attention should be prohibited. Heidegger will criticize Husserl for remaining trapped in the "theoretical" mode (and Levinas will support this assessment in his thesis on Husserl's notion of evidence). Heidegger later returns to the dilemma when he calls for a turn away from *Zerstreuung* toward the ontological difference, which on the surface at least comes dangerously close to attention once again. When he turns to the problem of method in the notes that become *Deskriptive Psychologie*, Brentano goes to the heart of the matter. He identifies *Aufmerken*, like other basic terms in contemporary perceptual psychology as well as in the ongoing traditions of German philosophy, as overburdened with will. And so, for *Aufmerken* he substitutes *Bemerken*. Apperception could never will a direct view of the object; this would turn apperception into attention, the same one-to-one perception of outer objects that positivistic science demands, only now turned on inner objects, which would, in turn, disintegrate under its fixed gaze. This is the mistake made by Wundt in his empirical psychology, in Brentano's estimation. Apperception had to be qualitatively unlike outer perception, since what was to be received, perceived, or apperceived was the specific mode of perception and not a free-floating object, independent of thought. This faculty could not be described as an internal, purposeful turning-toward of a direct intellectual gaze. This is the source of Brentano's later rejection of Husserl's *epochē*: it was too willful. As a tool of science therefore Brentano's *Bemerken* is quite subtle: "noticing" in apperception means barely noticing, virtually unwillingly registering the way in which something appears in experience. If it were attention, Brentano remarks, it would turn all experiences into objects of attention, which is exactly the mistake the science of experience is designed to avoid (*Psychologie vom empirischen Standpunkt* 41). All shades of vision are allowed: delicate impressions, blurred sights, the half-seen and the barely imaginable, error, illusion, art, and so on. Moreover, it is not only a spatial receptivity to modalities of appearance, but also a temporal one. An "inner attention" would pervert appearance because *Aufmerken* directs itself only toward present objects. The targets of this science will include memories, dreams, wishes, fantasies, as well as perhaps as yet unheard-of modalities of human sensibility.

Although the basic activity of the new science cannot be willed, it can be practiced, "geübt." A psychologist needs to undergo "an education in noticing" (*eine Ausbildung im Bemerken*) and perhaps this is the training on which Kafka drew when he wrote these points in response to Brod's articles (*Deskriptive Psychologie* 38). It was surely what the others in the circle were practicing and discussing. Kafka catches a problem in Brod's assertions about the psychology of aesthetics that recalls Brentano's rigorous exclusion of attentive thought. At the core of the new method lay a mode of attending to experiences without direct attention that was supposed to preserve their truth, the truth of the way in which they were experienced. The "clear sight" that Brentano wishes for the artist trained in *Bemerken* is in fact oblique. Brentano compares it to trying to see the edges of eyesight (*Deskriptive Psychologie* 38). As indirect as it is unwilled, carried out only after a strict apprenticeship, once it has become skill or habit, or occurring as if in a dream, the method should nevertheless not be confused with no method at all. As much as it cannot be willed, it also cannot be accidental or contingent on anything external to consciousness. This is to say that although it reduces will to a minimum, will cannot be done away with altogether in descriptive psychology. And this is where Kafka steps away from Brentano and from psychology. Without the ability to initiate a scientific act, if one were asleep or disoriented, the practice and its practitioners could simply disappear. This leads Brentano to make note of an important worry. "More important even than exercise in noticing is taking care that there is no exercise in not noticing." Not-noticing, if it were practiced, becomes a wall that a scientist breaks through with difficulty and continual effort; it becomes a kind of "second nature" and introduces the natural attitude back into the work. The highest danger is distraction with regard to "inner" events and a return to mere empiricism, invasion by the "outer" (*Deskriptive Psychologie* 39). In this way the descriptive psychologist balances on a tightrope stretched between apperception, willing to the smallest degree, and anapperception, drowning in *Vorstellungen* over which she has no control. Yet it is just such a lack of control and a return to "outer perception" that marks the reception of artworks for Kafka. Art is received, it seems, when it escapes notice completely.

It only counts as received when one has to look at it again at every turn and ask, perhaps, how is one supposed to think about it?

Keine Literatur

These very early notes on the incompatibility of art and consciousness, in the motivation for them and even in their object, seem to stand far from the famous reflections on literature that Kafka entered in his diary at the end of 1911. There, in three obviously interrelated but separately written fragments, he explored the relationship between literature and consciousness—in this case, what he calls "national consciousness"—in a tone that at first hearing seems quite positive. In the first fragment he says outright that literary work has the great advantage of setting minds in motion, drawing the often divisive strands of national consciousness together into a unity, binding together unsatisfied elements and restricting national attention to the interior of its own circle, such that anything foreign appears not as itself but as a shadow across the domestic image (*Tagebücher* 312–13). It is, however, somewhat surprisingly, "bad literature" that best accomplishes these things. "This kind of literature is actually livelier than one full of talented writers," since the great author hinders the widest distribution of literary activity (*Tagebücher* 314). Bad literature, in this fragment, may be equivalent to the "aesthetic beauty" that Brod equated with "the new" in the article whose premises Kafka challenged in 1906. And this is understandable, art that is new is new art, that is, it changes nothing in the idea of art and does not ruffle national consciousness. An aesthetic *Vorstellung* challenges neither consciousness's authority nor its underlying rhythm of change, absorption, rejection, alteration. . . . A nation's self-reflection in bad literature is not weaker but stronger in small nations, Kafka continues, where the national self-image depends all the more on the few works and even fewer literary figures it produces. Here the pressure for literature to aid and abet the small national consciousness in its David-like effort to resist foreign Goliaths is almost too great to withstand. This demand and this resistance is the "creative and happy-making power of a literature that is bad in its details" (*Tagebücher* 314). As often happens, a "power" that makes people happy makes Kafka anxious. The *Kraft* or power to create

"Litteratur" written here with a double "t," the power to create bad literature whose only task it is to bind a nation through consciousness of what is
its own Kafka handles here hesitantly, in ambiguous phrases like this, such
that one cannot say at first whether Kafka holds that the effects of "bad
litterature" are bad or good. We should remember that these diary entries
are exploratory, experimenting, in no way definitive, and not always representations of convictions or developed arguments. Like many other of
his diary entries and notebook fragments, he explores a set of ideas here in
their first outpouring, without editing; then he moves on, often returning
to the ideas later, but when they are often already transformed. There is no
doubt that the reflections are critical in nature, aimed at the institutions
and the process of institutionalization of a particular time and place. The
examples he gives, the Czech literature with which he is somewhat familiar and the Yiddish literature that his friend Itzhak Löwy knows best, seem
as though they would benefit the questionable political futures of their respective "small nations."

What becomes apparent in the second entry a few pages later is that
even for small nations bad literature has a deleterious effect on national
consciousness over time. Even more powerful when it seems to issue from
dead authors, old bad literature produces a "Befangenheit," a bias toward
the straightforward (*ehrlich*) that quickly turns to reverence and awe (*Ehr-
furcht*) (*Tagebücher* 321). From producing an uncritical attitude that easily
turns to worship, literature soon begins to narrow and stultify. In the end
literature becomes indistinguishable from politics, the primary proof of
this being the similarity between bad literary works and political slogans.
Polemical, direct, even aggressive speech, which Kafka compares to curse
words (*Schimpfwörter*), plays a small role in great literature; in bad literature it dominates. So hyperbolic does it become that every line of every
novel seems to present a life and death decision. What this exaggeratedly
and cheaply political literature forbids, in its all-out bid to win the attention of the nation through an emphatic tone and propagandistic style,
is the exhaustion proper to good art.[12] Bad literature lets "no exhaustion
arise" (*keine Ermüdung aufkommen*) (*Tagebücher* 321). A perpetual motion
machine at the center of national consciousness, bad art, polemical, propagandistic art has a stimulating effect. No one will ever tire of this art
form, the slogans, hot-headed headlines, thin words calculated to whip

readers into a frenzy—and this psychological attachment, really a lack of possibility for detachment, preserves the unity of consciousnesses that insures the nation's intensity and continuity.

Only in the context of these two entries can the third entry appear in the proper light. This is the famous "Schema toward a Characteristic of Small Literatures" (*Tagebücher* 326). What he calls here "kleine Litteraturen" are *keine Literatur*, or at least *keine Kunst*, according to his earlier definition in his rebuttal to Brod. "Small literatures" is another name for what he formerly called "schlechte Litteratur." The "creative and happy-making force" of bad literature that binds national consciousness becomes, over time and after its success, a universal pleasure at the literary handling of "small themes" that require no more than "a little enthusiasm" on the part of readers for upkeep of the intransigent mentality that depends on them. Small literatures comport perfectly with political slogans in a decadent age, and this is precisely the difference between Kafka's concept and its distortion by Deleuze and Guattari in their 1975 book. "Minor literature" may be a revolutionary force; "small literature" in contrast is the very bedrock on which the thoughts of a nation perpetuate themselves. And yet, the current situation is also the starting point for an art that transforms these relations. The transformation is literary, not social or linguistic, as Deleuze and Guattari envision. To this end Kafka makes a list of bad literature's "better" characteristics. That he intends to list effects (*Wirkungen*) here that are not simply "good," like the effects he catalogued in the other two fragments, but even "better," has to be understood—to risk repeating—as the betterment of a very bad situation from within its bad horizons. Good means bad, better means, in effect, worse, but worse is the way out, for Kafka. Out of an art that has become indistinguishable from consciousness, an art that no longer enters through distraction and so is no longer art, Kafka begins to catalogue existing good effects (from the perspective of consciousness) that point toward better ones (from the perspective of distraction, and re-politicization). In doing so he screws together the skeleton of another art out of the bones of the nation's desiccated cultural corpse. He writes a list of the potentially positive dialectical moments in the current aesthetic standstill.

No one ever tires of bad literature, just as today perhaps no one tires of television, and this represents its great potential. For many of the elements

that Kafka praises in small literatures—conflict, the prevalence of maga-
zines, unprincipledness, easy establishment of symbols (*Streit, Zeitschriften,
Principienlosigkeit, leichte Symbolbildung*)—flaunt their exhaustibility. No
one tires of television, maybe, but television's elements—shows, actors,
styles—exhaust themselves continually. These aspects could potentially allow the half-dead art underwriting national consciousness to actually die,
and to keep on dying: this after all is the major symptom of healthy art: it
dies, becomes unusable, goes off-kilter, makes you a foreigner in your own
city. Literature, the one that arises from the most worn-down elements of
ossified "small literatures," will carry its own exhaustion with it. A final
positive moment in the schema of small literatures that Kafka outlines here
under the rubric of "Popularität" is: "Belief in literature, the act of giving
it laws [*ihre Gesetzgebung*] is given over to it" (*Tagebücher* 326). Here the
schema breaks off with a comma. Before it does, however, it becomes apparent that the infallible law that Anton Marty, following Brentano, lays
down for the apperception of thought-acts is not the only law. After the
law of psychological consciousness, which is "always" true "without exception" (*ausnahmslos*), and after the law of national-consciousness in which
no one ever tires of the constant reflection on the same sentiments that
bad literature endlessly serves up to it—where the new is always already
old—another law follows, the law that literature, under the strictest limitation of its sphere of effectiveness, gives to itself. In its self-satisfied dormancy
national consciousness bears a strange fruit. With its defenses worn down
by tradition, it cannot help but believe that what has provided its unity and
stability—culture, literature—will continue to do so. At this moment, at
the height of its stability, consciousness is at its most vulnerable. Literature
undergoes an "unburdening" (*Entlastung*) of the demands made on it by
a national politics that it has supported and made successful—and which
places its full, complacent trust in its literature. In a state where literature has
become absorbed into the political-ideological processes, whereby it comes
to spurn principles and forgo strong symbols, in short, in the very pompos-
ity and reductionism of politics and the weakness and corruption of small
literatures Kafka sees the potential for a literary effect that is not simply
good—does not simply continue to work for the national good—but has,
instead, something better in mind, better than nation, better than mind,
better than good literature that in effect and over time is in fact the worst.

In the critique of Brod, Kafka suggests in closing that Brod think of an artwork as that which cannot be captured once and for all. Art does not correspond to aesthetics. Those interested in art's effects will not be able to simply think about art, since they will not be able to dispense with the next reading, the next work, the next experience. This is a halting and somewhat hilarious version of art reception, a Keystone Kops clip of thinking, complete with half-gestures, misunderstandings, wrong turns, unexpected cul-de-sacs, and the standing possibility of exhaustion. Something essentially empirical in an artwork escapes thought's machine-like digestion. In the schema on small literatures, Kafka proposes another way for art, or in this case literature, to circumvent consciousness. Literature can become inassimilable to consciousness by becoming so fully assimilated that consciousness no longer notices it.

In the Corner

Since at least 1906, Kafka had been interested in art's difference from consciousness and all consciousness implies: unity, permanence, banishment of the foreign, repetition of the old as the new, the primacy of will. Art and literature, as Kafka was beginning to conceive of them—if not also quite yet to practice them—acted as an antidote or a preventative blow against consciousness. Although he does not or cannot yet enumerate the consequences of such a conception, he does try to place art in a position where it cannot be studied by science or received in thought. For Brentano and Brentanists perception and apperception make up the closed system of human cognition. A sphere should be made available in which not-even-noticing can emerge. Through this sphere an object that is not quite an object might enter. Art certainly makes objects, for the young Kafka, but it makes them in an odd way; it makes objects available for release from consciousness, a mode that science cannot comprehend. Similarly, literary artists may take advantage of consciousness's complacency—the aim to fix the world to such a degree that consciousness can become complacent again—in order to turn bad literature into art.

Something like primal distraction thus marks consciousness's limits. There is activity at and beyond this limit; it is simply disunified or distorted, and thus unwanted. Most of all: it does not store, catalogue, maintain, distinguish, and so forth. In the stories he soon begins to write, the word *Zerstreuung* comes to describe this outer limit. You could call it an empirical a priori. Wherever *Zerstreuung* appears in Kafka's fictions—and it is scattered across them—it determines nothing essentially and everything thus finds its limit there. It is not part of the thinking or the action of the characters and plot. It is a side issue, barely mentioned, hardly depicted, and not surprisingly absent from the critical literature on Kafka.

Imagine a geography whose lines lose themselves in snow. In this way *Zerstreuung zerstreut sich* across his oeuvre. Only an eccentric science could map it out. In one tiny tale in the early collection *Betrachtung*, "Distracted Gazing Out" (*Zerstreutes Hinausschaun*) a figure contemplates a scene through a window at the end of a winter day. Everything in the scene is in motion. Spring is coming swiftly, the speaker notes—as swiftly as the shadow of the man that overtakes the young girl happening by outside the window. The setting sun lights her face, but the tension swells as the man approaches her. Then he passes the girl; she hasn't seen him, her face remains bright. Between the girl's childlike ambling and the man's intent gait there is no correspondence. One in the light and the other in shadow, neither takes notice of the other. The narrator either: his cheek leaning against the window clasp, he asks "what will we do in the spring?" This particular type of *Betrachtung* is called "Zerstreutes Hinausschauen" insofar as it does not capture what it sees, and what it sees is a failed encounter between disparate gaits (*Drucke* 24).

At the moment of the most extreme tension between father and son, when the strictly separated segments of the son's existence seem to collapse, Georg Bendemann becomes "fast zerstreut" in Kafka's first Kafkan story, "Das Urteil" (*Drucke* 57). "'But look at me!' the father shouted." The command is not only to look at his father on his bed—now standing upright—in the half-light of his dingy bedroom. The son, a modern day Atlas charged with holding multiple worlds apart—his old father, his friend in Russia, his fiancée, work, East and West, *Judentum* and *Deutschtum*—is forced to gaze on the source of paternal power. Standing on the bed, his father apes the fiancée, hitching up his robe like he imagines she pulled up her skirts for Georg, until he stood "completely free and threw apart his legs. He beamed with insight." The insight beaming in this resplendence for Georg is the blinding disjunction between regions of his life. The friend who promises a break with patrilineal commandment, the lover who promises a family of Georg's own, the eastern Judaism that promised to enliven the tradition, and the inheritance from Noah from whom the prohibition against looking at your father's genitals was first handed down. Between his father's legs Georg sees the origin of sin, or the original clothing of sin where the genitals should be.[13] He retreats to a darker corner. Unlike Freud's version of this biblical scene, in Kafka's version the primal material is not repressed to be repeated later. In *Zerstreuung* nothing is stored. Caught between potentially liberating love for the friend, the chance for generation with the fiancée, as well as an incestuous possibility with the father (psychoanalytic theory strenuously avoids homoerotic incest)—caught between genesis and other, non-genetic paths he barely intuits, Georg "freezes" (*Drucke* 57). From the corner he does not have a better view of the situation—this is no situation, no site; too many places interfere with one another in his father's darkened room. Becoming "fast zerstreut" suspends it all, or almost does. Endless intercourse of traffic over the bridge from which he drops himself soon completes it for him.

While the workings of the punishment machine are being explained to him, the observer who travels to the penal colony has trouble collecting his thoughts ("man konnte schwer seine Gedanken sammeln") (*Drucke* 206). In *The Castle*, K is "zerstreut" when listening to the schoolteacher and the mistress of the inn. When he arrives in the maze of corridors under the *Herrenhoff*, K. succumbs to distraction: "he looked around aimlessly" (. . . *er ziellos umherblickte* . . .) (*Das Schloß* 385). The servant who leads him down seems to be steeped in it: "the more one spoke to this servant, the more absentminded he seemed to become" (*Das Schloß* 385).[14] Georg enters distraction when he can no longer keep separate his disparate desires, but yet can not unify them. K., we could say, becomes a device for the propagation of distraction; wherever he walks thought disappears from the scene.[15]

No Address

Where the Bau—burrow, building, construction—that the creature builds begins and ends, its entrance and exit, its *Eingang* and *Ausgang*, we find a small labyrinth. The creature must snake through it to enter and again to exit. To the extent that it can be represented, described, thought about, conceptualized, or named, this construction lies about its nature; what looks like a labyrinth is not one. This is one of the unspoken morals of the fragment. Seeing it from above—the way in which we almost always picture one—reassures us that it is comprehensible; from a higher perspective it is only a maze, since a labyrinth is precisely the prohibition of a higher perspective. A maze may be an instrument of torture or a teaser for the intelligence. A labyrinth teases intelligence away.

In order to examine Kafka's thought of the labyrinth as expressed here at the beginning of "Der Bau," let us accept the following postulate, partly Kantian but in some aspects exceeding Kant. In the "Transcendental Aesthetic," thought determines space a priori, whereupon space determines all of our experience, insofar as it consists of representations, *Vorstellungen*, of objects in space. Thought contains this division; it is the division, you might say. In Kafka, thought and space are reciprocally determined, which is to say that thinking, what there is of it, is as susceptible to built spaces as space is susceptible to thought. No longer a relation of transcendence, the relation of space to thought and thought to space becomes a dizzying exchange that reaches a peak of complexity in the labyrinth. The tangled corridors of the court are their own kind of trial.

Given this reciprocity, given that space and thought are codetermined, what space would correspond to non-thought? If you refuse to represent it, a labyrinth offers an experience of spacelessness, a freedom in confinement that corresponds to distraction—*Zerstreuung*. It is the closest paradigm, the projection of a mind unable to construct itself, determined by and determining in turn a course without location and direction. Almost any one of the various images of thinking—the Greek brothers forethought and afterthought, but also planning, memory, reflection (*cogitare*), intention (thought-act implying an object, *noein*), calculation (*logizesthai*), the soul's silent conversation with itself, and apperception—becomes senseless inside a labyrinth. Here there are only walls; the path itself becomes a wall. One transcends a horizon, turns a corner, but one cannot pretend to transcend horizons or move beyond corners per se. What's more, a labyrinth teaches this empirically. One can never dispense with passersby.

In the early days of the Bau, the creature thinks that through planning it can build a labyrinth and place it at the entrance to its burrow.[16] Reflecting on this act later, it recognizes this was a cheap trick. "My building began there . . . and my first joy at working ran riot in a labyrinth, which seemed to me at the time to be the crown of all buildings; but today I judge it probably more correctly to be a far too petty patchwork, not truly worthy of the total building [*des Gesamtbaues*]" (*NS II* 586–87).

The Sound of *Zerstreuung*

Returning from the surface to the quiet of its lair, the creature finds, not surprisingly, "everything is unchanged" (*Alles ist unverändert*) (*NS II* 604). As we know, it measures the lack of change in decibels. Quiet is the proof of the integrity of the burrow and consequently of the creature itself. As long as the burrow is quiet, it is peaceful; as long as the peace is uninterrupted, the creature can judge that nothing has broken the peace. Its ear is tuned for interruptions and the quiet thus buzzes with anticipation. The logic of sound runs like this. Change and non-change make up the poles of this logic, and both assume the continued integrity of the underlying idea. A sound is something like a signal sent by the Bau to its owner to warn of a breach; at the same time, even in the event of a breach, it reconfirms the logic. But soon the logic itself will come under attack, and the creature will find this baffling. Despite the fact that "everything is unchanged" the continuity of peace will be undermined. "Everything remained unchanged, the—" is the last line of the story, where it breaks off—"aber alles blieb unverändert, das" (*NS II* 632). For it is not precisely a change that comes but a different monotony. Sleeping, it is awoken by a slight hissing noise.

"A hissing barely audible in itself wakes me" (*ein an sich kaum hörbares Zischen weckt mich*) (*NS II* 606). Thus begins the second part of the story; we have crossed the crease. As we soon find out, the Bau acts as an amplifier that sharpens the creature's hearing. If one had to assign it a shape and an emblem, it would not be a mind, but probably an ear, whose canals, the more they turn around themselves into the depths of the head, expose themselves to what is without. In the end, it is not its perimeter that determines the Bau. Like a true labyrinth, it has no exterior shape, only an experience, and not a transcendentally synthetic one or an "inner experience" that imitates an "outer" vision, but one that repeatedly turns thought out of its house.[17] Experiences, like artworks, correspond to distractions. The creature who builds, dwells, and thinks in the Bau cannot comprehend this logic, however. It has made a mistake, the Bau is not a territory—how could it be? It subsists within the terra. Made out of earth, it is subterritorial. Sight is not the privileged sense at all, and so observation of the Bau, either from without or within, is a gross error. Moles are virtually blind in any case, and in the subterritory there is no light source. When we allow our senses to be sharpened by the story, we notice that the fatuous talk of *Selbstbeobachtung* has to be taken, in the case of the nearly blind mole in a lightless cave, as risible. The Bau, despite its plan—or rather, because of it—is a giant ear; the more convoluted its canals, the more sensitive it becomes to vibration. At times the creature half intuits this fact. "The most beautiful part of my construction, however," the creature rhapsodizes, "is its quiet; admittedly it is deceptive. Suddenly all at once it can be interrupted and everything ends. For now, however, it is still there" (*NS II* 579). Here as well, however, it misinterprets sounds as interruptions to a preexisting, continuous silence. In its greed for booty and its will to total security, the mole, fat capitalist, increases the "monstrous extension" of its Bau, turning the structure into a panacousticon (*NS II* 577).

Yet, instead of becoming focused in the ear, the noise that wakes the creature disperses evenly through the corridors and chambers. We can no more ascertain what the pervading noise is than the creature can. The "hissing barely audible in itself" is spoken of in the strangest terms (*NS II* 606). Already strange is the fact that the hissing causes so much alarm, although it is barely audible. Stranger still is the qualifier "an sich." Throughout the wild "Untersuchungen" that fill the last pages, such naively prophetic utterances frequently escape the creature's lips. It utters what it cannot know, and irony begins to tear at the earnestness of its narrative. When the creature speaks now, it is no longer to narrate the process of construction or to lament its unresolved problems; the present seems to shatter, spilling the tightly held past into the sand. What remains is speculation, speculative digging and speculative arguments; it makes one assumption (*Annahme*) after another (*NS II* 609, 622–623, 627), trying in vain to fit the evidence it gathers, digging and harkening (*horchend*) (*NS II*

606), to the premises it invents. This at least was not in the original plan: the creature destroys the Bau. Destruction is, however, the culmination of the logic of building that we have been laying out.

Zischen is less than a sound. At the very least it cannot become a sound image; it does not represent anything. To make matters worse, the noise cannot be correctly described, sounding "one time like hissing, the next more like whistling" (*NS II* 607).[18] The creature gets "in no way nearer to the place of the noise, it always resounds unchangingly thin in regular pauses" (*NS II* 607). According to the creature's reasoning, no being that it knows of could be the source for the noise. In every guess it makes, some feature goes unaccounted for. The "Stille und Leere" of the Bau is broken by a being it can neither find nor identify, by a sound it cannot receive.[19] The creature remarks more than once, again with blind prescience, that the noise is meant for it alone: it is "only audible by the ear of the real homeowner who is carrying out his office," is its telling conclusion (*NS II* 606). How can it understand a thin, sourceless, continuously discontinuous noise made solely for the builder who dwells in his building, a noise that gives rise to no image, but instead leaps "out beyond all thinkability" (*über alle Vorstellbarkeit hinaus*) (*NS II* 623)?

In the fervor to find a cause, the creature ignores the noise itself, that which exceeds thinking as building. It alone cannot be captured or hoarded. It resists preservation by shifting and pulsing; it cannot be defended against since it is not a single, unified enemy; it comes in to the ear but remains unanticipatable. No better built Bau could prevent its penetration. Rather than penetrate like an enemy it permeates like a *Kleinzeug*, the small fry whose medium is the wall. The territorialist, if that is what the creature is, is terrorized by a previously unheard and unheard of possibility of its own territory, an extreme democratic possibility, we might call it—equally distributed: the sound of *Zerstreuung*. This does not mean that distraction caused it. The noise demonstrates the particular defenselessness one can experience within the most highly defended. Its reverberations dispossess the builder of its Bau while still in it, and in the process form a diaspora without members—a diaspora of one, as it were; an uncondensed thinker. And indeed, attempts to discover the animal that emits the noise, as a builder by dismantling parts of the Bau, and as a thinker by imposing new schemata, come to naught. A truth that escapes the creatures lips makes the stakes of the noise plain. It is like "a nothing to which one could, I won't say, accustom himself, no, to that one couldn't accustom oneself . . . " (*NS II* 615). The weapons of consciousness that Kafka has been imagining since at least 1906, domestication of foreign elements, ceaseless self-reflection, a will to convert the unexpected into the new, fail completely here.

"I am too distracted" the creature whimpers: "Ich bin zu zerstreut" (*NS II* 617). But this is not the moment of greatest distraction, for it can still speak. After this admission it goes on ruminating. Imagining the Hausmannization of the Bau, it plans to cut a single wide gangway through it, to do away with all doubts, and in the process, however, doubling or tripling the danger to itself and its fortress. Gradually the creature develops a messianic theory about another creature digging slowly toward it, whose cryptic plan our creature must now try to decipher (*NS II* 623). Only at the end of the text, where the discourse breaks off mid-sentence, can we say that it, and the writer as well, have abandoned themselves fully to not thinking.

Note on Allegory[20]

For a moment, just before the end, the creature thinks it has solved the riddle of the noise. The noise must in fact originate in a mirror image of itself, in another creature that does exactly what it does. There must be another Bau next door. In the Bau that is another and the same a creature hears our creature stop and start, searches out the cause, scratches at the walls, runs up and down, and stops and starts in its burrow in order to listen to the inexplicable noise of its neighbor.

It is easy to read the Bau as an allegory of the futility of the will to political security and the obsessive thinking that arises from its failure. To some extent this is also the lesson of the earlier story about the Chinese wall. The difference in the Bau fragment is indicated by the *Zischen* that snuffs out thought and reveals a third option, beyond the oppositions of building and destruction, enclosure and freedom, and beyond the equally false fictions of pure homogeneity and pure heterogeneity that support them, that is, beyond the creature's folded way of thinking. In the Bau, a noise drives the creature worse than mad; it makes its thought alternately coherent and incoherent. In distraction, one can no longer distinguish what constitutes danger and what constitutes protection. Now the creature becomes for the first time available for a future that is not only unexpected but more importantly not expectable—a community, a diaspora in the manner in which Kafka envisioned "er" might live. We could live this way too; perhaps we are already doing so.

But we shouldn't leap to conclusions, not based on a story without one. From the first pages of the Bau fragment, the creature's persuasive rhetoric tempts us into identifying with its situation. Faced with the obvious anthropomorphism of a thinking, narrating beast, we draw a personal lesson from the creature's experience.[21] Even now, at the very end, when its experience proves false and its thinking falls apart, we think we have learned a lesson about distraction. Perhaps. But maybe, too, to the very extent that we assimilate the creature to ourselves, we misread and misunderstand it. It sees itself reflected in the neighbor it imagines produces that noise. In the most extreme circumstance, it still assimilates the foreign to its Bau. The mole says: "my imagination will not stay still and I maintain a belief—it is pointless even to deny it—, the hissing comes from an animal" (*NS II* 622–23). It is pointless to deny it: the foreign, insofar as we receive it by thinking, and not in distraction, becomes equal to the same. The last line of the story, echoing a sentiment repeated several times earlier in the story, says: "but everything remained unchanged, the" (*NS II* 632).

The fragment ends here without a punctuation mark; not even an ellipsis to indicate how we should proceed. One presumes the writer could not or would not go on. Perhaps it was late and he was exhausted. The narrator, in this moment, thinks it has finally come into contact with itself: the other-same, its co-diasporist, with whom it remains identical despite and because of the walls that isolate and individuate it. Once it reaches this conclusion, it makes sense to end the search. The creature has come back, after all its wandering, to the beginning. After many circuitous arguments it arrives once more at the thought that the noise can only come from another creature like itself, a Bau builder and thinker that for this reason must also share its fear of the great enemy—one who thinks alike and will also protect its thinking with its teeth. With this image, the fragment stops. Stops, that is to say—but doesn't finish. To assume that this is the revelation toward which the story has been leading may be mistaken. Who can say? The creature comes face to face with distraction and assimilates it once again to consciousness. Perhaps it might have learned something from this if its narrative had gone on. It would have learned, perhaps, that the walls are covered in mirrors. It should come as no surprise then that we too, from the very beginning of the tale, see ourselves reflected there. What is a cogitating, planning, building, story-telling animal but a *zoon logon exon*, an animal possessing reasoned speech, as Benjamin noted? This is how the mole comes toward us, threateningly, where we cower in our closed constructions. As soon as we believe that the fragment is an allegory pointing to us, we are farthest from having experienced it. If we understand it, we build it into our Bau. Or, as we tend to like to do, we move in and make our home in it. Even the irregular, unsystematic, soft, rift-producing noise that triggers the creature's distraction can be made to refer to us and our concerns. Our highest task then, which I have undoubtedly not carried out very well here, is to read "Der Bau" distractedly, without appropriating it for the purposes of self-observation, without walling it out by likening the creature's experience to our own. Our task: to read without thinking, that is, to read it as if it had not been written for us.

CHAPTER 4

Dissipation—Power—Transcendence / Heidegger

It is logical—almost: incipient phenomenology sees consciousness as the unified ground of experience. Experience is experience insofar as it can be reduced to a relation within consciousness, that is, insofar as it can be thought. This schema will be critiqued by a few early students and readers, who begin a search for alternative faculties, dispositions, or modes of relation to appearances that avoid placing a transcendent source for experience in the mind. But this is where the logic of intellectual history—the order of problems and solutions, teachers and students, calls and responses, dogma and critique—begins to falter.

When Kafka denies the possibility of a phenomenological theory of art, arguing that art is received when it does not touch consciousness, he does not critique it. The critique of thought by thought is no longer appropriate. Instead he is intent on showing what can occur in distraction, in not-consciousness. Reception beyond awareness then becomes part of a larger project to discover and describe ethical and political relations not based on intimacy and perceived sameness, without a continuous medium. Reports of a non-conscious community, a diaspora not collected in thought, must be made in a medium that does not pervert its message, in a communication not intended to be cognized. To address it requires an unthinkable non-communication for a non-faculty. Only a kind of writing whose effect is to minimize thinking, rather than increase it, could correspond to the demands of a "life" lived in a dispersal so constant that no reflective access to it is possible. The one illusion about distraction that can be removed, in other words, is the illusion that it has a cognizable source, and Kafka attempts to remove this illusion in the late story fragment "Der Bau."

An interesting repetition of this problem, but also an inversion of it, occurs in Heidegger's writings of the late 1920s. In the analytic of Dasein, existence is dissipated and existents are distracted from dissipation, the source of existence. Dasein is distracted from the fact of having been originally dissipated and living in that dissipation. In *Being and Time* as in Kafka's fragments and "Bau" story, the fact of not-thinking appears in a mode that is other than or less than pure thought. Heidegger is not concerned specifically with art or fiction, but with quotidian modes such as circumspection, what "one says," chatter, curiosity, ambiguity—in more general terms, falling and thrownness. For Heidegger, existents find themselves thrown into a situation they did not make, dispersed into non-originary modes of relation to things, and falling into distraction about it. Heidegger's response to this scenario in *Being and Time*, however, is to seek a way out. Granted, the way out is to go more deeply in—into the phenomenal structure of existence. It is true: the process of philosophizing is supposed to reorient existents toward their dissipation, not in any way to deny it or remove it. This constitutes an advance over metaphysical escapes. And yet, although Heidegger urges readers to reorient themselves toward the dissipating tendency, this orientation itself, the main disposition of the philosopher practicing fundamental ontology, is supposed to be less than dissipated.

"And"

In the book that begins with the question of being and moves toward the response "time," one question is missing: the one that quests after the little word "and." For a method, Heidegger's, in which trivialities often indicate the most important structural elements, this little word should at least rate comment. Indeed it escapes Heidegger's notice for a time, and then in a lecture course the year following the book's publication, he acknowledges having neglected to consider it directly, and corrects this oversight. "Being is understood in relation to time, but the problem of this relation of being and time is the 'and'" (*Anfangsgründe* 182). Unobtrusive as it is, this most quotidian of syncategoremes provides the only link between the two projected parts of the book, as well as between the two perhaps most misunderstood concepts in the history of philosophy. All along, Heidegger admits now, the "and" was what had to be interpreted. An analysis follows. Even the missing third division on time does not threaten the coherence of the book as much as the unaddressed "and." Masking rather than illuminating, "and" is a place-holder for something that not only lacks an interpretation but moreover does not seem to need one. It marks the place where the transition from time to being would have to be explained. Because it could not be at the time, "and" receded almost completely, and receding, it attracts Heidegger's attention in 1928.

Ontology and its chief tool, the question, are fated to encounter the "and." And so, the question of "and" in *Being and Time* is now seen to define the book's "problem dimension" when Heidegger revisits it with students in the last lecture course he gave at Marburg, in the semester before his return to Freiburg to assume Husserl's chair.[1] Although not treated explicitly in *Being and Time*, one could say that the whole book is an attempt to interpret the little word, and the crowning gesture of the last Marburg lectures is to make this esoteric level of the book explicit. To approach "and," the "Lectures on Logic Starting from Leibniz" ask, among other things, how being can be earlier than beings. That is to say, they ask into being's relation to time, the relation that it fell to the modest "and" to signify and forget. A lot is at stake in this relation. Only when he can show that time is earlier than being can ontology proceed with its questions, with questions that imply an order of origination (being before beings) and an order of implication (beings lead us, by questioning, back to being). Priority and in particular aprioricity are, so to speak, prior to all the operations and thoughts made in fundamental ontology, and time is the guarantor of this order. Said otherwise, "and" names and conceals the problem of transcendence, an ontological (not ontic) operation by which Dasein disperses itself, in advance, among determinate ways of encountering beings. In the Leibniz lectures it has two other names, two synonyms or two co-originating operators, or rather, three. "And" is parallel in the lectures first with "Seinsverständnis," the understanding of being, and then with "Freiheit," the freedom Dasein has to make an *Umschlag*, a revolution in the meaning of being, also called "freedom to ground," "Freiheit zum Grund." Freedom and understanding, in turn, are ground- ed in, mean, or derive their ontological power from one rather mysterious descriptive term that played a clandestine role in *Being and Time*. This term is of course *Zerstreuung*, meaning both dispersal and dissipation, and more. In the last Marburg lectures, *Zerstreuung* becomes the main hope for, if not resolving, then at least describing the most intransigent and up to then invisible problem of *Being and Time*. *Zerstreuung* will become the mode or way of the transcendence left unexplained in *Sein und Zeit*. Thus a version of distraction becomes, paradoxically, the fundament of fundamental ontology. It is also that which conceals this fundament. And so it also has a direct relation to truth. Dispersing and dissipating, *Zer- streuung* indicates something like the movement of ontological dispersal *and* the interpretive modality—dissipation—hides the meaning of being from Dasein. Dispersal-dissipation says precisely how being is earlier than beings and how Dasein misses this fact. But there is a third operation: it also tells a thinker how to arrive at this insight without transcending exis- tence in a traditional sense. A figure of primal distraction, it would seem, becomes the key to philosophizing.

After reading the Leibniz lectures, one is tempted to revise the earlier book's title to something like: "Sein zerstreut sich als Zeit," or "Zeit heißt Seinszerstreuung," since "and" in effect comes to be interpreted as *Zer- streuung*. Being disperses itself as time, time means the dispersal of being, the dissipation of Dasein and its distraction from its fundamental situa- tion. Everything rests on the interpretation of *Zerstreuung*. If, by means of this word, Heidegger can justify the aprioricity of being over beings, then the priority of philosophy over the empirical sciences—or for that matter, art, dreams, fantasy, and so forth—will be assured. No less important and intimately interrelated with this objective: *Zerstreuung* insures the coher- ence and co-belonging of the existential moments that Heidegger describes in the analytic. Existence is *zerstreut*; this is its structure. Moreover, the fact that we are so distributed into our habits that they blind us to other potential ways of being, not to mention to our fundamental freedom for self-interpretation, our abyssal "freedom to ground"—all this can become apparent to us through a correct understanding of dispersal-distraction.

Mighty Dissipation

Let us proceed from this insight: a problem blocks the progress of *Being and Time* and the seminars held just after the book's publication. It is not clear at first that distraction caused the problem, but a German word historically connected with distraction comes up again and again alongside it. Derrida begins to unearth the connection in his reading of *Zerstreuung* as sexual difference, which the word and topos sometimes mean in the 1928 Marburg lectures on logic. Heidegger himself, as Derrida recognizes, is already on the way in these lectures to discovering the connection to distraction, which he finds lodged in the metaphysical concept of *Grund*, grounds, *causa*, *aition*, the *idée fixe* of logic that in these lectures he intends to destroy, or rather, to reinterpret.[2] *Grund* is a version of transcendence, and transcendence is connected in some as yet unspecified way to distraction, *Zerstreuung*. This is the order; these are the figures. The problem that Heidegger calls a "Problem," which he outlines in this part of the 1928 logic lectures looking back toward *Being and Time*, is whether one can transit between an ontic interpretation of existence and an ontological interpretation, between an everyday understanding and one that steps beyond the everyday, such that 1) the difference between the two interpretive stances is preserved, and 2) the difference can be precisely located, crossed, understood, and ultimately made useful for philosophy, without going beyond existence, that is, without *metaphysica specialis*. To accomplish both these goals, he had to find a way to think about a transcendence within existence, one that did not pin its hopes on a "beyond."[3]

Only on the basis of a fundamental, prior, self-attracting *Transzendenz* could *Dasein* have access to itself; only through transcending could its existential categories appear. To say this, moreover, is to approach tautology, since the words "fundamental," "prior," "self," and "access"—Heideggerian words and hopes—imply transcendence and may be versions of it. If transcendence must start from existence and transit to existence, what could transcendence mean? What position does it have within the existential schema? Is it an existential category? Can it appear? The worry is that transcendence may be the only existential category that cannot in fact exist. Going beyond without in fact leaving—a formula for the phenomenological ideal of transcendence—is similar to the Kantian transcendental; it also denies recourse to what cannot be experienced. Yet Heidegger in addition refuses to situate transcendence in the mind. Experience is not governed by faculties, knowledge, ideals, or—*pace* Husserl— idealities. The conditions for existing must also exist, be experiencable, be "merely" phenomenal. A shift in perspective must be all that is required for them to appear.

As it turns out, this is where the problem lies, in the middle of Heidegger's "Problem"; this is where Heidegger's interpretation of the "problem dimension" of *Being and Time* begins and the dilemmas of distraction multiply. It turns out that only on the basis of something like *Zerstreuung* is transcendence from and to existence possible or even thinkable. Dispersal-distraction names the attempt to conceive of an existential transcendence. Although it is seldom noted by readers, *Zerstreuung* is already something like the condition for the possibility of transcendence in *Being and Time*—the (or at least *one*) condition of all other conditions, including being, and time—and therefore it becomes a condition for philosophy as such. *Zerstreuung* is the movement of existence's interpretability. Existence stands out of itself; it transcends to its self-understanding and it has already done so, each time again forever, and yet this is true only if it begins in ontic dispersal and dissipation from the essence of its "da." This is also to say that its dissipation has been capable of becoming interpretable—of becoming interpretation—from the outset; indeed *Zerstreuung* is interpretation's degraded double: dissipation, distraction. Distraction-dissipation is thus, in *Being and Time*, the existential precondition of Dasein's interpretability, its "being," and as a result the basis for hermeneutic ontology's operations.

The problem, however, is not that dissipation-distraction plays such an important role—although to some it might seem like a revelation. Heidegger rarely shies away from promoting seemingly marginal phenomena to the center of his thought. What is most surprising, at least at first, is that *Zerstreuung* is neither a *Befindlichkeit* nor another kind of disposition or comportment; it is of an entirely different order than *Angst*.[4] Indeed, it becomes the condition for all moods and dispositions.

At first glance, Heidegger's transcendent or transcending distraction would solve many problems. Not least of these is the problem of conceptualizing and reevaluating the phenomenon of distraction. Instead of the lowest, meanest, least meaningful disposition, it would take its place among the pantheon of philosophical forces. One would also be able to say "distraction" with a clear conscience and point to a stable uniform idea through which its meaning would be guaranteed. Yet here the difference from other figures would begin to break down. "Thought" finds its way again and again into transcendence and transcendental discourses; when not God, thought fulfills the hope of moving beyond the world toward its intelligibility, permanence, stability, and so forth. This is the mark of philosophic and scientific modernity, the gradual substitution of thought for God, begun in fifth-century Greece. A transcendent or transcending thinking—one always assumes this; faculties transcend experience in order to unify and understand it. Experience means this unity, this understanding, this "going beyond." But a transcendent not-thinking, one that goes nowhere? Let us see how Heidegger has to modify "not-thinking" in order to apotheosize it.

Before he called for a "mighty" distraction in 1928, Heidegger had already fallen prey to a desire for *Macht*, though not in the political sense that he would fall prey to five years later. *Being and Time* discovers a way to make dissipation mighty. Not an intensified dispersal but dispersal turned against itself brings about the surge in power. By removing dissipation, *Zerstreuung* becomes mighty, becomes, as it is described there, *Entschlossen*, resolved. "The resoluteness that runs ahead [*die vorlaufende Entschlossenheit*] is not a way out, invented in order to 'overcome' death, but the understanding, following the call of conscience, that gives death the possibility to master Dasein's existence [der Existenz des Daseins *mächtig* zu werden], and to fundamentally dissipate [*zerstreuen*] every fleeing self-concealment" (*SuZ* 310). This is a complicated passage. The "might" that is needed in order to reinterpret existence appears, in the passage, to belong to another kind of dissipation, yet it is in fact the same one, employed against itself. Resoluteness in the face of being-toward-death is described as the dissipation of dissipation. Dissipation dissipated equals power. In *Sein und Zeit*, Dasein can take hold of the leveling and diminishing tendency that characterizes its relation to the world and its flight from death by diminishing it away. Where *Zerstreuung* is the degraded interpretation of the world in which we exist, philosophical *Zerstreuung*—almighty distraction—degrades degradedness. This second dissipation is a *gründlichere Zerstreuung*, an act in which distraction and dissipation become fundamental and generative.[5] This is, itself, an important twist on the philosophical tradition. One could extrapolate from it a new formula for attention. Instead of a primal, present, attractive force, attention would consist in distraction from distraction. Thus, in *Being and Time*, under one and the same name, dispersal-distraction both produces the world's self-concealment (as not attending to it *im Grunde*, but rather becoming lost, multiplying, and becoming diffuse) and provides the very power for modification *out of the same movement or essence*. In *Being and Time* one must pay careful attention to these duplicitous permutations. *Zerstreuung* designates existence's foliage as well as its hidden root, and as such it is a word divided against itself, containing the seeds for understanding and misunderstanding at once. "Dasein's being-in-the-world has always already dissipated or even splintered [*zerstreut oder gar zersplittert*] itself, with its facticity, in determinate ways of being-in" (*SuZ* 56). One would want to ask: is, then, *zerstreuen* (or even *zersplittern*) itself one of these ways of being in? The way he slips it into the analytic reveals almost too much. Heidegger never makes *Zerstreuung* into a keyword of the analytic; it is neither an existential, nor, strictly speaking, a phenomenon. Indexes of his texts and dictionaries of his thought contain no entry for it. The text itself conceals the word's importance in its use as an operative term.

Part of its duplicity can be explained by reference to its role in the *structure* of existence. Existence's wholeness lies in its dispersal, the paradoxical formula of being-in-the-world asserts. This means that Dasein is entirely dispersed into varieties of worldly involvements, with no remnant of unity or non-worldliness to spare. Existential categories such as fallenness, understanding, and thrownness give some order to these scattered involvements. And still, they are basically disorderly and changeable. Beyond the categorial layer, however, we find another layer of operative terms, which are fundamental to the reader's understanding but rarely thematized. These include "wholeness" (*Ganzheit*), "dispersal-dissipation" (*Zerstreuung*), and of course the indispensible yet almost wholly unaccounted-for word "structure" (*Struktur*). Wholeness and dispersal-dissipation are neither logical nor ontological opposites; rather, they compliment one another: they even perhaps overlap. In tandem they give the most basic assumption of Heidegger's hermeneutics, which is: meaning is always whole. Even *Zerstreuung* is subject to this assumption. Dispersal-dissipation is whole and wholly itself, our being is wholly dispersed into ways of being, and wholeness itself is whole and thus the sine qua non of interpretability. Find a whole and you can say you have interpreted something. This goes back to the Aristotelian argument: you cannot say what something is if it is more or less than one. In the regime of being that Heidegger inaugurates, nothing ontologically partial can be interpreted as something. And this implies that, no matter the extent of the dissipation, as a term, a movement, an ontologically fundamental concept, it is never anything but entirely itself; all existence is a product of dispersal, but dispersal itself is never, in a word, dissipated. By seeing this, Heidegger's operation in *Being and Time* becomes slightly more transparent. To dissipate dissipation means to see what has been wholly dispersed as the source of one's whole being. This dissipates the effect of dissipation, even if and precisely when we commit ourselves fully to dispersal among ways of being-in.

Zerstreuung is thus, in truth, "mighty" to the extent that it is existence's underlying structure; it is that which articulates its scattered elements into a unit. At times it is a kind of weakness, to be sure, but even then it is wholly weak. It is the weak force that unifies the most disparate attitudes, acts, and phenomena of existence. And so, when Heidegger modifies being from a seeming plentitude of presence into a full existential scattering, he conserves plentitude as the ontological fundament. This is the point at which the Marburg lectures will take up the thread again, to face what Heidegger considers a stubborn knot, the point or twist at which existence reveals itself to be dispersed. How do we—we philosophers, we Heideggerians, we existents—move from concealing dissipation to revealing dissipation? How does weak dissipation become mighty, turn against itself, become the whole it already is?

Modalities of *Zerstreuung* in *Sein und Zeit*

In each of the three main determinations of being-in-the-world—intimacy with things (*sein-bei*), coexistence with other existents (*mit-sein*), and being out of oneself toward oneself (ecstatic time)—*Zerstreuung* plays a "fundamental" role. First of all, it makes possible a variety of ways of be-ing-with. Dasein disperses itself among modes of *Besorgen*:

The multiplicity of such ways of being-in lets itself be indicated in an exemplary way through the following list: having to do with something, production of some-thing, commissioning and maintenance of something, use of something, giving something up and letting yourself lose something, undertaking, accomplishing, ascertaining, investigating, observing, discussing, determining. . . . These ways of being-in have the kind of being, still to be more precisely characterized, of taking care of [*des Besorgens*]. (*SuZ* 56–57)

One does not find oneself in the world among beings that are geographi-cally dispersed—this would be a trivial matter. It is not a dispersed mul-titude of objects among which Dasein is *zerstreut*, but a manifold of ways of relating to things, a manifold of ways in which beings appear. Multipli-cation of ways, delivery to a range of possible objectives, modes of action, and relationships are governed by this figure. Let us mention now that what we call "attention" occurs in only one or two of these modes: curios-ity and the theoretical attitude. The *Zerstreuung* at issue is not the contrary of attention.

This or that manner of intercourse with beings in the world, all there is for Dasein according to Heidegger, in a philosophy without soul or world-substance, happens on the condition that dissipation-distraction has already occurred. "The phenomenological display [*Aufweis*] of the being of the nearest being happens according to the guideline of the ev-eryday being-in-the-world that we also call intercourse in the world and with an inner-worldly being. The intercourse has already dissipated itself [*hat sich schon zerstreut*] into a multiplicity of ways of taking care of this and that" (*SuZ* 66–67). Our current ways of dealing with things, which of course includes not dealing with things, our *Umgang*, the most gen-eral name for a movement among associations to things is the result of a spreading out, multiplying, and depleting movement that has already happened. *Zerstreuung* is past, it seems, as well as whole.

But it is also ongoing and repeated, in Dasein's involvement in *das Man*. *Das Man* is a way of being with other existents that Dasein adopts by habitually avoiding interpretation, that is, by remaining distracted, diffuse.

The self of everyday Dasein is the self of the "they," which we distinguish from the self-owning self, which means the self grasped on one's own. As the self of the "they," the particular Dasein is dispersed in the "they" and must first find itself. This dissipation-distraction [*Zerstreuung*] characterizes the "subject" in the kind of being that we know as carried away in the nearest-encountered world by taking care of this or that. (*SuZ* 129)

This second version of distraction-dissipation is no longer constitutive of the world, no longer structural, but occurs in the world as one of its degraded *modi*. For this reason, *das Man* as the collective name for collective distraction offers a unique place to grasp the co-world, the *Mitwelt*. In contrast to the "they," the hermeneutic-phenomenologist is one who works with distraction—sees it, understands it, but does not give in to its seductive pull. This means simply that, instead of saying "we pay attention," the common wisdom that "they" affirm, the hermeneut admits: I am by nature diffuse and "world" is the sum of the ways of my distraction. He reads the manifold of interactions with inner-worldly entities as "examples," understands the demonstrative (*Aufweis*) (*SuZ* 66) character of the scattered modes of taking care and marks his difference from those mired in them by remarking on it. Diffuse as it may be, the hermeneutic position cannot be simply one dissolution among many. With respect to his partner-beings, those who are *zerstreut* along with him, the hermeneutic phenomenologist can distinguish the "self-grasped self" from the self lost in *das Man*. Marking the difference, finding what has gotten lost—making oneself remarkable amidst the unremarkable—these are the actions required in the face of this sort of dissipation.

Beyond the structural and hermeneutic uses of *Zerstreuung*, there is a third, one that is closely related to Heidegger's concept of temporality. "In their not tarrying, curiosity takes care of the constant potential for dissipation-distraction [*Zerstreuung*]" (*SuZ* 172). It is not only the case that intimacy-with-things, *sein-bei*, is structured dispersively and coexistence, *das Man*, is distracted from its being; it is also true that those who inquire into anything in an everyday manner in fact seek dissipation. Attention, in this sense, is dissipation. Curiosity falls under the existential category *Verfallenheit*, in the special case of everydayness, but here it leaks into and contaminates another existential: understanding (*Verstehen*).[6] A degraded way of "seeing" associated with an ontic

interpretation of the world, curiosity sees only things, never their interpretation (ontic as ontic), never things as already interpreted (ontological
analysis), and it certainly does not "see" interpretability per se (fundamental ontology) (*SuZ* 170). As such, curiosity would seem to have little
to offer philosophy. In distinction from the theoretical attitude, it does
offer something, however. It runs counter to the ancient view of the
philosophical attitude. "Curiosity has nothing to do with the wonder-
ing observation of beings, *thaumazein*, it does not care to be brought
into not understanding through astonishment, but rather, it procures a
knowledge, but only in order to have known" (*SuZ* 172). The desire "to
have known" hints at curiosity's temporality. Curiosity is already away,
leaping past its object to the next and the next, and this precipitous
leap over the present of theoretical reflection lands in a "has been," a
movement that brings to light Dasein's authentic temporality: ahead of
itself already in a world. Curiosity, although unphilosophical, indicates
the nature of existence much more precisely than philosophy with its
"wonder." In this regard, too, the hermeneutic character of *Zerstreuung*
proves crucial for Heidegger, insofar as it eschews what is simply present.
Curiosity is futural; it considers everything it sees passé almost before it
has seen it. Heidegger exploits the German etymology of *Neu-gier*. Its vision is greedy for the new, and this implies an expectation to stop seeing
what is merely present. When he returns to *Neugier* in Division Two, its
impatience with the present will become crucial. "Curiosity is constituted through an indignant making present [*Gegenwärtigen*], that, only
making present, seeks therewith to run away from expectation [*Gewärtigen*], in which it is indeed indignantly maintained" (*SuZ* 347). Holding
itself in not holding back (*Ungehaltenheit*), preserving non-preservation,
behavior in curiosity has secret affinities with *Entschlossenheit* (as holding
fast) as well as with the temporal figure, *Augenblick* (as making present).
Curiosity is the degraded version and formal indicator of the moment
of sudden resolution that transforms the relationship to interpretation.
In the dissipation-dispersal of the curious, which is really an attraction toward the next newest thing, a more fundamental (though not
the most fundamental) temporal disposition, *Gewärtigen*, expecting, is
concealed. As Heidegger puts it: "The ecstatic modification of expecting into a springing-after, through a springing-out making-present, is

the existential-temporal condition of possibility of dispersal-distraction [*Zerstreuung*]" (*SuZ* 347). This dispersal-distraction, a temporally deceptive relationship to entities, is highly derivative, far down on the chain of conditions, anything but transcendent or transcending, and nothing like truth, and this utter degradation makes it a true expression of existence; truth becomes legible in its extreme contrariety.

Zerstreuung as a) structural dispersal, b) hermeneutic dissipation, and c) temporal leaping out and leaping ahead of itself share a pattern. Each of these versions formally indicates that which has been degraded in them, providing a point at which a modification can begin, toward wholeness, interpretation, and time.

The essence or wholeness of *Zerstreuung* is not itself *zerstreut*. We have already recognized this as one of Heidegger's desiderata in *Being and Time*. This is perhaps a problem, perhaps *the* problem of *Being and Time*. Dispersal is undispersed. Underlying it is, rather, as we find out in Division Two, one thing: "care," the most unified of all phenomena. Late in the book, Heidegger says something highly equivocal, then, about *Zerstreuung* and this problem. He requires that the phenomenologist grasp "care," the being of Dasein, "in an un-dissipated [*unzerstreuten*], existentially understanding gaze" (*SuZ* 323). This might seem to be an offhand remark. We should not be too hard on Heidegger for slipping into a kind of unconscious metaphysics in a single line, one remark, an attempt—perhaps a bad one—at formulating something that elsewhere he formulates better. He wrote the book in five or six months, and by and large his terms strive to avoid metaphysical connotations. And yet, although "care" names Dasein's primary meaning, it also points toward a feature that would be difficult to consider merely phenomenal or worldly: unity.[7] All else can be received in dispersion and dissipation except unity. The alternative would be perilous: a look looking at dispersion that itself became dissipated, to the point of not seeing. This could produce a destructural dispersal with multiple interpretations, a dispersal-distraction that could only be understood distractedly or not understood at all, a dispersal whose meaning was not epochally unified, implying a world whose dissipation did not imply its fundamental potency—any of these, or perhaps all of them, could arise if "dissipation" were understood dissipatedly. In such a world, interpretation would perhaps be seen as a violation of disorder, a falsity, and a pernicious one, rather than world's unified ground.

Heidegger avoids any suggestion of this reading. And so, even though he reminds us quite strongly at the beginning of the second chapter that, for all its rigor, the existential analytic is only a primary finding (*Befund*), and, more importantly, for all its unity Dasein is ontologically always a plurality of "structural moments," Dasein's plural-unified structure must nonetheless never be thought of as merely "pieced-together inventories" (*zusammenstückbare Bestände*) (*SuZ* 53).[8] No, an ad hoc group is anathema to ontological plurality, which is distinguished by the fact that it never disintegrates, never aggregates more items, and never runs out of stock for its interpretive business. This is why, from the very beginning of the analytic, structural moments, when introduced, immediately announce their inner connections and declare themselves parts of the primordial unity. Structural moments are *gleichursprünglich*, usually somewhat inelegantly translated as "equiprimordial." Insofar as they originate at the same time and in a similar way, dispersed *Existentialia* are not items stuck together ex post facto, joined by external forces, empirically, or by accident, but structural moments that point back to their unity. Plurality seems to be, in Platonic terms, semblance; existence's being is in reality unity.

The Un in the Unthought

We must be careful not to say that *Zerstreuung* is "the unthought" in *Being and Time*. In order to say what it means to think what was not thought, we would first have to agree on what not-thinking means. Given the large number of possible negations, negativities, privations, refusals, denials, and so on, it would be incautious to immediately read the not in "not-thinking" as if there were only one indispensable way to dispense with or remove or depose a thinking or a thought. Without a doubt—this act, thinking not-thinking or non-thought, involves us almost immediately in a vertiginous whirl. There ought to be as many variations of not-thought as there are negativities, and at least as many negated, nullified, lost, or broken cognitive moments as there are modes of cognition. In order to proceed, one of the multitude must be selected.

Twenty-five years after the publication of *Being and Time*, Heidegger selects one, or resurrects it, and it subsequently becomes essential to what he calls "Denken."

Thinking is indeed dependent on one kind of not-thought. "The unthought in a thinking is not a lack inherent in a thought. The *un*-thought is there each time only as the un-*thought* [*Das Un*-Gedachte *ist je nur als das* Un-*gedachte*]. The more original a thinking is, the richer will be its unthought" (*Was heißt Denken?* 72). This kind of not-thinking—if negativities can be organized into kinds—should remind us of the powerful distraction of the twenties. For one thing, it is a rich not-thinking—the richest—that interests Heidegger at this moment, and so we can assume there are other poorer ones that Heidegger cancels in advance—a lack in thought is the one that he openly denies here, but there are others. At least we can say, preliminarily, anticipating our argument, that the difference, for him, is always one of degree of abundance, and lack would be the lowest degree, the least rich, and not to be applied to not-thinking. The richest unthought for him at this moment is also not absolute not-thinking. The richest unthought thereafter becomes a methodological *Kunststück* for philosophy, once Heidegger, permitted for the first time after the war to teach in a German university, offers the lectures in Freiburg in 1951–1952 that codify it. He returns to the scene of the crime to ask a more essential question as he sees it then: "Was heißt Denken?"

Upon returning to the site of previous revolutions, real and perceived, he insists again that the emphasis fall not on the negative but on the positive. Unthinking is not worth touching. Only the unthought should be saved, and then only with the stress on thought. Because, we can suppose, the stress in this word will not be obvious to his students and other spectators and readers, he resolves to demonstrate it typographically, and, we may also assume, in a special tone of voice, whose weight hits just so, on the last syllable, and not on the first: "un*thought*." Unthought is emphatically *not Un*thought. To carry the philosopher deep into the riches of the tradition, displacing him into its beginning, making plain its truth and its grounds, *thought* must be intoned, underlined, saved, even if through a certain negation. There are grounds for confusion here, but Heidegger avoids them with this typographical and intonational guidance. He does not advocate falling into an unthinking relationship to the tradition, but through a negation, constructing a well-grounded one. "We can only learn to think if we unlearn its previous essence from the ground up" (*Was heißt Denken?* 5). Unlearning is part of thinking, to be sure, and "we"—Heidegger deliberately does not exclude himself from the horizon of this pronoun, and of course his students and readers are meant as well—we will have to go through it all, the whole historical repression, the secret history of being, one more time. From this prescription it is plain, also, that what begins in unthought, unlearning, is designed to end in learning and renewed thought.

The return to Freiburg is thus a double return, a return to philosophy as "thought," an originary *Denken*, and a return to public thinking, which means prescribing what thinking should be.[9] Heidegger lays emphasis here. Rather than positive doctrine or method, "the unthought" is what is carried forward, preserved, even and especially where the public side of a thinker's thought would seem at times to forsake it. Despite the vicissitudes of empirical events, the unthought survives intact and is given to the thinker by the tradition that he wants, by means of it, to dismantle. There is a secret tradition, in other words, a higher one, within the debased one that presents itself as thought.[10] "The unthought is the highest gift that a thinking has to give" (*Was heißt Denken?* 72). This version of not-thinking is marked as the richest in degree and, at the same time, it is also marked as a thing, a product, fully determined and ultimately thinkable. Substantivized in a perfect participle, adorned with a definite article, italicized, the unthought carries, without loss, a definite thought for thinking now. It is not non-thought, it has just not yet been thought. Its a priori thinkability remains untouched by the fact that no one has thought it. Therein lies its limit and its power: it makes possible the future destruction of the thought that denies it, just as it aides in leading the whole manner and scope of thinking back to its roots, preparing for a different flowering. Unthought corresponds to the *noema* in Aristotle's theory of the soul, the what of an intention, the objective correlative in the thinking act, the product or induct of noetic action; equivalent to *anoema*, unthought is what has not been thought but is nonetheless already defined and possessed by *noēsis*. History carries these *parerga* with it—let us call them as Heidegger does elsewhere: overflows, surpluses, *Übersprünge*. They represent precisely that which is not *called* thinking, the denial against which a thought becomes meaningful. Although not yet named or called to thinking, unthoughts are fully thinkable, if only at another time or by another thinker. In this way, "un" means "not-yet," the not-yet-completed within what has already been called thought. A shadow epoch that tears at the epoch's horizon, and at the same time the great thinker's personal, internal, fixed, and forward-relaying fate, *Schicksal*, an unthought is the line at which the work goes over into what it has repressed in order to constitute itself. A relay race of unthoughts implies corresponding futures of epochal arrests and restorations by thinking—now in the Heideggerian sense—implying as well, no doubt, each time, a concomitant resending toward yet another *Schicksal*. This serious game of leapfrog constitutes the movement of history.

Thinking calls upon "the unthought" of a previous epoch in this one. And this is perhaps why, at what seemed like the end of an epoch, or the beginning of a new one, Heidegger first had to say what unthought meant. We must know what thought is, construct a history of thinking, in order to think. And so it is all the more surprising that we first learn what "unthought" *is not*. It is not a lack, not something that, by the addition of *je ne sais quoi*, would allow unthought to disappear. Immediately refusing lack avoids, or so it seems, giving the impression that Heidegger supports a form of positivism. He does not mean by "unthought" that it is our task to perfect not yet perfect thoughts. In any epoch thought is complete, the result of a historical *epochē*. Thought makes out and is made out by an epoch's scope and limit, its full range of possibilities for the meaning of being, within which thought orients itself. Beyond its wholeness, beyond and along with it, however, every epoch in addition produces a negativity that affects it hardly at all. An epoch's unthought nowhere impinges on its sense of sufficiency. At the same time, however, in brushing it off completely, this *un* determines a future in which it will come to be thought. Sufficient to itself, fully determined, lacking apparently nothing, not perfectible in a scientistic sense or dialectical in a Hegelian sense, thought at the same time nevertheless allies itself with a self-repudiation that it radiates forward. The unthought names the specific refutation that an epoch carries with it and that makes it what it is. The *un* in unthought, Heidegger stresses, is therefore not by any means a lack of some part or capacity. The unthought is what was not thought although it could have been. *In potentia* thinkable it calls for an actualization whose medium is not mind but history and whose actuator is philosophy, or, as it will now be called, *denken*.

In 1951–1952 philosophy received the gift of unthought—shall we call it that? It gave itself the gift of the one unthought through one thinker. Was it then his "unthought" that was being taught? Or was it the unthought of a whole generation or of all time? Let us respond to these puzzling questions by making one thing clear. Heidegger was not interested in his own unthought. Perhaps he thought that was for other generations, other thinkers, perhaps even other languages or disciplines that would not be German and would not even be called "thinking." Then, however, he was concerned with presenting the meaning of unthought. It may well be that, as he writes, "there is no bridge here" (*es gibt hier keine Brücke*). Since instead of a bridge there is "only the leap/cleft" (*nur den Sprung*), we would be remiss if we did not inquire how the leaper finds the proper jumping-off place and lands where he ought to land, at the right "un," not, negativity, negation (*Was heißt Denken?* 4–5). What concerns us is whether the leap to unthought is a thinking or an unthinking act.

This act, the restoration of an unthought to thinking, does not seem to be dictated by chance. To be sure, bringing in what it negates means that thinking changes from more traditional metaphysical accounts. It becomes *geschichtlich*, and eccentric; it pushes itself out beyond itself. No longer does it consist in operating within a system constructed by a genius or proofing the foundation of an inherited system. It will be a foundational exercise in showing what exceeds the foundation, and furthermore, that foundation itself is excess. As is no doubt apparent, this exercise in excessive thinking is highly, richly, intensely intellectual, requiring a "higher" power of thought, higher perhaps than any previously imagined, in order to receive the richest gift that a thought can produce, its indeterminate negation. To think what in any epoch remains indeterminate, excluded as the excess or surplus of the epoch, in order to think the excessiveness of epochs in general, one calls upon a super origin, the most abundant resource. Hyper-thinking is what is called for here and what is called thinking about unthought.

Unthought thus appears through an excess of intellect, and it should not be too surprising that an excessive thinking is there to capture it. This transcendence or surpassing is reserved for the few transhistorical thinkers who go beyond the one-track-mind, the "eingleisiges Denken" (*Was heißt Denken?* 56) of *Wissenschaft*, and achieve a multi-tracking reflection or at least a thinking that acknowledges the potential multiplicity of tracks.[11] In the first of the lectures, Heidegger signals the move to excessive thinking with the term "das Bedenklichste," which might be translated as: what is most in need of being thought (2, 3, 11ff.). Heidegger's rebellion against philosophy consists in seeing thought as historically limited and immanently destructible. Thought is finite. Where thought faces finitude, however, the unthought transcends. Where there is no bridge there is nonetheless "only," "nur," a crack or a leap, and the little "nur" indicates a super-historical movement. The crack between epochal boundaries provides, through the proper placement of the leap, contiguity with the past. An excessive thinker attuned to *dem Bedenklichste* of today thinks the unthought, which entails positing the non-being of the thing previously called thinking. What is called thinking is intercourse with the unthought. Thus the task with regard to Nietzsche, for example, as Heidegger sums it up, is to displace backward (*zurückverlegen*) his unthought into the truth with which he began to philosophize (23–24). The origin of his thought, which withdraws from the great thinker—in Nietzsche's case, Platonism—is the unthought that is, at another time, given to be thought.

According to Heidegger in 1951–1952, the essence of *Denken* is to divert itself from its "anfängliche Wahrheit"; it avoids inquiring into its roots, its starting point and the other possible beginnings that this one beginning conceals; this is the unthought of thinking. Perhaps this can be seen as a self-indictment, a revelation of the finitude of his own thinking of the 1930s. It would be nice if that were the case. Its often triumphant tone and frequent celebrations of arrivals at times call for skepticism. But it is also possibly an attack on public opinion, the "Öffentlichkeit" that had kept him out of the university for half a dozen years. None of this has been thinking; thinking is not that; it has yet to start; it always has not yet started. Yet, these empirical worries or regrets are dwarfed in comparison to the meaning of unthought, which is never mistaken, lost, or shameful. Not-thinking is always already thinking. "The proposition: what is most to be thought of [*das Bedenklichste*] in our thought-provoking [*bedenklichen*] time is that we are not yet thinking. This proposition says, however, at the same time: we are underway in thinking toward the essence of thinking" (60). All this not-thinking has been the detour that led away from the untold riches of the origin. That we are underway means "that we are not yet thinking" (*daß wir noch nicht denken*) (59), and, having said this, having made this claim without proof, *diese Behauptung*, in order to attempt a different beginning, a groundless one, one comfortable with delays and detours, for which the detour is both the sign and the substance of the way, in the same moment thinking becomes the way back to its essence; it appears as it is, as delay, and thereby assures itself that it has been coming toward itself.

What would it mean to propose, in contrast, *zu behaupten*, that in his lectures on the name and meaning of thinking, Heidegger has not yet begun to think the word, term, concept, inkling "unthought"? This is a dangerous proposition—dangerous, it would seem, since, were it valid, the task of thinking as well as the shape of history would be much less coherent.

Heidegger's unthought is caught in the horns of a dilemma that arises from the assertion of the unthought; for it is an assertion, as he says, and it can never be more. This is what is asserted: that the achievement of a thinker is really, seen historically, the production of an unthought. If, then, the present body of thought is in fact determined by and wholly dependent on a historical supplement, then the one thing that can never remain unthought is "the unthought" itself.

A single unthought produced by and exceeding an epochal thinking may be thinkable, but the meaning of "unthought" is and remains unthought in another sense entirely. It cannot be simply brought back into thought. As soon as we assert that Heidegger's "Ungedachte" has not been thought, we both reify the concept and render it meaningless. It becomes reified in repeating it—the unthought is unthought—and in this dumb repetition it loses its high, rich, full meaning. The unthought becomes, in this light, the self-lacking lack, the lack that lacks itself and thus is in a sense an excess, though not, in turn, a specifiable excess; either a shill that can stand in for anything, or a hyperbolic expression of the hyperbolic that, in exceeding itself, falls short of its hoped-for effects, the unthought produces, when one attempts to think about it, instead of a new lease on thought, an unhealthy swoon.

In these lectures, Heidegger doesn't seem to be able to infer, deduce, or reduce back to the inkling that unthought might simply not be anything like thought. The conflicting figures he uses to describe it, leaping, in the first set of lectures, and thanking, in the second, gesture toward this incapacity. Though both are attempts to come to terms with alterity in thinking, the two figures imply different paradigms. The first, the model according to which true thinking means abandoning the grounds for thinking, is theological. This suspension without telos adapts Kierkegaard's leap, without abandoning its iron grip on the leap's immanent starting point and transcendent endpoint, despite the purported vertigo between them. The second adapts Nietzsche's notion of an unthought debt and a concealed multiplicity in the origin. Such an economic model remains too much in debt to a metaphysics of the will, in which the greater and more powerful, richer and more excessive always wins out. In short, abandonment—the leap—gives up too little, and owing—thanking—keeps too much. In both of these formulas thinking holds fast to one of its most traditional "powers," the ability for ability, or transcendence.

Zerstreuung and *Sorge*

To will and to wish, to be inclined toward, captivated by, driven to, and all the manners of "Besorgen," including the more general modalities of *Zuhandenheit* and *Vorhandenheit*—in short, every one of Dasein's constitutive existential moments outlined in the analytic—are functions or derivatives of *Sorge*, which because of its ability to spread out into a variety of modes can be nothing other than Dasein's being.[12] The relationship is exclusive: Dasein *sorgt* and that which *sorgt nicht* is simply not Dasein. Ontological carelessness or a being that is transcendentally carefree has no place here; carelessness is but an ontic negation of care, and so it does not affect care in its meaning; it is a formal indicator, never more. "Such a thing is possible ontically only in the same way as 'being carefree' and 'cheerfulness' are, since *ontologically* understood Dasein is care" (*SuZ*

57). And so, the "Weisen des Besorgens" that we have seen distributed to the point of splintering, "zerstreut oder gar zersplittert," are in fact expressions of a single *Sorge* or care that transcends them and relates to each and all of them as their internal unity and their meaning. A transcendent not-caring, if we could imagine such a thing, would be a threat to the very idea of existence.

Yet the manner in which Heidegger came to think about care calls the coherence of the phenomenon into question. "Seven years ago already," Heidegger says, lecturing in Marburg in 1925, "as I investigated these structures in the context of the attempt to arrive at the ontological foundations of Augustinian anthropology, I stumbled onto the phenomenon of care" (*bin ich auf das Phänomen der Sorge gestoßen*) (*Prolegomena zur Geschichte des Zeitbegriffs* 418). In this seemingly offhand remark, we learn that it was not fate that lead Heidegger to the discovery of Dasein's essence—and even less, his own developing phenomenological method. Crossing an intellectual bridge to alien shores—Augustine's anthropology—he stumbles onto it.[13] Accident made it available to him, opened a vista, we might say, on the un*thought* in his own thought. Shall we try to understand this chance collision? Is it a purely trivial experience, or can we read something more fundamental off of it? It may imply of course that where he did not seek care, care sought him. Only an apparent collision, then, only the semblance of an accident, this event in fact indicates the transcendent necessity of care. One encounters the grounds of existence carelessly, but this carelessness is an expression of—what else?—the operation of care. It was not Augustine's understanding of this phenomenon alone, Heidegger goes on to explain, that led him to *Sorge*'s preeminence as the category of categories for Dasein. "Nachträglich," subsequently and as an afterthought, ex post facto, he stumbled again, this time stumbling onto this most central of Dasein's self-interpretations, and the second time was decisive. "After the fact, however, I stumbled [*stieß ich*] onto one of Dasein's self-interpretations, in which it sees itself as care" (*Prolegomena zur Geschichte des Zeitbegriffs* 418). The "self-interpretation" of Dasein he means here is the Hyginus fable that he later includes in Section 42 of *Being and Time*, a short tale about a peculiar divinity named "Cura" and the creation of human being. What first appeared as chance, now takes on the cast of fate. The Cura fable, he argues, is an exemplary ontic intuition of the basis for interpretating Dasein as care. Humanity was ahead of itself, already determined by care, when Hyginus writes or records its story, and, having been forgotten, it can only be encountered late and, at first, without full understanding.[14] The more originary, ontological formulation of this tendency that needs explaining and that *Sorge* explains is rather Dasein's temporal structure, "the unified fundamental structure of being ahead of oneself in dwelling within" (*die einheitliche Grundstruktur des Sich-vorweg-seins-im-sein-bei*) (*Prolegomena zur Geschichte des Zeitbegriffs* 420). Being ahead of itself in an ontic involvement, Dasein comes to itself belatedly, *nachträglich*—and just in this way Heidegger came to the understanding of *Sorge*. *Sorge* had him—*Sorge* made him—and he was drawn along by its movement toward himself as the philosopher of care.[15] It is not hard to see that the collision of the philosopher with the essence of existence was not accidental at all. And yet. . . .

Heidegger admits in this passage that there were two *Stöße* or collisions that finally and, fatefully, turned him toward *Being and Time*—one hit in the Augustine lectures of 1921–1922, another while reading a creation myth from imperial Rome, made popular in a poem by Herder and then by Goethe in *Faust II*[6]—and yet. . . . In fact, there are or were three concussions, three unexpected blows, and the third one cannot be a blow of fate. This is the collision that happens within the Hyginus fable, the accident by which care "creates" *homo*, which one could translate as human being.

Who is care, where does she come from, why does she arrive on this particular day at a bridge across a river, this bridge, this river, where is she going, what makes her stop, what impels her to look down and pick up a lump of clay, and what leads her to think so carefully about it in the midst of the act and then again right afterward? All these unknowns, and more, call for responses, readings.

Heidegger's reading of the fable in *Being and Time* is so brief as to seem cryptic. The special meaning (*besondere Bedeutung*) that the fable carries as a pre-ontological testimonial (*vorontologische[s] Zeugnis*) to the essence of Dasein as care lies in its double revelation (*SuZ* 198). Not only does a human being belong to *Sorge* during its lifetime, *Sorge* is moreover the condition for the unhappy and temporary union between spirit and material. That is, it accounts for the way substance-ontology has understood human being for millennia. Finally, Heidegger identifies Saturn, the god who decides on the name "homo," with "Zeit," and thus also sees in the fable an indication of the close bond between care and the "zeitliche[m] Wandel in der Welt" (*SuZ* 198–99).

To become aware of the assumptions underlying Heidegger's interpretation, it is enough to follow carefully the sequence of events in the first three lines of the fable, as Heidegger quotes it.

> Cura cum fluvium transiret, videt cretosum lutum
> sustulitque cogitabunda atque coepit fingere.
> dum deliberat quid iam fecisset, Jovis intervenit. (*SuZ* 197)

> While Cura was crossing a river, she saw muddy clay
> and, thinking it over, she lifted it up and began to shape it.
> While she was considering what she had just made, Jupiter
> intervened.

Cura's first gesture gets lost in Heidegger's reading: she goes across. She does not transcend, perhaps, but in at least one sense she does. Her crossing the river brings her over the top of the material, in a position to become the origin of humanity, by raising it up to her height. It may be easiest to see the assumptions behind this act through a somewhat idiosyncratic later reading of the fable, one that is in fact, despite appearances, quite beholden to Heidegger's.

Hans Blumenberg finds something wrong with the sequence of events in Cura's procedure. "There is something out of order in the course of the fable," he writes, and this insight seems to bear itself out—insofar as Cura stops short in the middle of her transit. Blumenberg adds: "and not only something incidental [*etwas Beiläufiges*]" (198). Following this remark we find ourselves, in Blumenberg's analysis, on the straight path of science, from which incidental matters are banished. What is missing from the fable, he argues, is the "central piece" (*Kernstück*) that has been "cut out" (*herausgeschnitten*). Not something merely tangential to the path, but its very center and the key to its meaning has been omitted, and Heidegger, Blumenberg insinuates, has not even so much as hinted at this momentous absence. Both Heidegger and the tradition have perpetrated a crime against the story's meaning. A model for *homo* is missing. At the center of the story readers should find, according to Blumenberg, an image after which Cura can model the clay she picks up. Lacking a mimetic core, the story cannot possibly show how care came to be the essence of human being. Unlike Heidegger, Blumenberg stresses the moment of form-giving. Through form, the clay is given its meaning, the impress of the divinity who created it, expressed in the outer shape or outline of the physical being. Not to worry, Blumenberg will supply the missing mimetic moment, the missing model. He suggests that, looking down into the river, Cura must have seen herself reflected, and, on the basis of her own image, she narcissistically reproduced herself in the mud.

"Care goes over a river. As the fable wants us to believe, in order to come across the piece of loamy clay, out of which something can be formed. How does it come to the formation out of clay that allows Care to contemplate what it may be? Is it only a game with an accidental outcome, with belated approval through Jupiter's gift of mind?" (198). Why this strange emphasis on what the fable wants? "The fable" wants it to seem this way, that Cura stumbles on the clay and forms it accidentally, but Blumenberg wants something else. A divine model must be supplied, something that guarantees that *homo* indeed is not the product of chance and whim, or, worse, something formless or without model. It seems implausible, however, that the new being's form would preoccupy Cura in this text. She seems, in fact, unconcerned with what she is doing. Cura asks "quid," what she has made, it is true, but she has to ask because its form is not apparent. What Care determines in this new being is not form—that is left for Jove, who does this under the name *spiritus*—but a relation to carelessness, accident, and afterthought, and the indeterminacy that they produce.

When Blumenberg concludes *"Cura* goes over the river, in order that she can be reflected in it" (199), it is less an absence in the tale he is filling than a critical violence he perpetrates against it. Without other evidence, the missing reflection can only be the projection of a critic who hopes to see his critical understanding, and his theological view of creation, reflected in the tale. And so he fills in its missing center. In doing so he "extirpates," to use his terminology, another possibility, one that Heidegger also assiduously avoids. Unlike Heidegger, however, Blumenberg at least hints at the other reading. What the theological center denies is the role of chance, which Blumenberg reduces to a semblance. He mentions "the semblance of arbitrariness that disturbs the factual situation that Care goes over the river" (198). It is disturbing, yes: a factual situation and the role of chance: these determine the invention of *homo* anterior to any of the traditional theological origins: form, spirit, name. To avoid this eventuality, Blumenberg and Heidegger seek a ground for care's actions beyond her merely happening across the river. In the text she arrives arbitrarily, crosses arbitrarily, looks down arbitrarily, and then in the midst of thinking, picks up the mud. The meaning of this thinking is significant. Care may imbue everything she touches with care; but this thing is clearly moulded on vacation from herself—thinking here means, just thinking, thinking it over (*cogitabunda*), without determining anything, yet. Only after the fact, *nachträglich*, does she even think to determine (*deliberat*) what it might be—but even then she does not give it a final determination, Jove does.

Care is discovered accidentally by Heidegger, but as we can see Care is also prone to accidents. And still, for Heidegger, the accidental encounter is immediately subordinated to the necessity with which care must operate in human existence—transcendentally, transmitted from higher to lower, with no difference, except perhaps some strategic diminishment. Care's meandering, in contrast, is inhuman and directionless. Care does not care what it does or where it goes. Like Heidegger, Blumenberg resists this aleatory reading. This resistance can be read in what now begins to seem like a neurotic tick. He begins his interpretation of the text by noting: "in stumbling upon the hole at the center of the fable [*Indem ich auf die Lücke im Zentrum der Fabel stoße*], it becomes unmistakable to me that . . . " (198). No one, it seems, can look for care intentionally. One always only stumbles upon it. Then, after stumbling upon it, one immediate tries to exclude accident from the interpretation of care. One hurries to conceal the freedom of the encounter and make it seem like fate. As a sort of unfreedom Heidegger and Blumenberg accept *cura* as the highest determination of the figure that comes to be named—*but not by her*—"homo."

Yet Blumenberg is on to something. In his text, Blumenberg hits upon and then avoids the fact that Cura might not have crossed the river at all if things had gone differently. There is no sign that she was fated to commit this crossing or directed by some force higher than herself. If *cura* is indeed the transcendent condition for the human, fate arises only afterward, once *homo curator* has been given into her possession. *Care crosses the River*—the title of Blumenberg's book is a distortion of the sentence. Blumenberg here transforms the imperfect subjunctive of the Latin into the present indicative, and he drops the little word "when," *cum*, making the transit seem intended or even ceaseless and divine. *When care was crossing the river, Cura cum fluvium transiret*, reads the Latin text that Heidegger quotes. This happened to happen, once, at one time. No one cares about care; even Care herself doesn't seem concerned—and in this way, although she begins cogitating while fingering it, the being she produces may be in fact a product of her shiftless dawdling and the accidental "creation" that emerges from it. Cura's attitude is *incuria*; she is carefree, and the muddy non-form may spring originally from this offhand impulse and contingent *stoßen*. Only when Jove intervenes, *intervenit*, between her and her inscrutable product—another collision, incidentally; this time, though, for the first time, by force and intention—does something like a ground and a name, not to mention a mental life, get added to the being. In their readings of the fable, Blumenberg and Heidegger both play Jove. To see from the perspective of care on its vacation day—to appreciate the stupor and the straggling that is care: this is the challenge of the fable. Jove adds *Geist* ex post facto to the thoughtless muddling in which *homo* begins.[17]

Zerstreuung "and" Transcendence

In the Marburg lectures on logic, Dasein's condition of possibility is no longer care that subsequently "zerstreut sich" into a multitude of concerns. *Zerstreuung* now comes to be seen as, in the order of things, higher than care. For, if *Zerstreuung* is the movement by which the condition of all possible ontic concerns—care—is translated or carried over into those possibilities, it in fact names the possibility of that condition, the possibility for further possibilities, and in this way it becomes a synonym for time. As that which allows care to become a condition for the possibility of other phenomena, it comes "before" care and is therefore directly associated in the lectures with the ontological difference, the meaning of being, time, and ultimately, freedom to ground. As such, it comes to ground transcendence itself, a freedom that underlies and perhaps undermines—we shall see—the necessity with which Dasein moves between untapped possibilities and standing commitments, the freedom, that is, for modification—or, history.[18] Without a doubt, dispersal-dissipation takes on an uncomfortably large burden here. We might well begin to worry. These reflections drive us to ask whether, as the movement of care, this word, concept, topos, movement, the transcendence of transcendence—whatever it is or represents—by which our cares and attachments become ours, whether we can ever come to have an *unzerstreutes* relationship to it. That is: is there a science, a method, a philosophy, a thinking, or even a writing that can do it justice? To avoid this worry, perhaps, when *Zerstreuung* supplants care as Dasein's originating reflex, it receives a new name, "Streuung."[19] How far it has come from the ill repute into which the word had fallen! Instead of naming an empirical nothing that intervenes in *noēsis*, a site for moralizing, a condemnation or glorification of technology or leisure time, Heidegger positions distraction-dispersal as an ontological fundament that is unshakeable in its ability to produce existence. For a short time in 1928, *Zerstreuung* becomes the ultimate term in which all existential terms are rooted, the source for fundamental ontology, and the interpretation of the transcendence problem left over from *Being and Time*, in short, the meaning of "and." But what can we make of the oxymoronic phrase "rooted in dispersal"?

At the midpoint of the lecture course, Heidegger inquires into the nature of transcendence and the grounds for fundamental ontology, that is, into the justification for his own method in *Being and Time*. In order for it to operate, transcendence both must and cannot itself transcend. It suffers the problem of anything charged with crossing uncrossable boundaries. There must be something here that can appear there, as well as something there that can appear here, despite the absolute exclusion of the two orders. *Zerstreuung* is an attempt to enter into this dilemma in a different way. It is much easier to explain why transcendence must be transcendent than it is to explain why it cannot be. If transcendence itself is transcendent—as concept, intuition, ideal—it remains coherent and dependable, notwithstanding the instability and blindness of the existence it produces, and thus it protects and preserves its own power. Existence may be *zerstreut*, unstable, half-thought, fallen, thrown, and so forth, yet these descriptors are made intelligible insofar as *Zerstreuung* stands, as their source, beyond its effects.

The path to this problem cuts through Leibniz, hence the title of the lectures. Leibniz makes the strongest modern interpretation of being as substance, and thus is the site for a necessary destruction. "The Metaphysical Foundations of Logic Beginning from Leibniz" makes scant reference to the monad; instead of his metaphysics, Leibniz's logical thought is Heidegger's object.[20] The question "Why is there something rather than nothing?" lying behind the principle of sufficient reason brings Leibniz's logic close to Heidegger's *Seinsfrage*. Through this Leibnizean question Heidegger demonstrates that the "principle," the logical corollary of substance for Leibniz, is not simply a logical proposition in the form of a predication; it is metaphysical, is, in fact, a formula for apriorism, which Leibniz's presentation of the principle both obfuscates and makes accessible for the first time. The metaphysical grounds of logic become accessible through Leibniz's formulation of the principle of sufficient reason. For something to become a predicate it first has to be something, and this insight leads Heidegger to conclude that ontology precedes the reduced philosophical notion of logic as the study of predicative judgment or as rules for thinking (*Anfangsgründe* 24). After passing through historical interpretations of philosophical logic, Leibniz's metaphysics and the theory of the monad, and a general overview of the way the relationship between logic and ontology has previously been understood, Heidegger comes, in the second main division (*Zweites Hauptstück*), to the "Problemdimension" of logic. Leibniz in fact offers two fundamental logical principles, the principle of non-contradiction and the principle of sufficient reason. To this double beginning of logic, Heidegger asks three questions. What is the relationship between the two principles? What is the true foundation of the principle of sufficient reason? And: what is the relationship between Leibniz's logical doctrines and his metaphysical doctrines? Two further questions are then appended: what is a principle? And is a principle fundamentally logical or metaphysical? In short, Heidegger asks into the principle of "firstness" by which a sentence becomes a principle, and through which either logic or metaphysics would show itself to be a primary mode of philosophy (*Anfangsgründe* 135). That Leibniz addresses the fundamentality of any principle in one principle, the principle of sufficient reason, makes it more than just one principle among many; it becomes, in Heidegger's estimation, the one that specifies the principality of *Sätzen* by interpreting firstness. Firstness, principality, is a decision on the somethingness of something; without the decision that it is something, a being, something would be nothing. Although Leibniz answers it from within logic, the question itself is not in essence logical, but, as Heidegger shows, ontological.

The situation is made worse, not better, with time. The intuition of the primacy of this principle in Leibniz is covered up in Schopenhauer's doctoral dissertation. Schopenhauer translates "nihil est sine ratione cur potius sit quam non sit" as "nichts ist ohne Grund warum es sei" (roughly, "nothing is without a reason why it should be") (*Anfangsgründe* 141). Heidegger takes him to task for erasing the "potius quam," the axiom's key phrase. Heidegger writes: "The principle of sufficient reason is the principle of 'rather than,' of the preference for something over nothing, this over that, for 'this way' over 'otherwise'" (141–42). In Leibniz's original formulation one can see the entire problematic of the analytic of Dasein—concealing-unconcealing being through whose each-time finite understanding being is given to beings. Defining the origin of the principle of sufficient reason as the problem of the "potius," which Heidegger translates as "Vorzug," "advantage," "precedence," and much more appropriately, "priority," the question of being as transcendence can be glimpsed. Leibniz's "potius quam" points to a non-logical beginning that precedes and determines the most basic principle of logic. How is any being uncovered such that it could possibly become the object of a judgment? Transcending is equivalent to this uncovering.

These issues are more complex than my cursory treatment lets on; nevertheless the sequence of claims leading to transcendence as the unresolved problem in *Being and Time* runs as we've seen: logic is grounded in metaphysics, and metaphysics is grounded in a more original problem, the problem of priority, which warrants the movement from one to the other. In the most general terms, one should ask: how does something precede and determine another? How does temporalizing displacement structure world? Who can explain the "condition of possibility" that determines transcendence, since the question is already conditioned by a notion of conditioning? Might we discover that the groundlessness of being, which has been established by means of the transcendental method, is, itself, a groundless assumption?

At this moment, the importance of *Transzendenz* is beyond question, although a year later it will already have faded. In 1928, Heidegger calls it ontology's "guiding problem" (*leitende[s] Problem*) (*Anfangsgründe* 187) and as such its "fundamental problem" (*Grundproblem*) (186). He explains the "problem of *Being and Time*" as the missing question of "Grund," a word brought into the analytic here in a decisive way. What does it mean to be a fundament or *causa*, reason or origin, *aitia* or *archē*? An explanation of these foundational phenomena is missing in *Being and Time*, although it is also there, hidden in the link between the title's two words. "But this is the problem . . . how being is earlier . . . being and time, that is the fundamental problem [*das Grundproblem*]!" (186). The mysterious link eludes even philosophical attempts to access it; ontology and its tool, the question, are fated to encounter it, yet each time to obscure it anew. "All ontological questioning is a question into and a determination of the 'Apriori'" (184). How to access this problem without assuming the answer in advance is the obscure problem to which he refers. But it is only apparently obscure. Or rather, the problem is obscure, but its contours can be discerned against the light of misunderstanding. The adjective "ontological" communicates no more or less than this problem: a desire to access and guarantee the apriori, and in accessing it (or pretending to) to interpret it and thus to determine it as prior. Aprioricity itself, however, has only abyssal priority, which is only priority by dint of a decision and an evasion of further inquiry. The prior must come before itself, and as such someone comes always afterward to decide that it had been, indeed, prior. Each time it is made accessible, each time an ontological structure or origin is desired for a certain region or reign of beings, the movement of aprioricity recedes from itself, leaving an image in its place, a determinate "before" whose beforeness has vanished into the *nachträglichkeit* with which it has been, yet again, asserted. In short, what seems most clearly to be the a priori of some category or phenomenon, is in practice the more deeply a posteriori.

Given: transcendence means nothing more than "going beyond" for Heidegger, a mode of prior distancing that constitutes the familiar nearness with which human beings have already interpreted the world in which they dwell. But this is never an ontic relation. "If according to this, the originary transcendence (being-in-the-world) makes possible the intentional relation, this is, however, ontic, and the relationship to the ontic is grounded in the understanding of being, then there must be an inner kinship between originary transcendence and the understanding of being in general; yes, in the end they are one and the same" (*Anfangsgründe* 170). Not just today's understanding by this or that interpreter and not just the fulfillment of this or that intention for consciousness, but something that moves beyond these limited goings beyond, an act or event beyond any single step beyond determines transcendence per se. "This original transcendence [*Urtranszendenz*] makes possible every intentional relationship to a being" (170).

In a passage that Derrida makes much of in his reading, Heidegger tries to describe the distinction between transcendence and original transcendence or "Urtranszendenz." Facticity, the tendency toward beings and the ontic is "Zerstreuung," but the transcendence of facticity, the "every time again" that characterizes it, Augustine's "trial without respite," in short, the unity and perpetuity of existence and the inescapable phenomenality of the world of appearances result from a prior and purer "Streuung." It is this second version of dispersal, which seems to have been cleansed of the association with dissipation and distraction, that gives philosophy its special claim to understand. "Self-understanding out of the 'for the sake of which' means self-understanding out of the ground. This must have already become multiple according to that which I call the inner strewal [*Streuung*] of Dasein" (277). Given that the lecture course is meant to both introduce and persuade students to adopt the phenomenological method, the turn from care to understanding heralded in this citation is critical. "Umwillen," "for the sake of which" names the structure of care that makes up being-in-the-world (276). This is no longer the "beyond" of Dasein, however. Urtranszendenz is equivalent, now, to a more general *"Freiheit zum Grunde"* (*Anfangsgründe* 276), Dasein's "capacity" to act for its own sake, to care, in sum, for anything, but to always be caring for something. Beyond the being of Dasein, care, a higher or prior freedom makes out "der *Grund des Grundes*" of being (277). The ground's own freedom to be a ground, that which transcends it and names the last step in the chain, is thus the "Streuung von Grund" (*Anfangsgründe* 278). So we follow Heidegger, ever backward, from the weaker to the stronger, more comprehensive, more inclusive. Here the problem has been addressed, but only by wiping away the paradoxical power of weakness that Heidegger had invented or discovered late in *Being and Time.* There is a similar distaste for thoughtlessness, however. *Innere Streuung*, he insists, should not be confused with "Gedankenlosigkeit," which is mere "Schein" (278).[21]

Release from Care

Where does the thinker's commitment lie, when he makes the case for care? In which *Erschließung*, toward what *explanandum*, proscribed by what former possibility, not thinking what unthought? Let us not be coy: *Sorge* is *besorgt* by Heidegger, in whatever mode of taking care you want to specify: thinking, lecturing, teaching, wishing, reading. Intellectual historians will continue to select the ontic commitments that seem to determine Heidegger's thought; and when not beclouded by cheap moralizing, this can be helpful. In the ontological terms of the analytic, however, we can say that the committed philosopher, buffeted by the *Hang und Drang* of his *Da*, carries care into his workshop, and, in so doing, sets awhirl a vortex. An illicit ontic involvement fundamentally alters care's explanatory or interpretive power; Heidegger might not in fact deny this. Tainted by this or that concern, and by its own principle it must be so tinged, care can no longer transcend the degraded and degrading form of *Zerstreuung.* To go forward, then, to sidestep those forces in Heidegger's philosophy that tend to obscure distraction rather than illuminate it, we would want to know what the thinker was thinking when he "bumped into" the root of all ontic commitments, to identify, if we could, the one determined, closed off, enthralled mode that made it possible for care to appear to him as pure dispersal, the opposite of thoughtlessness. It was not nothing in particular. What if it was, in point of fact, not so much a commitment to care as an aversion, which doubtless is also a manner of taking care, to a dissipation without cause?

CHAPTER 5

Time Wears Away / Benjamin

Kafka intuits the political stakes, Heidegger stumbles onto the conceptual problem, and Walter Benjamin tries to produce a theory of it. Of course, this makes distraction sound much too unified. In 1920 Kafka proposed an extreme diaspora without a homeland in thought and in 1923 he presented the most paradoxical consequences of this political arrangement in the story "Der Bau." In 1927 Heidegger exposed the dialectic of dissipation and care constituting existence in *Being and Time* and in the 1928 Leibniz lectures he showed its source in a higher, pure dispersing, that did away with most of the deleterious effects of distraction. Between 1934 and 1936 Benjamin brought to fruition a preoccupation with a highly deleterious *Zerstreuung* that went back for him at least to 1916.

While still very young, Benjamin took his departure not from Brentano or Husserl, but from Kant. An attempt to conceive of experience outside the tyranny of the transcendental structure of knowledge first pushed the 23-year-old Benjamin toward *Zerstreuung*, and even in these early texts, he does not shy away from the contexts in which *Zerstreuung* means something like "entertainment." Kafka's concern with art and Heidegger's concern with philosophy, the one's insistence on a lack of transcendence and the other's insistence on the need for it, come together and are transformed in Benjamin's theory of distraction. He too desires a milieu broader and richer than the intellect in order to account for social, political, as well as historical action, a chaotic ground available for the kind of uncategorizable, disordered, fantastic, and unanticipatable modalities that make up Kafka's "life," if not Heidegger's quite orderly "existence." Benjamin's transformation of distraction strikes in the meaning and in the temporality of *Zerstreuung*. Kafka and Heidegger associate distraction with temporal problems: an endless, unchanging, yet finite quality of life, a repetitiveness in existence—diaspora and dissipation, always again. Only Benjamin ascribes it a specific historical movement. Distraction is itself dispersed and dissipating; it appears only sporadically as a producer of and a response to historical turning points.

A Wayward Phrase

A phrase from Benjamin's essay on technical reproducibility that has provoked both interest and skepticism since it was written declares the central concern for art-theory around 1935 to be the "reception in distraction" (*die Rezeption in der Zerstreuung*) triggered by film. Interesting is the potential that the phrase seems to have—still today—to illuminate the structure and effects of the then new medium.

At least part of the interest in the phrase lies in the structure of the phrase itself: its form poses an obstacle to understanding. "Reception in distraction" cannot easily be received; at best it is a paradox, at worst nonsense. In 1909 Karl Kraus described the historical grounds of paradox: "A paradox arises when an unripe piece of knowledge crashes with the foolishness [*Unsinn*] of its time" (164). In the best of cases, then, as a paradox, "reception in distraction" will have ripened over the years between 1935 and today, surviving the "Unsinn" of its time, emerging now—or soon—at the moment of its historical maturity, no longer paradoxical. And yet, although the argument can be made that today we are closer to distraction than ever, the phrase seems to hold our interest in particular because it is still difficult to understand. The phrase seems, in fact, to be more closely related to "Unsinn" than *Sinn*, and not just if we refer to the senselessness of the Nazi era, when Benjamin wrote it, or the prejudices of the immediate postwar years, the sixties in France and the seventies in America, and so forth—the various epochs of Benjamin reception. Despite the hunger with which his work has been received over the past thirty years, the phrase continues to appear odd and somewhat indigestible. This is perhaps because the collision of an idea with the nonsense of its time—Kraus's definition of paradox—would seem to contain an appeal to distraction within it. A time's distraction and the premature idea that collides with it is an image of this very phenomenon. Paradox, in Kraus's understanding of it, is another name for "reception in distraction."

Insofar as it describes the historical structure of paradox, the phrase cannot hope to find resolution or understanding in another time, as though it were simply waiting for the right mind to come and think it. In fact—and this is the more revolutionary implication of the phrase—distraction is what accounts for intellectual transformations that accompany changes in "times." The basis for this historical notion of distraction is the following insight. "The manner in which human sensory perception organizes itself—the medium in which occurs—is not only naturally conditioned but also historically conditioned" (Benjamin *GS* I.2 478). The self-organization of sensual perception is liable to changes, or so Benjamin argues, such that its historical constitution also affects its operation. With this in mind, distraction can be seen as the stage in which the "Sinneswahrnehmung" is no longer organized and not yet reorganized, a break in which the reorganization of its elements should take place. This interval is not an outgrowth of the intellectual faculties, but rather the intervention of "history" into their natural operation. *Zerstreuung* comes to designate, for Benjamin, mind's historical transition away from nature; toward what, however, is not at first clear.

At the very least we can say that distraction cannot be seen as a new part that fits into an old apparatus. It is not a new perceptual order but the condition for its possibility. According to the third draft of the artwork essay, reception in distraction allows "new tasks of apperception" to become "solvable" or "soluble" (*lösbar*) (*GS* I.2 505). And yet the sense or senses of "reception in distraction" and the "new apperceptive tasks" that it makes possible remain problematic, insofar as they are neither reception nor tasks, but that which intervenes in a configuration of "Sinneswahrnehmung," halting its operation and dissolving its naturalized structure.

"The aura was originally (as long as it established cult-value) loaded with history" (*GS* VII.2 677). If history is thought of as the layered deposit of meaning onto a singular, temporally and spatially finite, authentic cult object—this is one of the ways in which Benjamin defines history in these writings, as the objective correlative of aura—if history is auratic, "Rezeption in der Zerstreuung" points to the moment in which that cultural deposit is blown away, that is, forgotten or ignored.

Aura is in Benjamin's definition the one time and in one place appearance of a distance—a theological structure. Distraction allows the distance to return to its place, to disappear, releasing it to remoter regions. Once the proximal distance—the symbol, the idea, beauty, or god—releases its hold on the local artwork, the cult scatters. This is the other way in which "Rezeption in der Zerstreuung" made sense to Benjamin in the thirties. It named a peculiar condition in which the "Sinneswahrnehmung" became disorganized, and at the same time it gestured toward the Hebrew "Galut," geographic and political diaspora; a non-unified cult, a non-cult. "Reception in diaspora," another possible translation of the phrase, hints at a positive diasporic theory in which no future synthesis would define present disparateness—a diaspora without hope or promise.

Skepticism about the phrase may in fact be a response to the almost impossible conditions necessary for understanding it. Such reception is highly unstable. In it, one receives an art object whose meaning is no longer guaranteed by art history, or by a god. It would not be too much to say that "reception in distraction" receives nothing. It may in fact only receive the destructive tendencies that lead to the tradition's demise. And the destructive tendency hinted at in the phrase was controversial from the outset. One of the earliest critiques of the idea arrived in a letter from Adorno in 1936: "And the theory of distraction [*Zerstreuung*] does not, despite its shocking seduction, completely convince me. If only for the simple reason that in the communist society work will be organized such that people will no longer be so tired and so dulled as to need entertainment [*Zerstreuung*]" (Adorno and Benjamin, *Briefwechsel*, 172).

Whether Adorno's criticism is convincing or not, his wordplay is suggestive. At the same time—in the same word—he expresses a thought about the effects of *Zerstreuung* on society and the effects of the "theory" in Benjamin's text. Distraction is "seductive" because it shocks its readers, shocks them into not thinking, just as Benjamin says that shocks produce distraction in film audiences. Several elements of Adorno's brief commentary are worth remarking on. First, he sees Benjamin operating with respect to *Zerstreuung* in a scientific or philosophical mode. The

"Theorie der *Zerstreuung*" is to be assessed here according to its effectiveness as an argument. Is the major premise "convincing"? Is the conclusion valid? While it is valid, it is not, in fact, true, since in the political society to come there will be no need for it. He doesn't mention the more puzzling philosophical aspects of the "theory," for instance the suggestion that anything could be "received" in distraction. He also does not ask for a definition of the term; instead he assimilates it to the then popular meanings, diversion and entertainment. Whether Adorno is just being "crude," as he says, or whether he actually believes that the revolution is coming, he still understands the phenomenon within a revolutionary framework, seeing in it a negative product of the capitalist system: a palliative for overwork and exhaustion by means of stupefaction. How could liberation come from the seductive, false image—entertainment? For these reasons then, Adorno rejects Benjamin's thought of *Zerstreuung* in the artwork essay: first because he expects to be convinced as though it were a rational argument, second because he interprets the word as amusement, with all the negative connotations that would accompany it for a certain type of Marxist.[1] He did not imagine that what is entertaining could also, at the same time, be revolutionary.

The "theory" did not appear completely "convincing" when Adorno wrote Benjamin in 1936 for one thing because, for Benjamin, the stakes of the text were not only intellectual. In a 1935 letter to Max Horkheimer, Benjamin complains about his own financial situation: "The paradox in this situation is that my work has probably never been closer to a public usefulness as it is now" (*GB* V 178). The "work" in question is the artwork essay, and the usefulness, as he writes in another letter to Horkheimer from around the same time, lies in the "informational value" (*informatorische[m] Wert*) that "this work" might have "for the avant-garde of the French intelligentsia" (*GB* V 252). What is paradoxical about the situation is that for his work on technical reproducibility to be publicly useful, for it to be given worth as information by the most advanced of German intellectuals and to achieve for art theory what film achieves for the artist, as Benjamin puts it in a note to the second version of the essay, "the liquidation [*Liquidierung*] of the difference between intellectual and manual labor," Benjamin has to produce something recognizable as work to his employers. For the newly resettled Institute for Social Research he had to produce something that could be categorized as intellectual labor (*GS* I.3 1051). How then, the question poses itself, could a work that would redefine intellectual labor per se be received as the labor of an intellectual whose work was worth fair recompense, in advance of the revolution it intended to produce?

There is no question that Benjamin took Adorno's objection seriously, as seriously as any worker takes the censure of his supervisor, even if he is also his friend. With not only his theory of intellectual work, but his survival as an intellectual worker at stake, Benjamin writes three versions of the essay, which he had called, in an outline for the first version: "an attempt to give the questions of art theory a true contemporary shape" and "a programmatic work [*Arbeit*] toward art theory." This essay seems to be among the most reworked of his writings: in the process of rewriting, Benjamin produces a plethora of notes, among which we find the numbered set of theses with the title "Theory of Distraction" (*Theorie der Zerstreuung*) that, he writes Adorno, add up to "paralipomena," things left-aside. And indeed, they are left aside: nothing of the "Theory of Distraction" migrates into the third and final version of the artwork essay.

Reproducibility–Distracting/Dispersing– Politicization

When Benjamin sets out to elaborate and clarify the "theory of distraction" that Adorno, among so much praise for the essay in his letter, dismisses so "crudely," he writes a spare series of premises outlining a possible response. The twenty sentence-like notes collected in the *Nachträge zu den Anmerkungen* in Volume VII of the *Gesammelte Schriften* establish the conceptual parameters for his so-called "theory." One line among the twenty lays out the theory's parameters: "Reproduzierbarkeit–Zerstreuung–Politisierung" (*GS* VII.2 679). These are the poles of Benjamin's thought of distraction.[2] "Zerstreuung" stands between two terms with which we are perhaps more familiar from Benjamin's oeuvre, terms that fall—or seem to—into common disciplines: art theory and political theory. To what discipline does the middle term belong? What role does it play in this trinity? Asking this question points to the significance of the dashes—*Gedankenstriche*—that connect the three. Do these dashes signify a thoughtful movement between concepts? Is there a dialectic at work here such that politicization becomes a synthesis of the two former terms? Perhaps, and yet the specific values—*Werte*—of the concepts in question would have to be ascertained in order to be sure. Two of them, as I've said, fall into well-known categories: they are the elements Benjamin presents us with at the end of the published version of the essay on reproducibility. There he asks: what is a relationship between aesthetics and politics that would be useless for fascism? This telegraphic line, a triode of terms, offers a solution. By means of *Zerstreuung*, reproducibility draws aesthetics away from fascism toward a different order—an order in which all relationships become "politicized."

The triode, then, is an elaboration of the less than convincing "reception in distraction" of Section 15. In this line we find an unequivocal statement about the relationship that Benjamin hopes to establish between artworks, mental and historical life, and politics. It is not simply a new mode of perception or experience that is envisaged here, but a catalytic event whose technical base determines and is determined—reciprocally— by a political grouping principle, in the medium of distraction-dispersion-diasporization. *Zerstreuung* is a mental, historical, and geographical medium at once. It corresponds to reproducibility, which makes it possible. And it produces not a fixed political structure, but an event or shift in the grounds for the political, a "becoming political"—*Politisierung*—whose process depends on a mental break up and the historical and geographical diaspora that ensues. One of the "paralipomena" to the first version of the essay sheds light on the concept of the political event at work here. "The technical reproducibility of the artwork leads to its literarization," but the last word is struck through, "~~Literarisierung~~," and replaced by "Politisierung." Many "-ierung" words come into play in Benjamin's writings around this time. The "liquidation of the difference between mental and manual work" marks film's mode of artistic production (*GS* I.3 1051). There is also the "refunctioning [*Umfunktionierung*] of the human apperceptual apparatus" (*GS* I.3 1049). "Liquidierung" is in fact the model for each "-ierung"; the suffix liquefies the state or institution to which it is attached.[3] With this in mind, the politics that corresponds to a fascist-proof aesthetics is not a politics that could be mapped out as a different program for group formation or institution building; instead it calls for a "liquidation" of existing political bonds toward their infinitization, the making, we might say, of politics into a medium for ongoing politicization. This does not mean of course a liquidation of members of already constituted groups: there is no confusing this with a genocidal principle—impossible, since it names a principle for the dissolution of all grouping principles. Whereas in the first type of liquidation an *ethnos* or *genos* is reified in order to annihilate its contents, Benjamin's "Politisierung" is an intellectual act that liquefies the grounds for any group, putting the elements into circulation again and raising them to a higher status, toward purity—pure dispersion—to use Benjamin's language. Once liquefied, the elements of politics and their potential to reconfigure are no longer secondary to a completed politics; released from their structure, they swirl freely.

"A Distracted, Spaceless Infinity of Pure Reception"

What gets marked as problematic or questionable in the phrase "reception in distraction"—it is a paradox *an sich*, as we've noted, and not merely a historical blind spot—is the word "distraction." Not only is it difficult to imagine any reception taking place in distraction, but it is also not clear why we should not do everything in our power to avoid falling prey to something like this. In all the worry about distraction, however, the concept of "reception" slips by without comment, as though its meaning were self-evident. It is in fact a precisely understood concept that appears in Benjamin's earliest writings as the highest aesthetic desideratum. To encounter a "pure reception" that would dethrone knowledge from its hegemony over experience is an early desire. A different kind of reception would offer a decisive weapon in his *Auseinandersetzung* with Kant over the concept of experience.

In a sketch not written later than fall 1917, "Über die Wahrnehmung," Benjamin specifies which elements of Kant's doctrine of experience should be kept and which should be discarded. He sets himself the task, which he will soon work out in more detail in "Über das Programm der kommenden Philosophie," to retain "the highest determinations" that Kant gave to knowledge, while challenging "his knowledge-theoretical constitution of the structure . . . of experience [*Erfahrung*]" (*GS* VI 33).

The highest determination that Kant gave to knowledge was its purity; however, when he conceptualized experience he did not allow it the same determination. Or, better said, in the *Kritik der reinen Vernunft*, "rein" means that experience is derived purely from knowledge, and not the other way around (*GS* VI 34). Experience is always "knowledge of experience." In this light the concept of experience is so empty that it comes to be no more than the "symbol of this epistemic context" (*GS* VI 36). The whole of critical philosophy, insofar as it does not go beyond this knowledge-critical totality, depends on experience's void.

This argument has two corollaries. First, from the assumption of an empty experience, worthless in itself, the richness of the transcendental world can be deduced. Experience is, thereafter, the shell into which transcendental knowledge—the categories, pure intuitions, and ideas of reason—can be poured. Following up on this intuition, in "Über das Programm der kommenden Philosophie," written slightly later than its prototype, "Über die Wahrnehmung," Benjamin rebukes Kant for having established his philosophy "on the zero degree, on experience reduced to the minimum" (*GS* II.1 159). "Flache[] Erfahrung" is the unwarranted presupposition of Kant's knowledge-critical philosophy, and constitutes a metaphysical remnant, a mythological element that needs to be purged (*GS* II.1 161). If flat, empty experience were gotten rid of, two cornerstones of pure reason's edifice would have to go as well: the difference between empirical consciousness and transcendental consciousness and, in turn, the "image of an individual bodily-spiritual I that receives impressions by means of the senses and on their basis forms its thought. . . . " Benjamin adds: "This image is, however, mythology" (*GS* II.1 161). In the destruction of Kant's theory of experience, then, lies a possibility for an experience beyond body and spirit, beyond the unity of consciousness as the unexperienceable transcendental ground, beyond—perhaps—transcendence per se. It is surprising to note how many of the motifs that ten years later Heidegger would explore in *Being and Time* are already sketched out here by the 25-year-old Benjamin.[4]

What does it look like "beyond" the transcendental? A rainbow. A child is free of the tyranny of transcendental knowledge in the experience of color, whose totality the rainbow emblematizes. As such the child's experience is infinitely rich—nothing like the "flat experience" of the adult (unless of course he or she is a "kindliche[r] Mensch" [*GS* VI 110]). Two relatively completed though short compositions and several more fragmentary notes explore the child's experience along two axes: looking like or seeing (*Sehen/Aussehen, Schauen*) and color (*Farbe*).

Soap bubbles are another emblematic focal point of childlike experience; the "movable passage of nuances" on their convex, watery surfaces fascinate (*GS* VI 110). This observation, drawn from Benjamin's composition "Die Farbe vom Kinde aus Betrachtet," is evidence of a highly discerning capacity in children. However paradoxical it may sound, children are discerning in an order in which no objects come forward to be discerned. Instead of beings with outlines, infinite subtleties corresponding much more to a "Vermischung" than to a "Verschwommenheit" are the basis of this "sight" (*GS* VI 110). Children are best at being distracted: thinking nothing means that they need think no object, no form. And yet the mental correlate of the infinite nuances of color's phantasmagoria is not a cloud; a child's thinking is not nebulous or vague—far from it. It is incredibly precise, as precise as a manifold of perfectly distinct hues can be. In the realm of color, mixture is never contamination. Where there are no things there can be no pollution of a supposedly "pure" substance by accident. Mixture without muddiness thus constitutes the "purity" of color. Mingling one color with another simply makes another color, and the result is no less colorful or distinct than any other. As a sphere of pure distinction, then, for children the order of color is "something mental" (*etwas Geistiges*), Benjamin notes (*GS* VI 110).

Only to visual experience do these reflections apply. Let me cite a line from the essay in full, since it contains *in nuce* much of the argument about "seeing." "The childlike perception of color brings the sense of sight to the highest artistic development, to purity, insofar as it isolates it, it [childlike perception] elevates this formation to an intellectual one, given that it looks at objects according to its color content and accordingly not isolated, but rather it secures for itself the interrelated intuition of the fantasy world in them" (*GS* VI 110). The mentality of the colored world consists in the fact that it brings the sense of sight (*den Gesichtssinn*) into the realm of the mental. More than this, however, it brings the experience of seeing, and not just the seen thing, into the mental sphere as that which can teach it to be otherwise. This is because color, as pure seeing, is not susceptible to other mental processes. One cannot think color; it is only a highly experienced "seeing" that can learn to distinguish many colors. "Color must be seen" (*Farbe muß gesehen werden*) (*GS* VI 109). And what's more, "colors see themselves" (*die Farben sehen sich*) (*GS* VI 118). There is no higher instance, no uncolored receptive capacity that could be the agent to this passive, that would receive it and know it while avoiding being tinged by it—colors continually order and reorder themselves. The child is colored into the world such that *Erfahrung* becomes "Färbung," a modality Benjamin calls "reine Empfänglichkeit," "pure receptivity," that is, reception purified of categories (*GS* VI 111). Subjectless and objectless "being-colored-into-the-world" does not give up the world when it gives up a mentalistic relationship and the transcendental assumptions that the relationship entails. Quite the reverse—experience enters into the mental and rearranges it, deranges it.[5]

This is not limited to children. Coloring-experience—*Er-fähr-bung*—may still possess adults, either in art or in dreaming. The relationship between the two is worked out in more nuance in "The Rainbow: Dialogue on Fantasy" ("Der Regenbogen: Gespräch über die Phantasie"), written around same time or slightly later.[6] At the beginning of the dialogue on the rainbow when the two speakers come together, although Georg would like to hear Margarethe's dream and she would like nothing more than to share her dream "images" with him, such communication seems impossible. "Georg—I see that I cannot do it. A dream does not allow itself to be told [*Ein Traum läßt sich nicht sagen*]" (*GS* VII.1 19). The dream analog of coloring-experience is not communicable, at least not insofar as the receiver would not also be dreaming or inside the other's dream. And this difference is in fact what Margarethe's dream was a dream *of.* "Thus it was in the dream, I was nothing other than seeing. All other senses had been forgotten, had vanished. I too was not, not my understanding, which unlocks things out of the images. I was not a seer, I was only seeing. And what I saw were not things, Georg, only colors. And I myself was colored into this landscape" (*GS* VII.1 19–20). The understanding that separates things from their "seeing" is forgotten in dreaming, and so the contents of the dream cannot be communicated in the language of understanding.

Margarethe's dream, in which experience is freed from knowledge and presented in a richer form, stimulates Georg, her interlocutor, to extrapolate this model to the sphere of fantasy and then to art. In Georg's formulation, fantasy has much less to learn about experience from art than art does from fantasy. Painting is the exemplary art form that Georg adduces to demonstrate the difference. Painting cannot make a claim to "pure experience" because it does not have color as its essence; its essence is rather "surface," "Fläche." Essentially surface, its principle is space and not color, and its mode is thus forming and not coloring; painting forms space for the sake of things, with the result that for painting color is always secondary (*GS* VII.1 20–21). Philosophy that has seen color as a secondary property falls prey to critique here, when Benjamin—like Plato before him—recognizes a secret complicity between the Western philosophical outlook and painting.[7] Outline and perspective, light and shadow, objects conceived as formed content—painting's ontological toolkit—impoverish color, whose strength lies in an uninterrupted variability of hues. As the critique of painting demonstrates, not just any art can take this eccentric "Farbenlehre" as its principle. Said another way, an art that would take color as its principle and not merely as a weak reflection or secondary property would have to accept the laws of fantasy. A fantasy law carries the special proviso, however, that it cannot be followed as though it were a paradigm, a "Vorbild." It must instead be taken as an "Urbild," a "prototype," a prefiguration of a similar but not identical variation that streams from fantasy into art. Georg expresses this strict requirement in a paradoxical formula: "and only where he [the artist] strives to make the prototype into a model [*das Urbild zum Vorbild*], where he wants to take possession of the mental amorphously [*des Geistigen sich gestaltlos bemächtigen*], where he looks at it formlessly [*formlos anschaut*], only there does the work become fantastic" (*GS* VII.1 22). The young Benjamin becomes a partisan here of a theory of un-formation, in contrast to a formalist or artist-centered theory of art. From this will follow in his writings a theory of history and art history seen not so much as a succession of forms or intellectual reforms, but rather as the repeated advent of the principle of unforming, of which color is an essential prototype—prototype not because it is an archetype against which each instance is measured and found deficient, but because it can become one origin of a configuration. A color manifold represents an absolute dissolution of form, a uniformly unformed array—a rainbow, and the rainbow is the appearance of the beauty of decay. Along with it, the intellectual order that corresponds to the reception of forms, objects, things, space, and time also disintegrates. In the dialogue, Margarethe utters a word that sums up in an experiential manner Georg's speculative remarks. She calls the pure reception of color "woolly." She makes this word even more distinct with the following lines: "a distracted [*zerstreute*], spaceless infinity of pure reception [*Aufnahme*], the artistic world of the child was so constituted . . . —Children's perception is itself dispersed into colors. They do not divert [*Sie leiten nicht ab*]" (*GS* VII.1 25). Her last remark opens up the difference between two concepts of distraction that are easily and often confused. It is not the case that children are always ready to be distracted. Children are in point of fact undistractable. They are undistractable from distraction in the spaceless infinity of pure reception. In other words, in a world without things, distraction cannot be confused with diversion. One can only be diverted from one predefined thing or state of affairs to another. Children are resistant to being diverted from the vision in which they alone see and are seen, in which they experience/color—*er-fähr-ben*. As we've seen, Adorno takes it for granted in his commentary on the artwork essay that Benjamin means *Zerstreuung* in the first sense, diversion, amusement, looking away toward illicit things. All its relatives and connotations—division, diversion, amusement, entertainment, dissolution, on the way to depravity—speak of a deficiency, whereas Benjamin's *Zerstreuung* gestures toward an untold abundance and fertility in which nature and human nature merge in a Technicolor kaleidoscope that no Hollywood studio could reproduce. We encounter here an entertainment without an entertainment industry. In this other sense, *Zerstreuung* names a complete deformation of the perceptual-mental order on the model of a color manifold. In pure reception there are neither beings nor primary properties, only free and freely combining hues for which painters—even though Benjamin insists that they occupy themselves primarily with the forms of things in space—have a term: "values," "*Werte*."

Mass and Massiveness

"Reception in Distraction" echoes the early work on color. In what we might call "Er-fähr-bung," the hold of form on thought loosens. Experience is made "higher" than knowledge, higher, that is, than transcendence, and so it is not "high" in any relative sense. Experience becomes absolutely high. Coloring-experience, it should be noted, "Er-fähr-bung," is not comparable to a "transcendental experience" (which in any case would be indistinguishable from transcendental knowledge), but repudiates the supposed need to "go beyond." With the dissolution of the form principle—and of principles as formative or forming—the intellectual and empirical worlds cease to conform to a topographical model. Fantasy is the palette on which the empirical and the ideal mingle and stain one another.

We have seen that experience can be liberated from transcendence in fantasy—for adults in dreams and for children in the reception of color. But, at least in these early essays, Benjamin thinks of little else that could qualify as pure experience or pure reception. The return of distraction in the study of film extends, at least in part, the attempt to generalize the experience of child and dreamer beyond childhood and sleep—as well as beyond fantasy, to art and technology, and ultimately to the political. The artwork essay again calls for experience to be purified of knowledge; it demands that what knowledge has emptied out be filled up again from experience alone. In the intentional structure of film Benjamin sees the possibility to extend his critique of Kant's theory of experience to political experience. Wanted would be a politics without knowledge, not burdened by governing transcendental or normative structures. It would be something like a politics of pure experience, which would be in a real sense unknowable. Although surrealist artists were experimenting with wider applications of dream images, and Benjamin studied these experiments carefully, it was not enough to enjoin the dissolution of the individual imagination into collective dream-images or of grammar into automatic writing, not enough to envision another reality above or below the rational order as a secret source for behavior and meaning. Surrealist doctrine did not venture to explain political community, although it may have enacted it.[8] In neither surrealism nor *l'art pour l'art* did art theory achieve, from Benjamin's perspective, a heat strong enough to melt the bonds of the traditional association of aesthetics and politics.

In Section 15 of the essay on technical reproducibility Benjamin returns to the topic; however, distraction emerges in a strange set of relationships. It becomes the grounds for the occurrence of any historical turning point. Out of this, in addition, there results a specifically political effect.

Mass experience is also not governed by knowledge, insofar as, although it is a form of experience that extends to an almost unlimited number of members, the communality of the mass does not depend on any predetermined self-knowledge or identity among its members.

A mass ensues when "quantity is turned [*umgeschlagen*] into quality," as Section 15 in the third version begins. A qualitative aggregate, "Masse" is the only political unit Benjamin discusses in depth in the essay. Other words that might indicate similar formations—*Menge, Haufen, Ansammlung, Partei, Fraktion*—are absent. There is something in the quality of "Masse" that Benjamin likes. One obvious difference from other grouping principles is the non-spatial definition of a collection, which mass borrows from physics. There are some hints toward the physical provenance of the political term in Benjamin's text. Reproduction and mass share certain characteristics, first of all. They both "vervielfältigen" without becoming quantifiably more, for instance, just like mass may increase without increasing the number of things it is a mass of. More reproductions is not more than the original number in the same way that more originals would be. Reproductions cannot be more in a numerical sense, since each reproduction is not quite one; it looks beyond itself for its meaning or essence, and thus a group of reproductions does not precisely make up a quantitatively numerable series. They are all in some sense "the same." Something similar is true for mass. "Insofar as reproduction multiplies it [*die Tradition*]," writes Benjamin in Section 2, "it puts its mass-character in place of its one-time occurrence" (*GS* I.2 477). Both the political unit, mass, and the art form that it receives depart from the "once-ness" of tradition as well as from the "one-ness" of members of a denumerable series. The way of being massive turns, as Section 15 announces, from quantity into quality. "Mass-movements of our time" (*GS* I.2 478) are to be explained, at least in part, according to this qualitative "mass-character." Mass is the contemporary "way" of the "human collective" (*menschliche[] Kollektiva*), and this explains the change in "the manner of its sensual perception" (*GS* I.2 478). A mass does not perceive like a group of individuals perceive. Furthermore, the changed kind and manner of sensual perception is "not only naturally but also historically conditioned." In mass, we might say, nature changes its course—history intervenes in the seemingly natural makeup of sensual perception and the collective that corresponds to it.

The "demolition [*Zertrümmerung*] of Aura" and the concomitant change in political group from cult to mass coincide with this basic change in the perceiver-receiver. When we mass up, our senses become massive too, transforming apperception. We should not underestimate the momentousness of such a transformation, Benjamin insists. "The orientation of reality toward the masses and the masses toward reality is an event of unlimited consequences, as much for thinking as for intuition" (*GS* I.2 480).

"Quantity has turned into quality" (*GS* I.2 503) means among other things, that the group that previously could be counted up as an aggregate of individuals, equally capable of grouping together as of being separated into constituent units, becomes indivisible, and for this reason it receives art differently. It has one eye and more than one eye at once. Its reaction to artworks is "massive," reactions of individuals are "from the outset conditioned by the immediately impending massification [*Massierung*]." The spectator/spectators become susceptible to a simultaneous "collective reception" that points once again to pure experience (*GS* I.2 497). In color, experience is loosened from the transcendental; collective reception of artworks receives without a subject to receive. It enters the non-subject and bounces around. For, how can a mass—if it is not divisible into individual members whose individual cognitions could add up to one public or "people"—how can a mass give itself transcendental unity as the law of its experience if the group that it contains is not denumerable? How can the apperception of an uncountable one-many be a transcendental unity that ensures the coherence and continuity of its thinking? A non-denumerable collective operates, according to Benjamin's line of thinking here, through a truly plural thinking, one that can as little be broken down into individual opinions as it can be counted up and added together into a political will. And so mass, when it turns away from quantity toward quality, is receptive in what Benjamin calls "an altered mode of participation" (*eine veränderte Art des Anteils*) that appears in a "disreputable form" (*in verrufener Gestalt*) (*GS* I.2 503).[9]

Kracauer's Cult

Given mass's strange essence, when Benjamin writes that the social classes that enter the cinema are "umgeschlagen," turned around and thrust out of the realm of quantity into quality, they are also thrust out of the social and made inaccessible to sociology. Exactly how one imagines the "changed sort of participation," the modified way that participants have of having a share in a mass becomes a crucial question. Roman *socii* established a reciprocal relationship between members, a partnership implying mutual obligation that made an alliance of individuals necessary for a particular purpose. A mass, however, does not seem to be organized around a purpose. We should ask: what relationship determines a mass? Do massables amass on the basis of something held in common, a worldview, an origin, an end? Is a mass a community? The observer who wants to see mass should not be put off, Benjamin warns in Section 15, simply because the changed "share" in the mass appears in a "disreputable form."

Whatever the difficulties conceiving of this new shapeless political unit, the way mass cannot be received remains unambiguous in Benjamin's presentation. A mass does not become visible to those who pursue it by optical means. A mass has as little to do with the temporal-visual complex of present-presentation-representation as it does with the contrary complex of absent-invisible-unrepresentable. It is neither present nor absent, but rather virtual, dispersed, resistant, massive. Those who have a passion for its "superficial side," Benjamin remarks, miss these differences. This is probably a jab at Siegfried Kracauer's passion for "Oberflächlichkeit." Those who want to look at mass in a conventional sense, become preoccupied by mass's "Gestalt." Needless to say, the concept of "Gestalt" falls under suspicion in and around a mass. Like coloring-experience, a mass cannot be explained through the concept of form. In the afterword to the artwork essay, Benjamin ascribes a horrific outcome to the desire to give mass form. There are only two possible results. Mass becomes "a" mass, a unit with a visible external form in the bird's-eye photograph that falsifies mass into an aggregate with an outline. That is, mass gets form from the perspective of a bomber. A second shape is given to mass by an army, which turns it into a group with countable members; this is accomplished by dissolving the mass into corpses (*GS* I.2 506). Both reduce mass to formed material.[10] Attempts to give mass form run counter to the tendency of reproducibility, however. Reproducibility caters to qualitative massiveness, a relationship that cannot be represented without destroying it.

Benjamin's stealthy but pointed critique of Kracauer in the first passages of Section 15 take issue with his view of *Zerstreuung*. Kracauer welcomed *Zerstreuung* with open arms, but for him it was the proper term for the representation of the new unit of social organization.[11] Mass joins the "Cult of Distraction" in order to catch sight of itself, in order to encounter itself in an "image" or "copy" of itself (*Abbild*) ("Kult der Zerstreuung" 316). With mass, that is to say, there is no change in the public's desire for self-representation. The relation of art and the political group that looks at it does not change. The represented object changes—but the reliance on representation remains constant. Kracauer's understanding of art in this essay is a copy of a Hegelian view. Art binds the individuals into a community, by tying the community to one image of itself, by offering it a representation; it gives itself an image, understanding image as a normative political instrument. Sociology, in turn, presents the new norm as science. The norm of mass, for Kracauer, is different in magnitude and kind, but not in idea. It is still a norm. Film's image captures a bigger, faster, more delirious collective whose experience in the world-city would be utterly lost if it did not find adequate representation in splinters, on surfaces, in flashing lights and endless illusion. As a theoretical term—as the theoretical moment of mass experience—for Kracauer, mass founds itself on an adequate view of its essence. That essence can then be presented in sociology, where the word *Zerstreuung* provides theoretical truth about a cult whose image is given to it by film.

In presenting this new form of "culture" as a "cult," Kracauer becomes a warning for Benjamin. In the theory of art that Benjamin is developing in the 1930s, cinema is precisely that technology and that art form which leaves the cultic model of spectatorship behind, not to mention the normative politics that some think accompanies it. "The technical reproducibility of the artwork," Benjamin reminds us, "emancipates it for the first time from its parasitic existence in ritual" (*GS* I.2 481). With the disappearance of the "here and now" of the artwork, and the dispersal of the patina that deposits the here and now onto the work and makes the cult portable, the cultic aspect of culture ought to vanish as well, so that a welcome barbarism takes its place. Art theory is charged with opening the door to this barbarism. Without a doubt, Kracauer's reading is an empirical gain, and Benjamin has learned from him. Kracauer describes the experience of distraction quite precisely: "stimulations of the senses follow upon one another in them [films] so densely that the narrowest cogitation cannot wedge itself in between them" ("Kult der Zerstreuung" 314). Here we have a description of what Benjamin will call the massification of thought. In Kracauer's hands, however, it is made to reinforce perhaps the oldest image of thought. Instead of dissipating when it is being entertained, mass fulfills itself mentally in cinema; it becomes intellectual, "geistig," again in its new form. Cinema that is "for" the masses is quite conservative. It brings the dangerous mass back to its senses. And this is just what the sociologist counts on, since his medium is thought. In this way, a mass is the new form in which the unchanging social substance presents itself, and sociology receives this form without having to change its own methods or challenge its intellectual status. As a good empiricist, Kracauer attributes the emphasis on form to his object, not to his own theory. "The more people perceive themselves as a mass, the more the mass attains formative powers also in the realm of the intellect" ("Kult der Zerstreuung" 313). But this seems like a displacement. The attribution of a desire for form to the mass is a projection of the theoretical underpinnings of Kracauer's sociological theory. What would sociology do if it could not claim to represent the newest social forms, if what the "new" society was lacking was precisely this, form? It is possible that a theory of politics without "the social" would be needed.

Kracauer's positive attitude toward distraction is thus double-edged. He glimpses its importance—he even describes precisely its advantage over thought—but he quickly reassimilates it to traditional schemata. Kracauer is open to the idea of distraction. Nowhere does he moralize or condemn. In this article, first published in 1926 in the *Frankfurter Zeitung*, where he was culture editor, Kracauer recommends that mass culture as he describes it be accepted and encouraged. He even urges that the lust for distraction be given the financial support it needs to develop. This is the moral duty of the sociology of modernity: to make "the disorder of society" visible and graspable ("Kult der Zerstreuung" 315). Such making-visible, he claims, is the preparation for the "necessary transition"; to what, however, Kracauer does not specify further in this brief editorial. In his earlier book on the foundations of sociology, he gives a fuller view of the society to come. In "Soziologie als Wissenschaft," Kracauer chastises a traditionally minded sociology and turns its face toward *Zerstreuung* as the hallmark of modernity. Sociology should take distraction as the key concept for an understanding of "an epoch full of sensation" (*einer sinnerfüllten Epoche*); and yet, once again here, he makes this claim in order to reconfirm science's traditional method, which he says consists in "disguising the truth as a copy of reality."[12] Although an epoch that is overfilled with sensual stimulation produces a "bad infinity" of worldviews, nothing of its badness can infect sociology's ability to represent it ("Soziologie als Wissenschaft" 29). In spite of the degradation of modern experience, then, in the midst of describing it and even praising it, sociology manages to preserve a non-degraded scientific experience by encompassing the totality of worldviews and becoming, itself, the unity of the bad infinity in a good principle—the principle of representation—in order to regulate it.

Toward a Haptology

In Benjamin's eyes mass representation means mass destruction, and therefore the theory of art will itself need a makeover in order to receive it. It will have to give up the normative, mimetic, and ultimately conservative tendencies of science, and perhaps become massive itself. And this is one of the more radical connotations of his attempt to think distraction. Theory cannot keep itself out of the fray. To be able to begin to conceive the changes to "apperception" required to receive mass in a massive way, theory has to give up the model by which it thinks it thinks; that is, it has to give up vision. Benjamin turns to architecture—not because it contains a crowd of visitors within its walls, but rather because in architecture optical reception cedes to another mode. In architecture optical perception gets retrained by touch. "There is no concept of such reception," Benjamin declares, and yet nevertheless it can be expressed as laws that are, for an understanding of mass and film, "die lehrreichsten," the richest in teaching (*GS* I.2 504).

Concentration has zero value here, since in tactile perception fixity translates into the most immediate loss. Touching must continually change objects in order to sense: "it takes place . . . as if in a noticing that is incidental/ running past [*beiläufiges*]" (*GS* I.2 505). Although the metaphors involved in the words "concept" and "attention" arise from or depend on touch—stretching to make contact and grasping—grasping is in fact death to tactile reception. Touch senses only in letting go. The instant it stops it begins to lose its object. "There is no concept of such reception," and for this reason no theory is produced in the mode of touch, only habit, "Gewohnheit" (*GS* I.2 504–5).[13] In addition, touch never produces an adequate perception of its object; because it cannot grasp or measure, it either loses by becoming accustomed to its object or else it continues to perceive it by passing by and failing to keep track. Thus there are two losses that surround touch. The first, when it stops and rests, is complete amnesia; the second is a positive loss, an active, moving letting go in which sensation flees behind the sensor, which rushes to keep up, to keep losing. The laws of touch are "rich in teaching," for Benjamin, because they teach in a future tense in which reception runs ahead of itself out of fear that if it stops for an instant it will lose itself and its object, becoming transfixed in a stupefied present.[14] For this reason, in the sphere of touch, to be oriented is utterly disorienting. Reception in distraction, the revised, non-quantitative share in mass, insofar as it can be conceived of on analogy with touch, prepares the way for historical turning points by letting go of concepts, of the conceptual gesture, to grasp, hold, stop, keep. It releases the grip on a present that it cannot sense and passes into a richer though highly indeterminate future.

Although it does not grasp what it receives, mass nonetheless thinks. Benjamin reports that the French cultural critic Georges Duhamel writes of film that it is a "pastime" that "demands no concentration, presupposes no faculty of thought [*kein Denkvermögen voraussetzt*]"; it is not as the "old complaint" about the diversion-seeking masses that Benjamin wants to base his investigation into mass reception on this faculty-less event (*GS* I.2 504). This is not merely anti-elitism or love of pop culture on Benjamin's part. What Duhamel intends as a reprimand, Benjamin raises out of the realm of intellectualism, reading there an inadvertent discovery of the structure of mass thinking. It amounts to a shocking proposition: in order to receive in distraction, apperception must temporarily set itself out of power, its presupposition, *Voraussetzung*, must become its suspension, *Aussetzung*. In this way, mass *Zerstreuung* can be seen as another working through of Benjamin's thoughts on the revolutionary general strike and other non-mental suspensions, in which structural transformations become possible.[15] *Zerstreuung* abandons—if only for an instant—an apperception that would have to presuppose its own structure in order for there to be thought. Groping absentmindedly ahead, thought abandons its objects and along the way itself. One thing must be very clear in all these readings: distraction does not remove thought forever, as madness or death are supposed to do. Then again, it does remove this structure of thought, and perhaps forever, for the sake of a future thinking that would operate differently. For this reason apperception's new task cannot be called revolutionary; that is, it is not asked to reorganize the world and retain an identical power for another regime or interest group. Benjamin proposes here a revolution in the conception of radical change in which apperception, instead of being given an upgrade to its operating system or a set of categories more in step with the times, has its structure, aims, processes, and product made responsive to difference, in a *Streik der Facultäten* that brackets the very routine by which apperception already, in advance, and without publicizing its commitments, understands itself as a faculty and domesticates an otherwise wild future.

Benjamin's insight is instructive and at the same time difficult to receive. Apperception, which in philosophy's view has always, one way or another, been in control of reception, must abruptly become receptive itself. In order for apperception to renounce its teaching habit and learn to learn, it will have to become susceptible to teaching. Like the Zen master who strikes the student in order to enlighten him, film shocks apperception into massiveness. Apperception and reception reverse roles in the cinema and mass thinking strikes against a future in which a present *Bildung* will be brought to fruition. The strike, however, is not carried out in the desire to end all work, in keeping with a utopian Marxist vision that today rings horribly false. Mind on strike does not imagine a "free spirit" that would do away with thought once and for all and replace it with leisure. Rather, the intellect withdraws from work in a gesture that, although it can neither be willed nor willed away, is reproducible: it can be trained for or gotten used to. "The distracted one can also habituate himself," Benjamin announces. In becoming a habit, distraction becomes a tool for dissolving regimes of thought, modes of understanding, by admitting an empirical moment into the transcendental structure of apperception.

The Distraction-Value of Art

It is not the case that after apperception has been put out of work by distraction, thought simply resumes its attentive activities, as if obeying an eternal law of alternation between attention and distraction. Above all, we must not think this. It is also not the case that attention, under the influence of distraction, is broken up and shared out such that afterward it pays an attention of a different quality, a fragmented attention, for instance, or a collecting one that would be the synthesis of the two terms. Distraction is a transitional phase toward another sort of relationship.

Zerstreuung carries a heavy weight in the reproducibility essay. It accounts not only for the change in the mode of reception that comes into being with mass, but also for mass's internal structure. Mass is, though dense, internally "zerstreut," that is, no matter how much pressure it is put under, it will not fuse into a unit. Participants give up their individual identities, but not for the sake of a group identity. Moreover, *Zerstreuung* denotes not only the internal structure of the mass, as well as the relationship between a particular artwork and a particular public at a particular time—film, mass, the early twentieth century—but also, and perhaps more importantly, it names the historical force that transforms that relationship. Cult-value cedes its hegemony over artworks to distraction-value because dispersion-distraction-entertainment, *Zerstreuung*, brought on by the artwork's technical reproducibility, scatters the cult internally. Distraction is the condition of possibility for a political event: a dense diaspora.

The audience for film is "zerstreut" because it no longer has to be tied to one place and time; it becomes plastic and mobile. This does not mean that the shock effect of film must act geographically: it also disperses a mass when it is in "one place," i.e., the movie theater. That is to say, the very unity of place flies apart in distraction. Mass is there and not there. This is the mode that Benjamin wants to make into a paradigm for historical transitions. Because of the change that it brings about, and its potential to bring about a change again at any time, *Zerstreuung* is a term that should belong to historiography as much as to the philosophy of mind. Furthermore, because of its position between nature and history, since it intervenes as a historical event in the natural structure of mind, it also calls for a different relationship to science. The science that comes to terms with distraction has to transform along with the artwork, mass, history, and the apperception that it seeks to explicate. "Reception in distraction" affects the reception *of* distraction in the theory that would account for it.

Several important historical differences accompany the advent of *Zerstreuung*, therefore. Art differs in its production and distribution, such that it becomes political and historical in a different way. Reception differs in its mode, such that it no longer means grasping, while remaining itself unaffected. Apperception differs in the tasks it can accomplish, which now include a revolution in its own structure. History differs—it learns how to dispense with tradition on the model of a fast-moving, forgetting sense like touch. And so, it should come as no surprise that art theory also has to transform if it wants to account for these changes.

This is the situation in which the reproducibility essay leaves *Zerstreuung*. There is no concept of it insofar as it designates a reception that tears apperception away from its traditional tasks, including the subsumption of intuitions under concepts, the unification of all mental experience, and the recognition that that experience is one's own. In short, what is received in distraction is the suspension of apperception. Mass, neither one being nor many individual beings, receives, but it does not understand what it receives in concepts, nor does it, if it can be said to have mental experience, undergo that experience as unified or as belonging to it. What it receives is received as disunified and not its own possession. Receiving in distraction, mass cannot identify a self to which the experience belongs, and this is perhaps the last victory in Benjamin's battle against Kant's theory of experience, in which the unity of apperception is the highest instance. Mass apperceives as anyone except itself. The model for this reception and this training is not optical but first of all tactile, given that touch has as its basic gesture letting go in passing by—in a "beiläufiges Bemerken." This is the "mass-movement" that Benjamin is after. Mass moves not geographically but intellectually, spreading into a diaspora wherever it may be, a *Zerstreuung* that resists being co-opted for the kinds of group action that fascism demands. As distracted-dispersed, mass becomes immovable by ordinary means.

The notes entitled "Theory of Distraction" that Benjamin wrote in or around 1936 in response to Adorno's criticism are an attempt to rethink these complex changes and to suggest some of their consequences. They can be divided, roughly, into three types.

Premises on Sociality

Attempt to locate the effect of the artwork in the elimination of consecration in it

Versuch die Wirkung des Kunstwerks unter Eliminierung der Weihe in ihr zu fixieren
—*GS* VII.2 678

This premise, the first in the notes, says what is wanted from the concept of distraction-entertainment-dispersal. It is important to note that the artwork is not explained in terms of its mode of production here, or, for that matter, its source in an artist or in divine inspiration, its structure or its formal elements, its place in a historical series, its genre, or even its ontological activity—by the kind of "world" it opens. The explanandum of any artwork for Benjamin in these notes and in the writings of the mid to late thirties in general is its social "effect," its "Wirkung." These notes focus, as Benjamin says elsewhere of his writings after 1933, on the sociology of art (*GS* VI 227).

A theory of distraction is thus an attempt to locate a change in an artwork's social effect. The change in effect is not as easy to place as it at first seems, however. Given Benjamin's understanding of aura, which this premise implies is the aspect of traditional artworks that produces their specific social effect, what changes is not only the effect but the historical basis of the social per se. Aura is an accumulation of history, and with its dispersal the shape of history changes such that sociality can no longer constitute itself in the same way. Nevertheless, amidst this shift, Benjamin still preserves the role of artworks at the center of the constitution of the social sphere. This much does not change when the aura blows away. Artworks remain at the center of historical shifts, but now, without aura, they operate otherwise. A separate note among the paralipomena reads: "Aura was originally (as long as it underpinned cult-value) loaded with history" (*GS* VII.2 677). Loaded up with history, an artwork became the focal point and origin of tradition. It acted as a historical substance, and although it lived through a multitude of changes in context, it remained the fixed reference point by which something like historical change could be cognized. Tradition meant the repetition of this reference point, this repository of historical sentiment—as the objective correlative of historical continuity: so long as one could view the immovable, datable artwork once more, history remained continuous no matter how distant its center. The consecration of the artwork by the priest and the consecration of ever more and ever more distant cult members through the artwork established the community's parameters. Now, according to Benjamin's premise, mystery, silence, ritual, sacrifice—the sanctifying acts of the cult—were rudely eliminated in the new art form, film. A theory of distraction would have to account for the elimination of consecration as the artwork's effect, and replace consecration with something else.

Two other premises elaborate on this one. First:

Parasitic existence of art on the foundation of the sacred. (*GS* VII.2 678)

This premise follows the previous one and makes it more precise. The divine presence in the artwork—its symbolic nature, if you will—grounds its ability to consecrate members. In order to theorize the elimination of the sacralizing process that happens in an artwork, the divine origin of artworks will have to be rethought. In the case of film, Benjamin has already begun to replace a divine origin with a technological one. In retrospect, he argues, technology intercedes even in the origin of the theological artwork already in Athens. The Greeks

could not reproduce their artworks. (*GS* VII.2 679)

This Feuerbach-style argument holds that it was not the gods that lent artworks permanence but the technical inability to reproduce them that lent permanence to the gods. God is a projection of a technical limitation. Rather than on the sacred, art is parasitic on the foundation of technology, and the gods cannot but submit to its historical power. All that is parasitic on the divine—eschatological fantasies, communities based on the dream of unchanging foundations, artistic inspiration, even thought—loses its footing in this change of perspective. It is no wonder that the theoretical attitude loses its preeminence as well.

A second premise that corresponds to the elimination of the sacred as the artwork's ground is critical to understanding the social change that Benjamin envisions. As in the Trauerspiel book, Benjamin's touchstone for demonstrating the change is Ancient Greece. The values of distraction need to be developed for film, he argues, the way the values of catharsis were for tragedy (*GS* VII.2 678). The contemporary art theorist should nevertheless still take Aristotle as a model and seek to develop what Benjamin calls "the values" of distraction. Although they are not specified by Benjamin in these telegraphic premises, we can imagine which values of catharsis he may have meant. His only comment is:

Distraction just as catharsis is to be circumscribed as a physiological phenomenon. (*GS* VII.2 678)

Without going into the myriad problems in understanding Aristotle's notion of catharsis, let us concentrate on the effects he describes. Purgation of passions through pity and fear seems to us more psychological than physiological, yet in fact for Aristotle the seat of emotions lay in the organs and blood. Benjamin will look for a configuration corresponding to Aristotle's analysis of tragedy's effects: a physiological response with political consequences. Catharsis is to be replaced, but the fact that political effects are produced by artworks is not.

Premises on Temporality

In film the artwork reaches the highpoint of erodability
In Film erreicht das Kunstwerk den Höhepunkt der Verschleißbarkeit
—*GS* VII.2 678

In this premise the basis for the artwork's new social effect is labeled *Verschleiß*. Inasmuch as catharsis was produced not as a one-time effect, but in a yearly return of the Dionysia, the cult festival by which artworks—in this case tragedies—distributed their physiological effects to the political body, it worked according to the Greek temporal signature—"Dauer," duration. Catharsis translated the Greek tragedy at the center of the yearly ritual into an enduring physiological change and thus became a producer of the political will to endure.

Just as Greek art was dependent on duration, so current art is dependent on wearing away [*Verschleiß*]. (*GS* VII.2 679)

But whereas Greek art, because of the lack of technical reproducibility, produced a time filled with duration, film wears time away. In order to help understand the new temporal mode, Benjamin offers an analogy, the same that he will offer in the notes that make up the *Passagenwerk*. The speed of film's deteriorability arises from its parasitism. Parasitic on fashion, a paradigmatic mode of experience in capitalism, film wears away in the way what we wear wears: through variable, unexpected shifts, according to the seasons of the market, a constantly inconstant alteration in the value of any stylistic element—cuffs, collars, hems: this modality of change occurs within the coming and going of film images. The temporality of film—its dependence on *Verschleiß*—is to be explained in two ways:

through its surrender to fashion or through its refunctioning into politics. (*GS* VII.2 679)

How can politics make the rapid wearing away of images in film its principle, as fashion has with colors, lengths, and fabrics? What is a politics of *Verschleiß* . . . a political practice or a theory of political practice in which the theory is allowed to erode? Benjamin does not say. One can surmise, however, that the political form that could absorb and make use of *Verschleiß* would be in some way similar to his conception of mass. That is, its fundamental unit would be a group not consecrated to the gods and made exclusive through controlled access to an artwork, not purged of strife-inducing passions, whose history was not comparable to tradition, and the temporality of whose relations was not parasitic on divine permanence; in short, it would take place outside the polis, and—for that matter—outside time. Benjamin thinks here the end of the polis and the end of politics in the Greek sense. But he also thinks the end of time, as a continuum of discrete durations. Greek art is art because it endures and promotes duration, tendering its physiological value in the currency of politics. The time of "Verschleiß," however, no longer operates as a sacred medium in which coming and going can be stilled or understood. Even the coming and going of time is permitted. As one of film's effects, time itself is allowed to "wear out." With the dispersal of aura, the de-sedimentation of history onto the artwork, time can no longer be thought of as a continuum by which events are meted out. When the auratic artwork no longer endures, time follows suit. After the erosion of time through film, we enter an epoch of "times." Politics would have to adapt to this, would have to, to be precise, remain adaptable.

Communicability of Effect

The criterion for the fruitfulness of its effect is the communicability of this effect

Das Kriterium für die Fruchtbarkeit ihres Wirkens ist die Kommunizierbarkeit dieser Wirkung

—*GS* VII.2 679

Zerstreuung—if it truly disperses the *durée* of history previously maintained by aura—will have to imagine for itself a theory, a mode of seeing, an understanding, something—something other than a theoretical intuition of its essence—some mode of communication that is as *verschleißbar* as its time is. If the change in art and history is as radical as Benjamin paints it in these notes and in the artwork essay, when film diverts history from duration, how can theory endure just as it was, in its golden age? What is a theory without persistence—indeed, what is theory without an original claim to the permanence lent it by its object? It goes without saying that along with the artwork, the cult, and the gods, theory is also Greek. A theory of *Zerstreuung* awaits development in the manner of Aristotle's theory of catharsis—but this does not mean that its mode of presentation will be the same as Aristotle's. Tragedy and theory are Greek twins. In the fifth and fourth centuries BCE, the "foundation of the sacred" that lay in the artwork (tragedy) was communicated by a *theoros*, the half-religious, half-political figure who brought the god's oracle, in translation from the priest's poetic verses, delivering to the polis the predictions that allowed political practice to continue as it was. When Aristotle defines the effects of good tragedy—it keeps the polis from succumbing to the deleterious forces of its own *demos*, at least until the next year's Great Dionysia—he also rings in the epoch of theory as an enduring attention to immutable things.

We should remember that according to Benjamin's analysis history is the product of auratic art and not the other way around. Correspondingly, as we've noted, film produces a temporal disintegration that can hardly be called history. If history in Greece is the potential to continue, in the age of film it becomes the potential to leave off, to stop. The art theory of the film age would have to correspond to eroding history. This criterion must be added to the other parameters in which it would have to operate: the massiveness of the mass, the technical nature of film production, and the wide dispersion made possible by reproducibility. *Theoretiké*, as Aristotle envisioned it, would no longer be possible since in *Zerstreuung* it would have to become wearable, along with the apperception whose activity it formerly guaranteed. Wearable theory, theory that wears out, theory as shifty as fashion: the shifty science that would go along with the *Verschleiß* of film, mass, technical reproduction, and dispersability is implied in this vocabulary.

The "theory" of the title, "Theory of Distraction," does not show up among the twenty or so premises. Instead the notes turn around a mode in which a science of distraction would have to operate. Theory undergoes a transvaluation of its values. The "Werte" of distraction-entertainment-dispersion that need to be developed on the model of catharsis for tragedy are "consumption-value" (*Konsumwert*) and "doctrinal" or "teaching-value" (*Lehrwert*). These correspond roughly to Marx's "exchange-value" and "use-value," the first "value" being quantitative, the second qualitative. Consumption-value, like exchange-value, is countable; the higher the consumption-value, the greater the number of consumers and the ease of consumption, and the wider the commodity spreads. Conversely, teaching-value describes the potential that the knowledge has as a doctrine to be assimilated, practiced, worn out, and, at some point discarded. The communicability of film's effects in these two dimensions—qualitative and quantitative—that is, the *Zerstreubarkeit* of art, history, and politics by means of film, is the criterion of its effectiveness. Since film, through *Zerstreuung*, has such a high consumption- and teaching-value, it is highly effective, that is—very communicable. Its effects spread and spread, and their dispersal is not checked by absorption and assimilation—on the contrary. Its unlimited effects derive from the fact that in *Zerstreuung* the two modes converge. Although they rarely come together in other arts, in film

Teaching-value and consumption-value converge. With that a new kind of learning is given. (*GS* VII.2 679)

Through distraction, more than through any other artistically or techno-logically produced effect, the potential for learning comes together with the capacity to be consumed. To give a counterexample: a book on the problem of distraction may have a high teaching-value, but its consumption-value is quite low. The intellectual and social requirements of receiving it remind us of the cult. The same could be said of auratic art, museum exhibitions, and so forth. Conversely, whereas the communicability or distributability of fashion is extremely high—before you know it everybody's wearing that hat—its teaching value is low. Film, in contrast, is easily consumed, widely distributable, and carries with it the potential to teach apperception and train the mass in massive thinking—distraction—which is, at least in theory, useless for fascism.[16]

What about distraction is so consumable? Benjamin offers several clues, and these are also the physiological effects he means to ascribe to it, on analogy with catharsis.

The relationship of distraction to incorporation must be investigated,

he remarks (*GS* VII.2 678). Part of the program, then, for understanding *Zerstreuung* includes an investigation into its capacity to be incorporated. This is because

Its actual humanity consists in its unbounded ability for adaptation. (*GS* VII.2 678)

Now the connection between the three elements, *Reproduzierbarkeit–Zerstreuung–Politisierung*, shimmers into view. This premise, one of the last in the so-called Theory of Distraction, constitutes an esoteric doctrine of political diaspora. The politicization that Benjamin seems to intend in these notes is a translation of mass onto a planetary scale. Distraction-entertainment disperses the polis to the four corners of the earth, because with distraction it disperses an unlimited capacity for adaptation. This for Benjamin is the essence of the human, the ability to become what you are not[17]—and thus *Zerstreuung's* "real," "effective," "wirkliche" humanity consists in its ability to aid human beings in dispersing and adapting, not to new homelands, but to dispersal itself. The release of tradition and the dispersal of the cult is but a preparation for adaptation to other contexts, providing tools for future liberation from those as well, a prophylactic against any future accumulation of history. "Lehre," teaching, doctrine, allows a discourse on distraction to accompany and not annul the dispersive movement of mind and mass.

In what position do we find ourselves now, when we are, at least putatively, receiving Benjamin's transmission? The advent of film falls one hundred years in the past. Have we become well trained? Have we absorbed its shock effect? Or have we assimilated its lesson to the point where we need to depart from it again? The true test is the following: for the revolutionary promise of film as Benjamin tried to interpret it to have been fulfilled, we would have had to abandon it. And perhaps this will soon be the case. Art critics certainly have not dispensed with theory—quite the contrary, theory seems to have become the sine qua non of our dealings with art. This is perhaps the reason why "distraction" has not become a permanent addition to our theoretical vocabulary. From the perspective of the structures of science and culture in which we still operate, a doctrine that is as *verschleißbar* as the history it inaugurates would quickly become a liability. Yet, in the revolution in apperception wrought by film, theory should not be able to hold itself above cognition's disintegration, clinging to a universal image—even if it is an image of distraction. Film teaches us to let go of images. And so, after apperception's hold over reception is broken by film, once popular experience is "freed" from knowledge, theory—even critical theory—cannot continue to function in the same way. *Zerstreuung* enters experience as a doctrine subject to the *Zerstreuungen* of experience. In this way it is an open question whether it ever was or will be convincing, with what intention we should receive it, or whether we are still living under its historical sign. If we receive it theoretically, we nullify its effects. If we receive it as doctrine, we miss its essence, since it will have already become outdated.

Distraction and Politics

There is no distraction today, even though—and perhaps because—there are too many distractions. Nonetheless a barely visible figure—*le distrait*—continues to look like us, to look at us, although we do not look back or reflect on him or care. Who are we, then, suddenly to care? This is just one of the many irksome questions left unasked at the end of this book. There is still the question of import: what does this revivified thought of primal distraction mean to us? What can we expect to change now that we have begun to think about distraction? "Think about" has the sense here of reflecting on an already understood object, but it also means to lend meaning to: to address something that we believe addresses us. To some extent at least, any attempt to affirm distraction carries with it the tendency to erase it and replace it with cognition, reflection, concern, address, meaning, and so forth. But this may be a false problem, since, precisely insofar as thought reinstitutes itself so fiercely when faced with this affront to the source of its powers, to this very extent—if we are right—primal distraction will accompany it—precede it and follow it—anyway.

There also remains a second question, the question of the effects of this other distraction, the parameters of whose indeterminacy we have been trying to divine. What are, as Benjamin asked, adapting a Marxian vocabulary, its specific values, its "Werte"? What effects does a moving "unmover," as we derived it from Aristotle's demand; a distracted, untimely acosmopolitan like La Bruyère's *distrait*; a reflecting mole that hears the noise of not-thinking; *Zerstreuung* as pure transcendence—that which steps beyond everything, even traditional understandings of transcendence—and a new collective without mind, mass: what effects do these produce and in which arenas?

Replying to this question is complicated, for one thing because distraction is not one thing. In the ragged history of the scant attention paid it, its iterations vary considerably, and so, of course, do their hoped-for effects. Moreover, the thought of distraction plays a different role in each of the texts in which it is addressed. For Aristotle, not-always-thinking is a threat that allows him, by excluding it, to build an ontology, a politics, and an ethical theory on the basis of idealized, continuous intellection. The effects he thinks not-always-thinking will have, if it indeed exists, are perhaps not fully understood by him, since not-thinking remains a matter internal to the construction of his system. His concern is more with the cause of not-thinking than with the phenomenon itself. It does not come up in his empirical studies, when he describes beings, but rather in his metaphysics, when he tries to describe being. Something like the reverse is true for La Bruyère, but contrary to expectation this is where he is in fact the most similar to *his* classical ideal. Aristotle demands that the cause be found, and when it can't be, he abandons it as a mere semblance of a problem. La Bruyère seems also to know that distraction is not a metaphysical matter. A foible of the times, a mere phenomenon with the shallowest roots, a fashion or manner of the moderns that never afflicted the ancients, something like pure manner, distraction is then free to become the basis for all other moral foibles. It is, for him, something like the universal source for immorality, since it names the opposite of what is moral: moral is intellection. Moral slips are made, as it were, in distraction from the truth of the soul. Beyond the logic of La Bruyère's argument, however, the antics of *le distrait* also have effects on his immediate surroundings. Social and political effects, though not desirable, happen.

Cutting across these texts and arguments, as well as those of Kafka, Heidegger, and Benjamin, are two separate but related tensions. First, there is a tension between the concepts of distraction at work in these texts. At one pole, distraction is understood as the absolute and causeless suspension of intellection. At the other pole, it is understood as—you could call it, roughly—a movement of disunification, a scattering, spreading, dividing, or diverting. The tension between these two poles, between suspension and disintegration, can be found to one degree or another in almost every conceptual articulation of distraction. The tension may diminish if we consider that the rather abstract notion of a "suspension of thought" is usually envisioned as the suspension of thought's unity. Thought is suspended insofar as it cannot collect itself, insofar as it cannot form a unit or a temporal continuum, insofar as it is no longer like itself or no longer stands above the experience it claims to synthesize, and this is why it is most often envisioned as disintegration or dispersal. This leads us directly to the second tension.

In the history of the thought of distraction—this ragged yarn—one finds a tension also between its envisioned effects. In the main, distraction is shown to have effects in two spheres: in the intellectual and also in the political sphere. Of course, in political philosophy these spheres are often inseparable. One is constantly being made the basis of the other, thought of politics, politics of thought, and perhaps no right order can be found. In any case, the relationship between the two tensions that traverse the non-history of the thought of distraction—suspension/dispersion and thought/politics—can for all intents and purposes be formulated like this: in a theory of politics in which a metaphysically unified and temporally continuous intellect is made into the foundation of political structures, of political action, and of the stability of the polity, distraction names the moment when the foundation crumbles under the edifices built upon it. When thought is suspended, its unity ruined, action becomes dispersed, vague, ineffective, silly. Institutions deteriorate, groups become diasporic. This seems to be the effect produced by La Bruyère's figure, insofar as he can no longer keep the social hierarchy in mind, mixing up nobles with farmers, kings with servants. There is also little doubt that, in Aristotle's political theory, intellection is the ground of politics, and a gappy polity on the model of not-always-thinking would be unacceptable. The thought of distraction may itself, then, more often than not, be an effect of a political fear, the fear of an internal attack on the political order by a domestic enemy that cannot be preempted or repulsed.

If this is the case, then we could call what usually occurs when primal distraction is addressed an inversion. The thought of distraction springs from a fear that a fully coherent political structure may not be possible. As a response, doubt is laid at the feet of thought, whose unity was supposed to have guaranteed the coherence of the political sphere in the first place. Afterward the order gets reversed. Distraction is made into something like a blight on politics, the cause of political disintegration, and distraction's effects are then considered to be derivative political effects. The presupposition of this way of thinking, is, however, first of all the idea that temporal and geographical unity is originary and anything else is a degradation of that origin.

The fear of political disunity and the consequent conceptual inversion don't seem to occur only in theories of mind, morality, or the soul. Outside the somewhat esoteric narrative of not-thinking in philosophy, literature, and cultural critique, political theory itself shows scars of an inner war over the meaning of distraction. There too, distraction reflects a worry about the relation between thinking and politics. In discourse about politics there seem to be two main intuitions of distraction's effects. It should go without saying that the "politics of distraction" that our hyper-mediatized democracy broadcasts as truth, alternately celebrating and decrying it, is only one version of the phenomenon. In this all-too-widespread interpretation, distraction means the seduction of the collective by a weapon wielded against the people's visual apparatus, in order, ultimately, to bend their will to leaders' wishes. In this way it is but a more contemporary version of Hobbes's sword, a violence against the people used to maintain the cohesiveness of the commonwealth. An antidemocratic potential latent in democracies, such a policy of diversion may in fact grow out of the need for a missing sovereign moment, which some continue to contend determines our moment. Deception is wielded against the general will so that leaders can act—in the best interests of the people, as the case may be, but hidden from view. Diversionary tactics can perhaps be explained as an excrescence of the state of exception in which we are quoted as living. Perhaps they are a response to the need for sovereign decisions, in a society that will not accept this need. According to this reasoning, the extreme autocratic moment in the midst of democracy has to be covered up, dissimulated, if only to protect the image of democracy, which might otherwise be tarnished. Diversion would thus be one of several possible tactics for preserving both the belief in democracy and the ability to make the necessary sovereign decisions in secret and in complete "freedom from the laws" as Hobbes puts it (*Leviathan* 242). In a polity convinced that its legitimacy streams from a general will, which is in fact nothing more than an aggregate of individual wills (a majority of them, at least), where each will is attached to a thinking, deciding mind, the way to circumvent the general will and supersede the intellects that support it is to divert the collective mind through individuals' senses. It goes without saying that the media are an arm of the state in this regard. Distraction-diversion seduces away from the ugly Schmittian truth through beautiful semblance, in service of an ultimately beautiful state. This account takes quite a low view of the *demos*, however. In order for a policy of diversion to become the *explanans* of either a democracy gone awry or a democracy in a state of exception, the *demos* has to be sorely demoted. The thinking-willing collective becomes like a child, susceptible to bright colors and flashes; a general divertibility is posited, which rivals and at times supplants the general will.

A striking alternative to the power games of diversionary politics is another distraction, thought to disrupt power politics altogether. Hobbes is remembered for his articulation of the fundamental position of sovereign authority in the modern state, and yet along with this he envisioned quite clearly the disruptive effects of a more primal distraction. He broaches distraction as one of the most pernicious "Of Those Things That Weaken or Tend to the Dissolution of a Commonwealth" in Chapter 29 of *Leviathan*. Distraction is not perpetrated against a people; through it the people breaks up the polity. Or rather, savage nature returns in the midst of the *civitas*. Yet it is not the same "miserable condition of war" arising from self-interest and competition that was supposed to obtain in the state of nature, but a new war—a civil war, with one single enemy, although an unintentional one. A different *bellum omnium contra totum* breaks out within the commonwealth and turns against the structure of sovereignty itself. The subject of distraction in these passages from *Leviathan* is not an individual person or an aggregate of individual citizens or even the sovereign, but the commonwealth as a whole. When the commonwealth becomes distracted, the sovereign unit simply evaporates. The commonwealth is, we recall, imagined as "one person," and so it shouldn't surprise us that it is as liable to the ailments of mind as any meager person is. In a distracted commonwealth, we find nothing like a politics of distraction that seduces a subjugated, childlike citizenry out of its rights. In this regard, Hobbes has much to teach us. A thought planted ten years earlier in *De corpore politico*, the idea of a distraction with directly political effects blossoms in *Leviathan*. Insofar as "the sovereign is the public soul, giving life and motion to the commonwealth," any resistance to the soul is tantamount to regicide (*Leviathan* 249). And so, where it forms part of a policy of a government and its media, distraction may be a weapon wielded against the people for the sake of preserving the state's autonomy, when it has to act quickly or confront something it presumes the people cannot understand. When it is politicized, in contrast, distraction becomes a threat to this structure, the commonwealth, by subtracting the common denominator, mind. Hobbes, at least, sees a structural threat here. Any movement that is initiated outside the soul is not a movement of the commonwealth, but a movement that hampers its ability to move, a foreign movement, originating in but still not of the collective, the apogee of which is civil war. A swarm of souls replaces the one soul, an immanent and dispersed repulsion reigns, when "the commonwealth must needs be distracted, and no man dare to obey the sovereign power farther than shall seem good in his own eyes" (*Leviathan* 241). One does not have to celebrate civil war to appreciate the implications of the moment when a mass of "private judgements" replaces the otherwise single-minded polity; this contentious group looks something like a radical democracy.[1] This is not a question of zombie-like acts on the scale of individuals. Instead, the limbs of the people-man defect from the common head. Once the sovereign soul has been dethroned in this way, it is seen to be "expiring," and "the members are governed by it no more than the carcass of a man by his departed, though immortal soul" (*Leviathan* 249). First of all, this distraction is primarily collective. Yet it is the opposite of the "hive mind": it resists collecting itself. The corpse of the commonwealth moves perhaps, but this is not motion as classically conceived, since nothing moves it and it does not move itself. Moreover, this new, more intensely "mortal god," so bound to the earth that it cannot rise up enough to walk, will not be resurrected. In this kind of distraction there occurs a death of political life within the polity—the demise of sovereign politics, for sure, but not at the same time the end of interactions. The corpse of the state, although no longer animated by one soul, staggers around. It is a different state—a disintegrated body politic that would not only not be able to, but also would not need to face and decide on an exception. No state is left to protect and preserve against and for the sake of the future. Leviathan stumbles, turns, falls, like a sleepwalker who does not even dream where he is headed. The overt anthropomorphism of politics that represents the collective as a body with a head, the covert theomorphism of the modern state, abandons its projections and hopes.

What is this frightening phenomenon, at the heart of the most authoritative theory of sovereignty in the seventeenth century? (A historical question could also be asked: why the seventeenth century should become the epoch of primal distraction, why writers as diverse as Pascal, La Bruyère, Leibniz, and Hobbes, unlike writers of other centuries, could have it so acutely in mind . . .) Let us note that this fright is different than another. Hobbes makes it clear that distracted politics is not to be confused with a divided sovereignty, where there is a contest for power. This can also lead to the dissolution of the commonwealth, to be sure, but, we could say, it operates from the head down, preserving the head's position. Hobbes writes " . . . powers divided mutually destroy each other," but they do not usually affect the structure of sovereignty (*Leviathan* 243). The battle of sovereign with sovereign has little effect on the idea of the commonwealth or the structure of sovereignty, since sovereignty, according to Hobbes, cannot be divided. Rival claims to the position are always possible, likely even, but the authority and power vested in a sovereign are indivisible. Leviathan will always have, even after the agon between sovereign claimants, one head. More importantly, Hobbes also distinguishes the advent of distracted politics from another scenario: an all-too powerful commonwealth that tries to subject the sovereign to the laws of all. This, as he says, only displaces the instance of absolute power, since there will always be a judge or executioner who will assume the highest position once again. According to this logic, though state attack state, sovereign battle sovereign, or ambiguity beset succession, the sovereign moment remains inextirpable.

Primal distraction, we can see, has this place in political theory; in the most canonical theory of sovereignty it names the most destructive enemy of the state. This is because, in that theory, it challenges the theomorphism of man that underlies the anthropomorphism of the state. The alternative is one and grim from Hobbes's perspective: civil war. One could reduce his worry about distraction in *Leviathan* to a personal response to the English Civil War, but it is obviously more than that. Hobbes began to develop the idea two years before the outbreak of the war, in *De corpore politico* (1640).[2] Let us call this state-disintegrating political distraction one of the elements of law, even though it is not strictly a part of the law or obedient to the force of law. It hints at a threat that circulates around the highest contract, the covenant through which chaos becomes body. Bees are one kind of threat to covenants: they do not need a law to bind them. For Hobbes bees have a natural ordering principle: they are bound by appetite (*Leviathan* 127). Distraction is slightly different: it produces a multiplication of covenants, a general disorderliness of principles. All potential principles of order, natural, historical, intellectual, and so forth—including appetite, sovereignty, thought, non-thought, interest, will, whim—for a time have equal claims to priority. Hobbes's experience in the 1640s does seem to color his view of the results of distraction. One can imagine that it need not result in war: it could just as easily result in receptivity to difference and transience, an epoch of debate and disharmony, a mass, or a shifting set of orders not yet subsumed under a universal principle of order.

Hobbes's image of primal distraction's political effects could be developed in a historical direction. Following Benjamin, we could look into "mass" as the quintessential political actor at moments of crises, when politics needs to be repoliticized, that is, dissolved once again into a war of elements against wholes. Or we could develop it geographically, laying out an idea of a diaspora without a homeland in thought similar to the one that Kafka tried to formulate and also to produce. These, along with Hobbes's attempt, should count as precursors and counterparts to the communities out of work, with nothing in common, and without a head (*acéphale*) of Jean-Luc Nancy, Maurice Blanchot, and George Bataille. The question, you could say, in all these cases is whom you decapitate, how you decapitate him, and where the corpse is allowed to wander.

Whatever else it does and doesn't do, a revitalized concept of primal distraction seems to offer solutions to two theoretical problems in politics: inclusion and demise. In the first place it suggests not just the possibility but the existence of an infinitely inclusive collective without the need to count out its members or represent itself, on the model of the communality of *le distrait*, which is furthermore neither revolutionary nor utopian. It refuses the time signatures of both these dreams; it is something less than a dream, to quote Kant. It is not "to come." Although we cannot know this, it is already here. It does not require, for its grouping principle, any ground for being-with, since it is infinitely dispersed historically, conceptually, and perhaps also geographically, even if it concentrates in a small space. In the second place, it suggests a way to think of structural change in politics that does not depend on the fiction of a historical continuum, or even its interruption. Distraction breaks the contract between thought and time, even though it says nothing about what steps in if and when people regain their senses.

Notes

1. For a penetrating analysis of attention's inability to ground itself, see Werner Hamacher's "Bogengebete" (17–19).

2. Husserl describes the method of the *Logische Untersuchungen* as a "zigzag" movement between clarity and unclarity. "Die Untersuchung bewegt sich gleichsam im Zickzack." Because the clarity of the science follows and does not precede the investigation, a zigzag movement is necessary between the originary analyses and the "begriffliche Unklarheiten" that block the way (Husserl 22). Freud makes a similar requirement in "Ratschläge für den Arzt bei der psychoanalytischen Behandlung." The psychoanalytic clinician should practice a "gleichschwebende Aufmerksamkeit." A hovering attention is required, Freud argues, before attention can be paid to the right objects. The goal of this technique is not so much correct interpretation, however, as protection of the analyst from overstraining his attention (Freud VIII.377).

3. In his essay and introduction to the volume "geteilte Aufmerksamkeit," Thomas Schestag questions the assumptions that underlie the use of this phrase. He wonders: "welche Philologie wird dieser Überschrift—'geteilte Aufmerksamkeit'—gerecht? Eine Philologie der Demarkation? Oder erst die Demarkation der Philologie?" Schestag goes on to uncover, within the philologist's "love of words," an almost hateful act. An act of gathering a word out of a graphematic dispersion of letters, and letters out of marks, precedes even seeing the word, let alone reading it. Seeing, and then reading, consist in repression of an original dispersal of attention/marks. "Geteilte Aufmerksamkeit," if the phrase could be read, would suggest an a priori dissemination of marks that only through a negation enables a word to become a word (11).

4. In the last ten years there have been two significant "cultural" studies of attention, both of which are largely Foucauldian, both of which, as a consequence of their method, unduly narrow the understanding of distraction. The first is Crary's, the second Bernard Stiegler's.

Crary reifies attention in order to historicize it. But this is perhaps too simple a way to describe it. Among his rather frequent rhetorical negations, Crary denies that he believes attention is a thing. "I use the term *attention* not to hypostatize it as a substantive object, but to refer to the field of those statements and practices and to a network of effects which they produced" (23). It is hard to see how attention could become "a substantive object" in any normal sense of the phrase (it would be a faculty perhaps or a capacity, which is neither a substance nor a thing), and the phrase is already less than precise, but I take it he means he would like to suspend the question of whether attention has existence outside discourse about it. And yet, throughout the text there is a steady equivocation between what he calls, following Foucault, "techniques and discourses about visuality" (6) and phrases like "our attention" (30) and "the management of attention" (33), which make little sense unless there is such an entity called attention. Unless attention were a natural entity it would be hard to "manage." At times Crary argues that power creates attention, at others that it supports and shapes a preexisting attention. The more Nietzschean line would argue that attention need not exist, but could be an ideal or an utterance or a claim to knowledge that has the effect that people believe it. To accept this view would leave Crary in a conflict, however. In order to critique attention he has to show it is a construct, malleable, producible. In order to historicize it, however, he needs to reify it, to make it seem like a fixed constituent in an actual historical change. When he does this, attention becomes virtually a physiological truth. "Capital, as accelerated exchange and circulation, necessarily produced this kind of perceptual adaptability and became a regime of reciprocal attentiveness and distraction" (30). Here, for example, he argues that capital in fact modifies physiology.

The naturalization of attention stems from Crary's reliance on the concept of perception. In order to make his "historical" argument, Crary has to assume the unity and stability of both a phenomenon and a term, "perception," which is then susceptible to transformation by power. Where attention can be thought of as discipline, perception is the eternal criminal, that which can be disciplined. It can be reformed, but it never abandons its fundamentally receptive nature. There is no essential change. It is for this reason that throughout the book, history is associated with contingency and externality. Crary's theory of history, deduced only from this book, may be summed up in several theses, some of which are in clear tension with the others, if not in full contradiction:

A. Technology drives historical change, but what drives technological change remains mystified. This implies a kind of materialism, which is contradicted by the argument that:

B. concepts (constructions) determine "activities of the body" (46).

C. The change in perception is a one-time break, never before seen; i.e., history is homogeneous before and after, and this is because:

D. history is conceived of as the uniform ground against which change can be seen.

His view of history corresponds almost exactly to his understanding of vision. It too is a uniform ground against which change is marked. Vision can disintegrate or be made coherent, but it always remains vision, that is, reception of what is by an encapsulated subject.

There are, however, moments in which the idea of attention is allowed to fall apart. For example, Crary tells us that Manet knew "that a sustained looking at anything will relieve vision of its fixed character" (126). In other words, the act of attention may imply moving away from itself. And he does offer counter-concepts to attentiveness that are not diversion. He evokes "creative, intensive states of deep absorption and daydreaming" (4) and goes on to discuss daydreaming in more detail with reference to its colonization by media (77). He calls for a perception in which objects occupy "qualitatively different strata" instead of being flattened out (7) and the exploration of "creative possibilities . . . amid new technological forms of boredom" (78). And finally, and perhaps most interestingly, he sees "a singular countermodel of attentiveness" in Freud's "gleichschwebende Aufmerksamkeit" (367–68). These revolutionary suggestions appear sporadically in the text, but are never elaborated. Yet even these suggestions are conservative, opposing the extensive and superficial to the intensive and absorbed, re-inscribing the very logic of the subject that he seems to critique.

More recently, Bernard Stiegler has begun to publish a trilogy of books entitled *Prendre soin*, which has been rendered "Taking Care." The first volume, *Prendre soin: de la jeunesse et des générations* (2008), performs a consistent and rigorous critique of what Stiegler calls "psychopower" (*psychopouvoir*)—consistent in that it does not hypothesize a radical break in which this power came about from nothing, rigorous in that he analyzes the phenomenon of psychopower by precisely distinguishing his terms. And still he "diagnoses" a disintegration of attention as our current illness. The major social change that brought about the crisis in attention, which in turn has provoked technologies of control, for Stiegler, is the lowering of the age of minority, which has an exact analogue in consumer culture. There is no longer a strict difference between minors and adults, such that adults no longer "take care" of minors. Instead, minors are abandoned to the vicissitudes of capital's forces of attraction. Attention, however, is neither essential nor physiological. It is neither an epistemological "construction" nor a modification of a natural capacity such as vision. Rather, it is the product of the sedimentation of an intergenerational symbolic milieu (20). In other words, attention is historical, where history is written (104), and it is through an impoverishment of history that attention, which is analogous to reading, becomes impoverished. Attention meant the interiorization of inherited symbolic representations (23). Earlier, it manifested itself in the book, the psychotechnique at the basis of monotheism (35). Thus previously it was not necessary to "capture" attention; instead attention was formed, through education, by learning to read

(37). Stiegler identifies writing as a form of critical attention, thus the role of technics in attention-formation is clearly spelled out (49). The crucial distinction for him is between the material-technical attention, which he calls psychotechnique, and psychotechnology. Psychotechnology and its offshoot, nootechnology, remove attention from the realm of signs and history and insert it into the realm of biology, what Stiegler calls an organological interpretation (of which Crary is often guilty) (69), and this in turn opens the possibility of a pharmacological response (71–78). The rest of the book describes in detail the ills of this interpretation and response.

Throughout the argument, however, a single opposition is operative—between "une attention critique et rationelle" and an attention "dispersée et dissipée" (147–48).

The great contribution of this analysis is the suggestion that attention consists in something utterly unlike perception, that is in history and writing. One does not pay attention: it accumulates through social and technical acts. A community of educators and adults, decides, collects, preserves, writes, and reads the sedimented signs, but this means that they sift them and allow them to settle again. And yet, with this explanation, the term attention has become so big and baggy that almost anything can be described as attention—indeed it articulates "dans *un très grand circuit* l'histoire universelle de l'humanité" (104). In this way a furtive humanism enters the scene, one that prefers adults over children, collection over dispersal, preservation over wearing away. Preservation and wearing away, majors and minors, humans and animals, *pharmakos* and *pharmakon*—these antagonisms strictly delimit the field of inquiry. Distraction thus comes to mean either an attention deficit or a hyper-attention "comme une attention non seulement distribué, mais dispersée, disséminée et dissipée" (145). In response, one might inquire: what is reading? what is writing?—if not a kind of dissipation, another kind perhaps, one worth dallying with. Within the logic of this argument, the sedimentation of history stands out against the dispersion, dissipation, and dissemination of the new hyper-attention against which Stiegler argues. One keeps and holds, the other lets go and loses.

5. This is as true for psychiatric diagnoses as it is for cultural theory. For the history of the invention of ADD and ADHD, see the opening chapter of Barkley, *Attention-Deficit Hyperactivity Disorder* (3–75).

6. Avital Ronell discovers many of the problems of distraction while writing about one of its partners, in her book *Stupidity*. To name only one: the improbability of actually encountering it. "It turns out," Avital Ronell comments while writing about Musil's stupidity, "to be as elusive as it is somehow present" (71).

7. Ronell reports on an analogous prejudice: "The consistent untimeliness and out-of-placeness of the question, 'What is stupidity?' is only intensified by the fact that it admits no resolute literary or scientific rejoinder. Barely philo-

sophical, a detached satellite to meaningful discourses, the question orbits on its own" (72).

8. Empirical consciousness is "in itself distracted" (*an sich zerstreut*) (*Kritik der reinen Vernunft* B133). For an exposition of the fine lines between "Aufmerksamkeit," "Abstraktion," and "Distraktion" in Kant's critical writings and in the *Anthropology*, see Gasché, "Über das Wegsehen." In the notes to the *Anthropologie* collected under the heading *Reflections*, Kant makes a record of several disjointed thoughts on distraction:

> *absence*: durch innere Ursache
> distraction: durch äussere Empfindungen. Arbeit zerstreut. Zeitkürzungen zerstreuen, Geniessen.
> Damit man nicht ausschweife: Hauptaufmerksamkeit. Wovon wolte ich reden. *protensio*.
> (*Kants handschriftlicher Nachlaß*, #524 p. 27)

And then:

> Man dissipirt sich willkührlich, man wird distrahirt unwillkührlich (Verliebt. Besorgt. Intriguen im Kopf. Bey sich selbst seyn.) Durch vielheit verschiedener in kurzer Zeit auf einander folgenden Beschäftigungen. Alles, was das Gemuth unwillkührlich beschaftigt, wenn es auch blos der hang zu Einbildungen wäre, zerstreut. Durch Krankheit zerstreut, hypochondrisch. Habituel zerstreute (scheinen Narren) Leute sind in Geschaften nicht brauchbar. Newton, der glaubte, gespeiset zu haben.
> Das nichts Denken (Gedankenlosigkeit) bey der Zerstreuung bedeutet den unwillkührlichen Lauf der gedanken. (ist eine Art von Traum. Solche Leute, vornehmlich Frauen, taugen nicht viel.)
> (*absentia animi, dagegen praesence d'esprit*.)
> Seine Gedanken sammeln 1. Nach einer (lebhaften.) willkührlichen Zerstreuung der Lustbarkeit oder Gesellschaft gibt neues Leben. (*boudoir*.) 2. Nach der todten Zerstreuung der Gedankenlosigkeit ist schweer und giebt einen Matten gebrauch. Abstrakte Kopfe sind zerstreut, empirische gut bey sich selbst. Zerstreut seyn beym Rechnen. Geldzählen. Reisen. In Gesellschaft. Bey einer Rede. Beym Lesen. Schwächt das Gedächtnis.
> (#525 pp. 27–28)

These remarks reveal a precise knowledge of various phenomena that go under the name distraction; at the same time they show its effects, even on the experienced philosopher. Notice in the first set of notes how distraction seems at one point to overcome him. He interrupts his thinking to write: "Wovon wollte ich reden."

9. For an account of Kant's hypochondria, see Fenves's *Late Kant*, particularly chapter 7, "Revolution Is in the Air."

10. Hegel classifies "Zerstreutheit" with "Blödsinn" (imbecility) and "Faselei" (blather), in the section on anthropology of the *Enzyklopedie, Dritter Teil*, under "Die fühlende Seele." In fact there are two *Zerstreuungen*, a pernicious and minor one, and one that is a breather from the heavy exercise of the spirit. The first "besteht in einem *Nichtwissen* von der *unmittelbaren Gegenwart*. Oft bildet dies Nichtwissen den Anfang des Wahnsinns; doch gibt es auch eine vom Wahnsinn sehr entfernte, großartige Zerstreutheit" (172ff.).

CHAPTER I

1. The long story of *nous poiētikos*, productive intellect, better known by its Latin name, *intellectus agens*, begins in *De anima* 3.5, just after the appearance (and disappearance) of not-always-thinking. Richard Sorabji has collected ancient commentators' views on the subject (*Commentators* 102–18). Wedin makes a strong argument for understanding Aristotle's sketchily introduced concept as equal to the notion of thought thinking itself (*Mind* 168). Productive mind is the mind that produces itself as thinking, as the form of itself. This, in turn, should be understood with reference to the definition of the producer (*to poioun*) in *De generatione et corruptione*. The producer is like an artist who makes something, that is, who introduces something foreign but remains himself unaffected by what he produces and by the act of production (*Mind* 173–74).

2. Two important, though brief, studies support this argument. Jean-Pierre Vernant's *Origins of Greek Thought* describes the flattening and consolidation of the landscape that took place under the name of "thought" in the fifth century. Writing of Anaximander, Vernant elaborates on this thought: "With one stroke he obliterated the mythic image of a layered world, where the absolute opposition of high and low marked the cosmic levels that differentiated the divine powers, and whose spatial directions had contrasting religious meanings" (121).

In an equally short but no less potent study of the transition between archaic and classical Greece, François de Polignac locates the change from myth to thought in a movement of geographical consolidation. The coming into being of *poleis* was a consequence, according to his somewhat controversial theory, of the community's changing orientation toward sacred architecture. From the eighth century onwards, sanctuaries began to function as points of orientation for communal activity, although they were located outside population centers. The wall or limit, *temenos*, that determined the bounds of the religious site came to order existence; a boundary sanctuary, according to Polignac, always bordered on an uninhabitable, wild area of sea or mountains, or stood at a border with an unfriendly populace. "The social space was thus constructed around two poles: the inhabited area and the sanctuary, the separation/combination of which formulated a new definition of community on a territorial basis" (39–40). The definition was not only territorial, however. The city was also defined, if we accept Polignac's thesis, around a theoretical or cognitive distance from divine violence.

3. References to Zeus's fateful principle alternate between his plan, *boulē*, his diaphragm, *phrēn*, and his mind, *noos*. See *Iliad* 1.5, 10.45, 13.524, 12.173, 14.160, 5.242, 16.103, among other passages.

4. Part of the fragment is quoted in Jan Bremmer's survey of the motif of "the living soul" in Ancient Greece and other cultures in *The Early Greek Concept of the Soul* (49ff.).

5. For a description of the motif of the boy-medium and the hieroscopic sacrifice of boys, see Daniel Ogden, *Greek and Roman Necromancy* (196–200).

6. The verb *plēsso* in the middle and passive often means to be struck by something intellectually, to be struck dumb or amazed.

7. Why *nous* must be shown to be separable is discussed in Kahn (375–79). The difference between the Platonic separability of the ideas and Aristotelian separability of *nous* is discussed by Wedin in "Tracking Aristotle's Nous." Plato's mistake, according to Aristotle, was to conflate noetic separateness with ontological separateness (153).

8. Myles Burnyeat argues in the published lecture *Aristotle's Divine Intellect* that the description of active intellect at *De anima* 3.5, *Metaphysics* Λ, and *Nicomachean Ethics* 10.7 are not only of a piece, but refer to the same thing, to the divine intellect (33–43). Wedin criticizes this view (*Mind* 209–54); for him, Aristotle considers the intellect a finite, functional, image-producing system, and so the comparison with the mind of God amounts to hyperbole.

9. The treatise focuses on the intellectual part of the *psuchē* comparatively briefly and on the productive aspect of the intellect in a truly telegraphic manner. Although there is some agreement among classicists that the intellect sections or perhaps the entirety of Book 3 were written later than the preceding two books—despite the fact that the section divisions as we have them cannot with any reliability be attributed to Aristotle—there is little consensus on the dating of the section on the intellect or the order of composition of all the sections. A good summary of the debates and methods on the order of writing all the works is "Aristotle's Works and Thought" by Georgios Anagnostopoulos, in *A Companion to Aristotle* (14–27). On the *De anima* and other works on the *psuchē*, the standard text is still Irving Block, "The Order of Aristotle's Psychological Writings." Evidence, for him, indicates that the *nous* section and Book 3 as a whole was composed later than the first two books (73–75).

10. In the long-running controversy over whether productive *nous* is or is not to be identified with Aristotle's god, Brentano, for one, was determined to prove that *nous poiētikos* was not divine, but the active principle of human thinking (*The Psychology of Aristotle* 110–11). More recently, Burnyeat makes the more controversial claim not only that the thought thinking thought of *Metaphysics* Λ

and the so-called active intellect of *De anima* 3.5 refer to the same thing, but that Aristotle's own intellect, when producing these thoughts, is also godlike (9, 38–43). Revisiting "the theory that Brentano dismissed as 'prattle without all sense and reason,'" Burnyeat revives it by saying: "The Active Intellect is God" (42). It is not clear, however, whether there are significant differences between the contents of these two views, or whether in fact what we mean when we say divine is what Aristotle, Brentano, and Burnyeat mean when they add together "separate from body," "active," and "a system of absolutely correct concepts" (Burnyeat 41).

11. For the late, seemingly coordinated development of the sections on the intellect in these works, see 328–327 BCE in Rist's chronology (286). On *nous* as the basis of psychology and ethics, see chapter 9. The importance of developmental interpretations of Aristotle's writings for understanding conceptual distinctions within the texts is argued admirably in Charlotte Witt's "The Evolution of Developmental Interpretations of Aristotle."

12. The passage from the *Ethics*, in W. D. Ross's translation revised by J. O. Urmson, reads: "This element which is thought to be our natural ruler and guide (*archein kai hegesthai*) and to take thought (*ennoian*) of things noble and divine, whether it be itself also divine or only the most divine element (*en hēmin to theiotaton*) in us, the activity of this in accordance with its proper excellence will be complete happiness. That this activity is contemplative we have already said" (*The Complete Works* 1860).

13. Aristotle recalls the common analogy between *noein* and *aisthanesthai* at 427a19, and then again at 429a13. He complicates the analogy at 429a29ff. For discussions of the analogy and its limitations, see Burnyeat (19–28), Wedin ("Tracking Aristotle's Nous" 134), and Kahn (364–72).

14. Whether this is said of the human or the divine mind is disputed (see Note 8, above). Ross, to make his interpretation clear, inserts the word "divine" (which is not in his Greek edition) before "thought" in his translation of the passage's first sentence (*The Complete Works* 1698). Yet it seems clear from the preceding discussion of intellect in general that this refers to anthropic *nous*, albeit in its most godlike aspect.

15. Joseph Magee categorizes the differences between perception and intellection in *Unmixing the Intellect* (117–44). *Nous* differs from *aisthēsis* in the wide range of its objects, in being unmixed with body, in being impassive toward the strongest intelligibles, and in receiving non-sensibles. Ronald Polansky works carefully through Aristotle's distinction of *nous* from *aisthēsis* in his commentary on *De anima*, lingering over the vexed question of where *phantasia* belongs (403–33).

16. For a summary of Anglo-American responses to Aristotle's psychology, see Christopher Shields' "Some Recent Approaches to Aristotle's *De anima*," in Hamlyn's edition of *De anima, Books II and III* (157–81).

17. A scrupulous discussion of the meanings of *aition* throughout Aristotle's writings can be found in Monte Ransome Johnson's *Aristotle on Teleology* (40–63). It is important, he argues, to distinguish *aition* from "cause" in later English philosophy. Cause implies, among other things, an empirical event. Johnson favors the translation "explanation" or "causal explanation," which leaves the hermeneutic or epistemic aspect of *aition* audible, where English "cause" tends to conceal it (41). Burnyeat has a similar reading of *aition*, as related to *ousia*, which means for him "a first principle of explanatory demonstration" (24). *Nous*, he argues, is no more than the "achievement" of grasping a form (as cause) (27). This makes it particularly paradoxical when *nous* is asked to grasp the cause of its own dysfunction. Can deformation have a form?

18. Among modern philologists, Ross believes not-always-thinking is an actual problem for Aristotle, although for whatever reasons Aristotle neglects to resolve it. "A. does not appear to discuss this question anywhere," Ross writes in the commentary to his edition (*De anima* 295). Hicks simply repeats it, while demoting the demand to "a parenthetical remark." As an aside, it poses no problem for the theory of *nous*. "Why then," Hicks continues, "if τὸ νοοῦν and τὸ νοούμενον be always present, should there be any intermission in the process of thinking?" (32–33). Hamlyn accepts the problem as a problem, yet denies its importance. "The remark about why the intellect does not always think is parenthetical, suggested presumably by the previous remark about the identity of that which thinks and its object. It is not obvious that Aristotle does consider the question later, except perhaps at the end of Chapter 5" (*Aristotle's De anima, Books II and III* 129). Polansky, in his recent commentary on the text, seems more willing at once to imply that this idea is a problem and to leave it as one. In a note he rejects Mary Luise Gill's conclusion that intermittent thinking belongs only to the passive mind. Polansky writes: "This will not be the interpretation of this commentary. The question of iii 5 is what is the agent intellect, i.e., that which acts on the mind to cause it to think, but in answering this question Aristotle is also explaining why humans do not always think (esp. when iii 7 and iii 8 are included)" (455, n31).

Among ancient commentators, the impulse to fulfill the insatiable demand is strong, although the responses remain largely unsatisfying. Here is Themistius on the passage at *De anima* 429a13–15, translated by Robert B. Todd: "For it is said in a stricter sense that [the intellect] would be 'perfected' rather [than affected] by being advanced from potentiality to actuality. And it is obvious that [it is advanced] from potentiality. That is why we do not always think, nor even always think the same objects rather than different ones at different times. This is, in fact, a sign that this intellect exists in potentiality, as there can be no transition from one activity to another unless a potentiality remains to display the different activities" (Themistius 94.12, 118–19). But Themistius here misses the point and with it the urgency of Aristotle's demand. If not-always-thinking were simply equivalent to potential thought, Aristotle would have treated it as part of passive *nous*. He deals with mind's passive latency and intermittency at great length and in many places (*Metaphysics* Λ 1074b15ff., *De anima* 3.4, 429a10–b9, b29–30a9).

Philoponus states the problem precisely, but then misreads it in a familiar way. Here is the translation by William Charlton and Fernand Bossier: "But we should consider the cause of its not understanding always. Aristotle here interposes another problem. If the intellect is both intellect and intelligible thing, why does it not understand all the time? Since the intelligibles are always in actuality, how is it that it does not understand them all the time? And if it is both intellect and intelligible thing, why does it not understand itself all the time? Such is the problem or difficulty. Aristotle did not, as some have thought, omit to provide a solution; he will give it later, as we shall make clear when we get there" (60–61). Philoponus sees 430a25 as the answer to this question, where Aristotle states that "without this [always-thinking] it thinks nothing." But this is simply to say again that all not-always-thinking must be potential thinking, and active, actual thinking operates continually.

In the commentary on *De anima*, written before becoming involved in the Averroist controversy over the materiality of the *psuchē*, Aquinas rejects any natural change in the intellect; its only motion is that from potential to actual ("non est mutatio secundum esse naturale") (§160). And since thought has its unity in succession, as an operation unified in time, not in magnitude, any interruption would be less like a disintegration of a faculty than like a suspension or break in the number series (§111). As for our sentence, the demand that not-always-thinking be thought all the way back to its origin, Aquinas's comment is complicated. He takes it as an element of the question "how can mind think itself?" Yet the difficulty for him lies in the nature of potentiality. For *intellectus*, as the pure potential to become any object, in order to cognize itself, must translate or transform its potential into an actual. The form of the potential intellect, that which the active intellect desires to know, is also potential. *Intellectus possibilis* is a variety of *materia prima*, base matter (§725). Among intelligences only God is perfect actuality, as intelligible as he is intelligent (§726). Thus, given that the unity of thought is time and the only non-time is eternity, why a particular thinker might not always think remains obscure (§727).

19. Richard Sorabji divides ancient theorists of time into those who believe *aei* and *aion* mean infinite duration and those who believe they mean timelessness. For Aristotle, according to Sorabji, nothing in time can last until the end of time or outlast it; this is why time is called the destroyer. A second class of beings, which Sorabji mentions but does not investigate further, are those too quick or too divided to count as taking time, such as "coincidences, relations, processes, points" and

so forth. Thirdly, there are beings that relate to time differently than any other be-ing; they are not in time although they are not technically timeless. Stars, for ex-ample, are not in time and yet they are for all time. Finally, there is that which lies beyond the farthest sphere of heaven, God's eternity, *to aion* (*Time* 126–27).

20. The most complete discussion of the law of contradiction is in *Metaphys-ics* Γ, 3–6.

21. On the notion of a counter-time or "untime" in Kant and Hegel, see Wer-ner Hamacher, "Des contrées des tempes."

22. Aristotle has an eminent precursor who also envisioned a breakdown of thought—or more radically, a prehistory before the reign of thought began. Par-menides, in his philosophical poem, addresses the *akrita phula*, the uncritical tribes, driven by a *plakton noon*, a mind that wanders like planets or children's un-controllable limbs, on a non-path between deciding for being and being deceived by non-being. Fragment 6 of the poem presents a primordial collectivity called *brotoi*, which means roughly "mortals," before the imposition of critical thought. The goddess who narrates this part of the poem, in order to convince the traveler of the importance of the union of thought and being, tries to scare him with a vision of distracted ones. Here is the recent translation by David Gallop:

> It must be that what is there for speaking and thinking of *is*; for it is there to be,
> whereas nothing is not; that is what I bid you consider,
> for [I restrain] you from that first route of inquiry,
> and then also from this one, on which mortals (*brotoi*) knowing nothing
> wander (*plattontai*), two-headed (*dikrannoi*); for helplessness (*amechanie*) in their
> breasts guides their distracted mind (*plakton noon*); and they are carried
> deaf and blind alike, dazed, tribes without judgment (*akrita phula*),
> by whom being and not-being have been thought both the same
> and not the same; and the path of all is backward-turning. (Parmenides,
> *Fragments* 61)

There is much to read in this passage. Crucial for our purposes is the character of distraction: it is not diversion. What are called here *brotoi* are not those who naively believe opinion to be true; that is, they are not the ones who simply and blindly follow the path of non-being. Rather, they vacillate between making a distinction and not making a distinction between being and non-being.

CHAPTER 2

1. La Bruyère carries on this cliché. Portrait 49 in the chapter "Of Women" lists the details of women's "weakness of temperament, or laziness of mind" but attributes it to decidedly social causes, including "the distracting effect of their household responsibilities" (*Characters* E 64, F 219).

2. Nonetheless he quickly spawns a set of copies, testifying to a sudden relevance, including the main character of a popular play by the same name, *Le Distrait*, by Jean-François Regnard, first produced in 1697.

3. Roland Barthes formulates La Bruyère's relationship to past and future slightly differently. He describes the "uneasiness" with which our modernity—Barthes' modernity of 1963 (yet another crisis of the modern)—receives *Les Caractères*: "the world of La Bruyère is both *ours and different*," he remarks. It is ours because we (we French, in this case) are so familiar with seventeenth-century stereotypes that "we circulate quite comfortably among these old figures from our childhood." It is different for the very same reason; its topoi are too familiar, and so they are untimely, too worn out and anachronistic to represent "ourselves." His solution is unexpected—but nonetheless correct. "Let us discuss everything in La Bruyère which concerns us little or not at all" (222–23; emphasis in the original). Although Barthes doesn't spend much time on him, Ménalque would be an archetypical aspect of *Les Caractères* that "concerns us little," since he is everywhere among us, since he is us.

4. To abandon time is to abandon the possibility of moral judgment as well. Mores to be depicted must be current, or at least "of the century," or else the moralist will be thought absurd. La Bruyère rethinks this problem in the section on fashion. There he worries that, under the sign of fashion, characters will change before the moralist has a chance to depict them (*Characters* E 258, F 512). The name of this slippery character is the hypocrite. With much more élan and without a theory of history, La Rochefoucauld expresses a similar sentiment: "At times we are as different from ourselves as we are from others" (#135).

5. See the fourth chapter, "The Destruction of the Hero" in Bénichou's *Man and Ethics* (98–115).

6. Marc Escola, editor of the critical edition of *Les Caractères*, discusses the morality of the figure in similar terms in *La Bruyère/ 1, Brèves questions d'herméneutique*. In Escola's reading, Ménalque never coincides with a fixed and determined moral quality (318).

7. One origin for this ideal of an all-encompassing abjection can be found in the Jansenist ideology. See Bénichou, chaps. 3–5 (75–137).

8. A subtle analysis of this process of thinking is given by John D. Lyons in his *Before Imagination: Embodied Thought from Montaigne to Rousseau* (97–98).

9. Marc Escola traces the development of section 7 of "De l'homme" through the additions and changes made by La Bruyère across many editions (*La Bruyère/ 2, Rhétorique du discontinu* 255–67).

10. For a reading that investigates this lack of self-presence as a question of representation and a linguistic question, see Marc Escola in the chapter "*Ménalque* tel qu'en lui-même." There he proposes: "'*Ménalque*' est un objet que le

discours se propose comme le lieu de sa propre mise à l'épreuve. Telle est la proposition qui va a guider notre lecture: il s'agira de voir comment le discours affronte cet objet, comment La Bruyère tente de rendre présent au discours un être qui ne saurait jamais être present à lui même" (*La Bruyère/ 1, Brèves questions d'herméneutique* 319).

11. Various keys to *Les Caractères* claim that one model for this figure was "le comte Charles de Brancas" whose blundering does in fact make Louis XIV laugh (*Caractères* 726, n7). For a complete list of possible keys, see Escola, *La Bruyère/ 1, Brèves questions d'herméneutique* (325). La Bruyère himself was rumored to be the butt of ridicule in the house of the duke of Bourbon.

12. In her study of the epistemological cousin of distraction, *Stupidity*, Avital Ronell writes: "The stupid cannot see themselves. No mirror has been invented in which they might reflect themselves. They ineluctably evade reflection" (18). The distracted one does see something reflected in the mirror, but there is no inkling that the image belongs to him.

13. On the close relationship between these English journals and *Les Caractères*, see Turner, "The Influence of La Bruyère on the 'Tatler' and the 'Spectator.'"

14. One of the few intuitions of this problem can be found in a youthful exercise by Jean Paul, entitled "Schilderung eines Zerstreuten." At the very end of the piece, the protagonist-narrator, who at the outset had announced his intention to investigate his own distraction, describes its failure: "Aber wahrhaftig ich vergess' es in den Tod, das Bild eines Zerstreuten dem denkenden Leser zu geben und es ist sonst wider meine Art" (753).

15. The debt to Hegel is made explicit: "Madness is placed in a zone of exclusion from which it will only escape in part in Hegel's *Phenomenology of Spirit*" (46). Whereas in Hegel, madness only partially escapes its confinement, in Foucault through an intensified Hegelianism it will be fully liberated.

16. "Absentmindedness, indeed, is not perhaps the actual fountain-head of the comic, but surely it is contiguous to a stream of facts and fancies which flow straight from the fountain-head. It is situated, so to say, on one of the great natural watersheds of laughter" (Bergson 68).

17. This line is repeated verbatim at Luke 11:23 and so has been considered among the authentic sayings of Jesus.

18. Jean Mesnard argues that to attribute Pascal's theology to a single source in Port-Royal Jansenism is first of all to ignore the broader Augustinism that circulated in his day, and second of all, to ignore the fact that Port-Royal does not represent a unified intellectual stance (138–43). Debates over whether Pascal was a heretical Jansenist (because he defends those accused of following Jansenius) or an anti-Jansenist, because of many remarks and *pensées* that contradict tenets attributed to Jansenists and followers of Port-Royal, are ongoing.

19. This trend can be followed back to Aristotle. Anthony Levi gives the Aristotelian provenance of moral intellectualism, following its path through ancient stoicism to Aquinas and Pascal (27ff.). On the passion for reason in literature of the age, see Jeanne Haight's *The Concept of Reason in French Classical Literature, 1635–1690*. Chapter 5, "Human Reason as Empirical Reason" distinguishes the historical senses of *experience, raison* and *raisonnements, esprit, connaissance,* and so forth (100–117). She does not discuss *penser* or *pensée*. Shapes of a nonuniversal intellect are presented in readings informed by Deleuze in *The Movement of Thought: An Essay on Intellect in Seventeenth-Century France* by Herbert De Ley, see especially chapter 3, on the thinking process in Montaigne and Charron (26–38). The meaning of *esprit* in La Bruyère is described in the first two chapters of Marine Ricord's *"Les Caractères" de La Bruyère ou les exercices de l'esprit* (13–74). The persistence of the idea of reason as a principle of social order, the nature of man that lifts him above nature, is discussed by François-Xavier Cuche in *Une Pensée Sociale Catholique: Fleury, La Bruyère et Fénelon* (147–54).

20. From the entry on "penser" in the *Dictionnaire de l'Académie Française* (first edition, 1694) ("ARTFL Project").

21. To understand the meaning of the trivial in Pascal, flies are critical: "la puissance des mouches," the paradoxical strength of flies defines triviality (E #22, #48; F #56, #81).

22. A commonplace in the epoch with regard to the passions. La Rochefoucauld puts it this way with respect to love: "Constancy in love is perpetual inconstancy, inasmuch as the heart is drawn to one quality after another in the beloved, now preferring this, now that. Constancy is therefore inconstancy held in check and confined to the same object" (#175 p. 59).

23. In this way his foibles give the appearance of all moral failures at once. "Sa distraction semble faire de Ménalque un parfait incivil. Et l'incivilité, dans une éthique de l'honnêteté, est le défaut des défauts: celui qui les résume tous" (Escola *La Bruyère/ I* 332).

24. Blanchot's "other attention" comes close to what I mean by "distraction," although it has little to do with the customary opposition between the two words. He exposes the idea in *The Infinite Conversation* during a complaint about Simon Weil's discussion with herself in her notebooks. What she calls a "hidden God," the truth that must be kept secret and at the same time perpetually sought out, Blanchot separates from traditional theological terms. Weil's secret deity sought by thinking is better expressed this way: "It may be (and are we not continually having this experience) that the further thought goes toward expressing itself, the more it must maintain a reserve somewhere within itself, something like a place that would be a kind of uninhabited, uninhabitable nonthought, *a thought that would not allow itself to be thought*" (119). The thought that does not allow itself to be thought is like an affliction (Plato says something

similar in the *Sophist*) on the "hither side of attention." "The other attention is as though idle and unoccupied" and as such it is "the reception of what escapes attention" (121). Werner Hamacher brings to light a related "gegen sich selbst veränderte . . . Aufmerksamkeit" ("Bogengebete" 21) through a reading of a favorite line of Benjamin's from Malebranche, "Attention [*Aufmerksamkeit*] is the natural prayer of the soul." Attention is a prayer, prayer is language, and so attention is language directed toward a future other that might receive it and an other language that might translate it. Attention prays not in secret to a personal God but in public, in every utterance, to a future that empties attention of its fixation on the present.

25. A brief investigation of political equality in the book can be found in "L'Idée d'Égalité dans Les Caractères," by Corrado Rosso (Dagen, Bourguinat, and Escola 245–48).

26. A contrary view is taken by Marc Escola in *La Bruyère/1*. He argues that, since the moral value of any of the fragments in the book is up to the reader to decide, this footnote represents an extraordinary attempt by the author to dictate the value of this one character (318–19). This view derives from the same insight, however, since it would be the extreme valuelessness of *le distrait* that causes La Bruyère to react with a footnote that tries to control how readers read him.

27. That this inclusive community already exists has been observed by a twentieth-century Ménalque and prophet of middle America, of the middle class, and of the middling part of the soul. Homer Simpson recognized that distraction has become so inclusive that the word no longer has meaning. "Distracted, that's a funny word. Does anyone ever get 'tracted?" ("Diatribe of a Mad Housewife").

CHAPTER 3

1. "Gedanken" "denken" 584, 587, 592, 599, 601, 613, 616, 623–24, 626–27; "Verstand" "verstehen" 579, 583, 586, 590, 606, 610, 615–16, 620, 631; "Überlegung" 598–99, 602, 630; "rechnen" 577, 582–83, 594, 601, 627; "Plan" "planen" 581–84, 586, 591, 600, 616, 620, 623–24, 629, 630.

2. As if it were the story's—or even Kafka's—greatest mystery or secret, the problem of the fragment's ending has bothered interpreters—and not only interpreters. Endings bothered Kafka, for obvious and less obvious reasons. The editor of the *Apparatband* to the critical edition, Jost Schillemeit, indicates that, of the 16 sides, recto and verso, that the manuscript comprises, "eine ursprünglich vorhandene Fortsetzung vermutet werden kann" (*NS II* 142). An ending, says the editor, was most likely present, but accident intervened. How does he come to this conclusion? From the observation that the text extends down beyond the comfortable writing area of the last page, "bis zum Ende der untersten Zeile"

(142). The manuscript is thus poised at the tipping point between certainty and doubt over the ending. One thing can be surmised. Choosing a missing ending over one that was never intended removes the burden of thinking what a story would be that does not naturally, constitutively, following its own internal path, or the writer's genius, find a proper end. Only a force working against ending, a demonic force, the assumption goes, only something like accident or death could have denied a story so ripe for a finish its proper ending. The assumption Brod makes in his afterword to the first edition of the fragment has had a long life. Basing his opinion on the authority of Dora Dymant, he states with certainty: "Die Arbeit war vollendet; es fehlt in den erhalten gebliebenen Blättern nicht mehr viel bis zum Schluß gespannter Kampfstellung in unmittelbarer Erwartung des Tieres und des entscheidenden Kampes, in dem der Held unterliegen wird" (Kafka *Beschreibung* 314). There are more recent, and more nuanced, versions of this decision for a heroic conclusion. Having decided that the creature's enemy is "Death," that the creature is "the Thinker" (Boulby 176) and that the Bau is "his tomb" (Boulby 179), Mark Boulby goes on to surmise that the non-ending is intentional, because Kafka could not write convincingly "about his own death (who can?)" (Boulby 181). The story's end and the author's death become conflated here, and for this reason the Bau is in fact finished, even though and because it is incomplete. In all these cases, just as it is for the Bau creature itself, completeness is the goal, and the obsession.

3. In the early collection of essays introducing the reading of Kafka to an English-speaking audience, Malcolm Pasley takes note of a few of the many possible metaphoric readings. "The burrow as Kafka's work" (Pasley 419) and "the burrow as Kafka's inner self" (420) are two rubrics under which he sketches out potential approaches to the fragment. Heinz Politzer emphasizes these two interpretations as well, calling the fragment "the tale of Kafka's work at the moment of his dying" (Politzer 321) and "a place of some timid inner security, a frail Castle Within" (333). More importantly, or at least, in an interpretive gesture that is less biographical—or ergographical—and more allegorical, Politzer, subtly insightful as he is throughout his reading, despite certain blind spots, argues that Kafka finally enters the Castle in this story. Whether we agree or not that it is "Kafka" or even "K." that is at issue here, the suggestion that the creature builds and dwells in its Castle is suggestive. The creature is *Herr* and *Knecht* at once, worker and planner, memory and speaker, destroyer and questioner, and its Castle is likewise everywhere and nowhere. Politzer describes the attitude in the creature that corresponds to this predicament as "extreme doubt" (322). This does not quite capture the situation of the animal who "cannot live within the cave and likewise is not able to bear the thought of leaving it" (324). To bear a thought, this is what the creature must do and cannot, and so he arrives at an unbearable thought—that he will have to let thought go. That this is not nihilism Politzer

also understands. He denies that the "forces at work" in the story are purely "self-defeating," although the conclusion he draws from this insight, that Kafka finds security at last, however precariously, in this *Bau*, seems untenable (331).

4. A very different view of the relationship of building to thinking, with both based in a concept of inhabitation, can be found in Heidegger's 1951 lecture, "Bauen Wohnen Denken." Clearly Heidegger's association of "Wohnen" with "zufrieden sein," being satisfied and at peace ("Bauen Wohnen Denken" 143), is just the beginning of the differences with Kafka's attack on inhabitation, on the logic of *Stiften*, and his almost opposite concept of freedom.

5. In his study of Kafka's relationship to and critique of *Wissenschaft*, Paul Heller cites the crucial passage from *Brehms Tierleben* on the perceptual capacity of the *Maulwurf* that he calls the "Keimzelle für Kafkas Erzählung 'Der Bau'" (120). I quote it here in its entirety: "Das Gehör ist vortrefflich. Wahrscheinlich wird es besonders benutzt, um Gefahren zu bemerken; denn der Maulwurf [. . .] hört auch jedes ihm bedenklich erscheinende Geräusch mit aller Sicherheit und sucht sich dann so schnell wie möglich auf und davon zu machen [. . .] in der Erde wirkt ja der ganze Körper gleichsam als äußeres Ohr [. . .]" (*Brehms Tierleben*, 1912, Bd. 10, s. 313. Qtd. in Heller 120).

6. The genre in which the mole is called upon to demonstrate a certain scope and movement of thought extends at least to Kant, who in the first book of the "Transzendentale Dialektik" admonishes us "den Boden zu jenen majestätischen sittlichen Gebäuden eben und baufest zu machen, in welchem sich allerlei Maulwurfsgänge einer vergeblich, aber mit guter Zuversicht, auf Schätze grabenden Vernunft vorfinden, und die jenes Bauwerk unsicher machen" (*Kritik der reinen Vernunft* A319, B76). Already in Kant the "transzendentale Gebrauch der reinen Vernunft" is contrasted to the work of an eternal mole, that makes any majestic edifice teeter on its foundation. Nietzsche in the Preface to *Morgenröthe* cites the genre with scarcely concealed irony, emphasizing the solitude of the earth-digger: "In diesem Buch findet man einen "Unterirdischen" an der Arbeit, einen Bohrenden, Grabenden, Untergrabenden. Man sieht ihn, vorausgesetzt, daß man Augen für solche Arbeit der Tiefe hat . . . fragt ihn nicht, was er da unten will, er wird es euch selbst schon sagen, dieser scheinbare Trophonios und Unterirdische, wenn er erst wieder 'Mensch geworden' ist. Man verlernt gründlich das Schweigen, wenn man so lange, wie er, Maulwurf war, allein war—" (Nietzsche v. 3, p. 11). On the larger semantic field of molework, see Winkler (145–46).

7. Giorgio Agamben, at one of the *Thor Seminars* in the late 1960s, asked Heidegger whether he had read Kafka, and in particular what he had thought about the Bau fragment. According to Agamben, Heidegger replied curtly: "the last gasp of Western subjectivity" (related in conversation, April 2004). The assess-

ment is possibly correct if applied to the Bau creature, but an unfortunate mis-reading of the story as a whole.

8. Brod chronicles the rediscovery of the manuscript containing the points, along with a sketchy memory of the occasion for writing them in *Der Prager Kreis* (93–95). There he censures the "jugendliche[n] Leichtsinn" with which he had equated beauty and newness, having taken the notion innocently from Herbart and Wundt. His remarks are followed by a transcription of Kafka's original let-ter to Brod.

9. For a summary of Louvre Circle activities and the cultish relations among Brentanists in Prague at this time, see Smith, "Brentano and Kafka." Kafka adopts his portrayal of consciousness, Smith argues, from courses at the universi-ty and lectures in the Louvre Circle; and he goes on to interpret several of Kafka's fictions using Brentano's psychological and ethical theories as interpretive keys. For an introduction to Marty's activities in Prague and excerpts from one of his lectures on descriptive psychology, see Marek and Smith, "Einleitung zu Anton Martys 'Elemente der deskriptiven Psychologie.'"

10. A rare mention of this early fragment can be found in *Kafka's Clothes* (99–100). Anderson reads it as an aspect of Kafka's concern with being in motion, while I see him critiquing Brod for this commonplace view of "modernity." The modern and "new" Kafka sees as passé.

11. Barry Smith and Johann Christian Marek have transcribed and edited several sections from the 1903 transcript of Marty's lectures on descriptive psy-chology, although Kafka seems to have attended them in 1902. Nevertheless, giv-en the orthodoxy with which Marty followed his teacher's doctrines, and the fact that he taught the same course on descriptive psychology in Prague for more than three decades, it is likely that the lectures for which we have the manuscripts are similar, if not identical, to those that Kafka heard.

12. In his study of Kafka's relation to Prague intellectual milieus, Arnold Heidsieck acknowledges the larger context for the relationship between apper-ception and fatigue—"Many of Kafka's works of fiction offer some observation concerning the dynamics of apperception and fatigue," he writes. Yet he consid-ers exhaustion a mere interruption of the "mysterious power" of apperception that he claims Kafka explores (33). For as much as Kafka does put characters in situations that test their ability to notice, and Heidsieck catalogues some of the most important of these (34), more and more—according to the program out-lined in the notes on Brod's article—Kafka in fact experiments with ways to put noticing out of operation.

13. A discussion of this passage and its relationship to "the traffic of clothes" can be found in Anderson, *Kafka's Clothes* (88–89).

14. Absence of thought could be said to intervene in many places in Kleist's texts as well—in the dash in *Marquise von O*, at crucial junctures in *Prinz Fried-*

rich von Homburg—but the most schematic passage, which Kafka undoubtedly knew, would be the last lines of the pseudo-essay "Über das Marionettenthea- ter." Here too it is a reaction to what is said, the final reaction of the narrator to the friend who has been speaking to him in parables. The narrator confesses, at the very end of the text, that the whole story has left him "ein wenig zerstreut" (Kleist 345).

15. There are other moments of distraction in Kafka's fictions. Although he takes *Verwirrung* as a synonym for *Zerstreuung*, a decision with which I do not agree, Christof Hamann demonstrates the amphiboly of distraction and diaspora that animates the earlier novel, *Der Verschollene*. In his dispersal into America and his mental distraction, Roßmann participates in a "Fremdwer- dungsprozess," according to Hamann, that leads him to become a "befreites Sub- jekt" (141). More apt, I think, would have been to take as distraction's synonym the title, even though it was attached to the text posthumously: *Der Verschol- lene*. In being "not heard from," Roßmann is in fact freed from subjectivity in *Zerstreuung*-distraction-diaspora.

16. In order to protect Kafka from accusations of nihilism, Winfried Kudzus places the meaning of the story in the prestory, in events before the narration be- gins. "Die Veränderung im Bau ist schon am Anfang geschehen" (316). He rea- sons that as soon as one enters the Bau, one has missed the point, reading is in vain, and all there is to gain from the words of the text is a fall into a bad infin- ity. "Der Eingang in den Bau ist gleich zu Beginn verstellt." This may be, and the creature almost admits this several times. Yet it only applies if you fall into the other trap and accept the almost irresistible analogy between the Bau and the text. A text is not a Bau, reading is not "going," unless, that is, you prefer to ig- nore the words that otherwise slow up your progress.

17. A paradox punctuates Deleuze and Guattari's complicated and ambitious book on Kafka, one that calls at least part of their project into question. A para- digm they cite over and over again to describe their method compromises their ability to use it on Kafka. They claim at the outset that they do not intend to rep- resent Kafka's "imaginary" with a set of "archetypes," and yet the archetype that comes back again and again to describe the whole complex of his works as well as particular aspects of it is the Bau. In their hands the Bau becomes a rhetorical device, a metonymy used to depict aspects of Kafka's writing. Slippage between the functional, political, "experimenting" reading that they announce and a fair- ly traditional hermeneutic one concentrates itself in this figure. The metaphor is deployed in the very first lines. "How can we enter into Kafka's work? This work is a rhizome, a burrow" (3). I will set aside the troublesome apposition of bur- row and rhizome, in which the differences between vegetable and animal intelli- gence, between organic growth and artificial construction are elided. To present an "oeuvre" as something that can be entered is not simply to use a metaphor but

to be overtaken unthinkingly by the main figure in one of Kafka's texts. Thus they imagine a set of texts as a building, and as a result reading comes to mean moving through rooms, looting the treasures found in them, and organizing them in a castle keep. Deleuze and Guattari go on to clarify, still in the first paragraph, that Kafka's "work" is not at all like the Bau in the story. Unlike this one, the other burrow, the burrow-as-Kafka's-oeuvre, has many "entrances." Because of this it is not open to interpretation but only to experimentation. And yet, as I have begun to point out, the logic of their rhetoric works against their claim to an anti-hermeneutic. Entrances and impasses, maps and modifications—the vocabulary belies a vacillation between Aristotelian and Cartesian desires to place obstacles and then remove them, and to chart an absolute position in three dimensional space. Thus, through a set of substitutions familiar to those who work with what Deleuze and Guattari call "the Signifier," although they denigrate it (also in the first paragraph), the burrow comes to signify everything Kafka is and all they want to find in him. The only thing it does not come to represent is itself, a coordinated set of tunnels in the ground, dug by an obsessively thinking mole. See pages 3, 7, 8, 10, 13, 17, 18, 33, 37, 41, 46, 59, 75 in the English edition for uses of the Bau as a figure. We might ask, what in Deleuze and Guattari's assumptions allows for this all-too-easy escape, this conversion of a trap into a procedure?

18. Noise murders, music saves: this is the main insight in Jacques Attali's analysis of music in political economy. Music sacrifices noise, the destroyer of order, and thereby reestablishes the orderly trade routes of capitalism, communication, the stratification of classes, the normative force of moral codes and law (Attali; see esp. "Noise and Politics," 6–8). Kafka, who confessed to having a tin ear, might have been well situated to "hear" noise, although, as Attali rightly points out, noise is not a positive perception that can be simply received. If it were, it would be communication. Because it is, rather, an interference and thus not a sound at all, but rather a violence to the systematic alternation of sound and silence in music, speech, and communication, a violence done to their constitutive opposition, it cannot properly be heard. What calls for more thinking in the relationship between Attali's historical analysis and Kafka's fiction are the differences in their receptions of Nietzsche and Schopenhauer. Despite his disagreement with Nietzsche, who wrote that music was the "expression of truth" (6), Attali's understanding of the tension between music and noise as a tension between order and disorder echoes Schopenhaurian strains in *The Birth of Tragedy*. Kafka seems deaf to these strains. To the Bau creature, silence is order, music absent, and noise is less disorder than the suspension of the opposition between order and chaos, which is a product of the desire for order.

19. Hansjörg Bay traces the figure of the "penetrator," the "Eindringling" in several of Kafka's works. In general the figure represents for him a "Zersetzung" of the reigning order (50). If this is so, it is even more significant that in this late

story the *Eindringling* never in fact appears, and thus the reigning order, in a coup de grâce, is not in the least disturbed—and in this way it is disturbed irreparably. Bay evades the absence of any actual invader by considering the hissing noise itself the most extreme version of the *Eindringling*. This certainly changes the terms of the argument. This invader, according to him, "deterritorialisiert in seiner Ortlosigkeit den gesamten Bau" as "reines . . . Geräusch" (63–64). Although he is right to say that the noise is "sinn- und subjektlos[]" (66), he does not identify it as the *Sinnbild* der *Sinnlosigkeit*, that changes nothing but also leaves nothing the same.

20. This note follows the pattern of the note-like series of propositions in Günther Anders' 1951 book, *Kafka: Pro und Contra* (The English translation is entitled simpy *Franz Kafka.*) His notes are warnings to the reader. The first in the chapter entitled "The Literal Metaphor" counsels that Kafka's stories are neither allegorical nor symbolic. Neither of these two terms is adequate to describe Kafka's rhetoric, not, that is (although Anders doesn't make this distinction) as the terms are traditionally understood. Walter Benjamin's theory of allegory, which might have been available to Anders in the early edition that had been helped toward publication by Anders' former wife, Hannah Arendt (who was still in touch with him, and specifically about Benjamin's *Nachlaß*), does not, however, find a place in the discussion. Instead, allegory as a representation that follows conventional rules and symbol as a representation that follows natural rules are the modes Anders finds inadequate to Kafka's fiction. The second term, "symbol," is the model for both. It is inadequate because Kafka writes in "the absence of that community of belief which gives birth to and sustains symbols" (43). There were certainly communities around Kafka, both political and literary, for whom symbols were important. In any case, Anders' historical-political assessment reintroduces the natural-symbolic back into the heart of Kafka's fiction. The unnatural, nonsymbolic means he employs in his fictions become, for Anders, the natural representation, the symbol of his historical condition, the lack of a natural community. Kafka's writings are not symbolic but "Kafka" is. Allegory faces the same problem, except, instead of a shared nature, "Kafka" and his community lack the shared conventions in which allegory could function. Moreover, in Anders' estimation, Kafka avoids the paths taken by Wagner and Nietzsche; he does not re-mythologize the world by inventing new symbols (whether Nietzsche in fact does this seems doubtful). Instead, taking existing images, Kafka illuminates the literal substrate of metaphors to "yield a new insight into the reality of our world" (45). After Anders, literalization of metaphor has been written about eloquently by Henry Sussman (105–9). Ritchie Robertson makes the case for allegory as a useful exegetic term with regard to Kafka, and comes to the conclusion by means of it that the late animal stories are not animal stories but references to humans (268–72).

21. The question of anthropomorphism in Kafka is vexed. Roy Pascal, in his study of Kafka's narrators, devotes only a few lines to the protagonist and narrator of "The Bau." In them he calls the creature incapable of reflection and compares him unfavorably to the other thinkers among Kafka's beasts: dog, ape, and mouse (192). The creature's incapacity for reflection occurs, however, within what looks exactly like reflection. It is perhaps the most rabid and unstoppable thinker of any of Kafka's characters, human or animal. And it is certainly not the case, as Pascal says, that the creature is stuck in the present. Its thoughts run back and forth along the Bau, which is as temporal—the work of a lifetime—as it is spatial. Some of the story is retold as memory, some cast toward the future as anxiety. In an early book, Hartmut Binder anticipates this reading. Extrapolating from the present tense verbs in the creature's narration, Binder contrasts the style of narration of the Bau fragment with other stories. Whereas elsewhere first-person narrators speak in internal monologues, "Der Landarzt" is the example he gives for this, the Bau creature offers *"geäußerte* Gedanken" (340–41). The narrator of "The Bau," he adds, is positioned within the events that are spoken about, and furthermore he argues that the creature's position "sich während der Erzählung dauernd verändert und diese Veränderung sich in der Erzählergegenwart spiegelt" (341). While there is a curious relationship between past and present in the text, and it is true that the narrative and the narration are intertwined in a manner that does not approximate speaking aloud—it is perhaps more like a transcription of his thinking, as Binder says—it is also probably true that the question of time is not only to be answered in the tense of the verb. Time is somehow the medium for a repeated return without change. As Henry Sussman writes: "the ability of such suggestive moments of insight," on the part of the Bau creature, "to subside into oblivion before reaching a logical conclusion is fundamental to the story's temporality of obsessive repetition" (117). The most intricate presentation of time in "The Bau" is that of J. M. Coetzee. "The relations between the *time of narration* (the moving *now* of the narrator's utterance) and the *time of the narrative* (referential time)" are "baffling," he admits. "Representations of an idiosyncratic feel for time," is his phrase for it (557), idiosyncratic first because neither German nor English has an iterative aspect for the verb, and so Kafka has to contort his language to express this, and secondly because the story tries to move not simply in repeated or habitual occurrences, but rather in repeated occurrences of urgent, unrepeatable interruptions of habits (559–60). In "the extraordinary time structure of 'The Burrow,'" time is nothing less than the iteration of the non-iterative, in short, the return of the singular. I quote Coetzee again: "The key notion here is *without warning*. A warning is a sign of a transition from peace to its opposite. . . . In 'The Burrow' however, time does not move through transitional phases" (574). Without transitions, time skips. On the whole it moves "away from universe-time [by which he means countable time

that beings can be "in"] toward event time" (576). The loss of universe-time is experienced as a "continual crisis . . . signaled by the whistling that comes from its point(s) of rupture" (579).

CHAPTER 4

1. The significant place that these lectures hold in the rethinking of *Sein und Zeit* that culminates in the thought of *Ereignis* in *Vom Ereignis* (written 1936–1938) is affirmed by John van Buren (367–68).

2. In the first chapter of *Heidegger and Leibniz: Reason and Path*, Renato Cristin sketches out a genealogy for Heidegger's interest in "Grund," leading back to Leibniz. In subsequent chapters he follows Heidegger's reading of Leibniz up to and including the influential essay "Der Satz vom Grund." Cristin's call for further study of the important intersections between the two thinkers has not, as far as I can tell, been heeded.

3. Among the many treatments of transcendence throughout Heidegger's oeuvre, we can mention but a few. On the relationship between the ontic-ontological difference and transcendence, see L. M. Vail, *Heidegger and Ontological Difference* (47–54). On Heidegger's rejection of Kant's transcendentalism and the proximity of his concept of transcendence to Husserlian intentionality, see David Carr, "Heidegger on Kant on Transcendence" in Crowell and Malpas, *Transcendental Heidegger* (28–42). In the same volume, Dermot Moran takes up the latter relation again in his chapter "Heidegger's Transcendental Phenomenology in the Light of Husserl's Project of First Philosophy" (135–50). In this chapter see especially pp. 140–41 for a an identification of being-in the-world as a response to Husserl. Transcendence in *Being and Time* and its sources in Heidegger's reading are also treated in Klaus Opilik's *Transzendenz und Vereinzelung* (see esp. 107–19 on transcendence and time). For a discussion of Husserlian transcendence (in opposition to immanence), see Jacques Taminiaux, *Heidegger and the Project of Fundamental Ontology* (9–10). In *Transzendenz und Welt*, Markus Enders explicates the "inneren Zusammenhang[]" between transcendence and world, covering as well the most important philosophical theories of transcendence to which Heidegger implicitly responds. Chapter 7 offers a methodical reading of transcendence in the Leibniz lectures.

4. As a structural and basic hermeneutic-phenomenological element, *Zerstreuung* has little in common even with the main *Befindlichkeiten* and *Stimmungen* as they are presented in *Being and Time* and in the courses given after its first publication. The Heideggerian topos closest to this breakdown in the structure of existence may be *Langeweile*, analyzed in *Die Grundbegriffe der Metaphysik: Welt–Endlichkeit–Einsamkeit* (117–260). A thorough description of

Heidegger's analysis of boredom with a summary of the critical literature on it can be found in Boris Ferreira's *Stimmung bei Heidegger* (188–260). Boredom comes close to distraction in Miguel de Beistegui's eyes, because it is profoundly historical (66–80).

5. In the essay "Geschlecht: Sexual Difference, Ontological Difference," Derrida shows how Heidegger's desire to step beyond a binary understanding of difference reproduces it, insofar as *Zerstreuung* and related words determine the ontological difference on analogy with sexual difference ("Geschlecht" 71ff.). Binary sexual difference and the generative potential traditionally associated with it are reintroduced into the very movement of ontological difference, which is thus not, in this one respect, different from traditional philosophical conceptions of difference. In fact, Derrida suggests that the entire project of fundamental ontology is limited by a covert reliance on sexual difference or duality as the model for all difference. The very movement of producing possibility—*Zerstreuung*—the fundamental ontological movement that constitutes the radical departure from substance-based metaphysical notions of foundation, is limited and biased in a most traditional way by Heidegger's understanding of *Zerstreuung*. Insofar as he critiques it in his reading of Heidegger, Derrida's text becomes a new model for writing about *Zerstreuung*. To the extent, however, that he interprets *Zerstreuung* as a different type of movement, "dissemination" ("Geschlecht" 75)—however temporary and contextually constrained the interpretation is to this particular reading—he places a bet similar to Heidegger's.

An inter- and an intra-linguistic proliferation accrue on "Zerstreuung" in Derrida's text; it comes to be synonymous with dissemination, and, in Derrida's writing, the word itself disseminates, such that other words—both within and cutting across the language, German, and angling toward language itself or at least toward "languages"—attach to or associate with the word: "*Zerstreuung, Zerstreutheit, Zerstörung, Zersplitterung, Zerspaltung,*" he writes. Derrida punctuates his text with lists such as these, in italics, in German, to remind readers of the disseminative cloud that trails the word, and this means, as well, in his own treatment, that *Zerstreuung* has also already been disseminated into French. In the French text a parallel "série" is given as "dissociation," "distraction," "dissémination," "division," "dispersion" ("Geschlecht" 425), and this appears subsequently in the English translation as "dissociation," "distraction," "dissemination," "division," "dispersion" ("Geschlecht" 75). None of these lists is merely equivalent to the other, or for that matter to itself, nor are the individual members of each list capable of being ordered into a lexicon according to their history or normal usage. Derrida's study of *Zerstreuung* is neither an etymological nor a semantic survey, of course, but a grammatological exploration, a gesture toward further derivations, producing what he calls—or he with his translator, a former student of his, Ruben Berezdivin, calls—a "lexical hive."

In order to make the type of critique he does, he translates *Zerstreuung*, where translation means multiplication. In order to critique Heidegger's genetic notion of the production of difference, and the prejudices or assumptions that underlie it—binary sexual difference—Derrida multiplies *Zerstreuung*. This is his task and this is the way his text operates. He brings Heidegger's interpretation back to its linguistic conditions of possibility in another *Zerstreuung* that would transcendentally precede his *Zerstreuung*. Yet the critique or deconstruction that takes place here requires that the German word be assimilated to the French "dissemination," to one meaning or analogue, and therefore, as the word through which the critique or deconstruction operates, this is the one word that cannot be deconstructed. Dissemination gives possibility but cannot be given any other possibility—especially not the lack of possibility that *Zerstreuung*, if it were allowed to mean not-thinking, sometimes brings to word. To be sure, like *différance, dissémination* is meant to raise more questions than it answers. It should be read as a problematic name for a differing difference, a difference that gives itself possibility, if not continuously then at least without any final end. And yet, there is a sense as well in which, unlike *différance* and *dissémination, Zerstreuung* can also be understood as *not making any difference*, as the evacuation of possibility and as a stumbling block to differentiation, variation, mutation, infection, contamination, dissemination, and so forth. It can, in short, withhold possibility, and it can do so without any strategy. This is the negative possibility that the translation of *Zerstreuung* as *dissemination* forecloses. As one of *Zerstreuung*'s possible, if not probable, semiological disseminations, it seems rather to withdraw the potential to differ or defer, to freeze distribution, to make being—even the being of language—impossible, to remove the hope of future understanding, and thus to reveal any attempt to make sense of it as arbitrary or violent. It names, in short, the possibility that there be no future, at least none from which talk of the "to come," *l'avenir, Zukunft* would derive authority. Whatever may come, we will not be there to receive it. This is the impotency that *Zerstreuung* could utter, although in both Derrida's and Heidegger's texts this interpretation is omitted.

6. As John van Buren notes, *Neugier* translates "curiositas," whose connection to "cura" is much clearer in Latin (179). A similar pattern arises in Kierkegaard, to whom Heidegger was attracted through Karl Jaspers' treatment of his thought in *Psychologie der Weltanschauungen*. In Jaspers' book the association of *Neugier* with *Zerstreutheit* is already established (182).

7. Toward an understanding of this unity, Françoise Dastur writes: "This unitary phenomenon, however, is not an *arkhé*, or an origin, that would enjoy

the simplicity and uniqueness of an ultimate structural element, a foundation in which the manifold would come to disappear. Far from being excluded, the multiplicity of items is, on the contrary, required by the structural unity of the being of Dasein and by the whole it represents, one which, as an articulated structural whole, cannot be 'rent asunder'" (20). A fascinating analysis of the number (or rather, the non-number) "one" in Heidegger's early writing can be found in Michael Roubach, *Being and Number in Heidegger's Thought* (8–39, esp. 15–17).

8. "'Care' is a formal indication of a manner of being, in which what is at stake is the respective manner of being itself, an individual's own being-in-the-world" and not "a collection of various human cares and troubles or even an exemplary form of them," according to Daniel Dahlstrom in *Heidegger's Concept of Truth* (288).

9. One can follow the path from the Kategorien-Lehre of Duns Scotus through the value-laden terms of the 1920s such as "Existenz" and "Philosophie" to "Denken" in Otto Pöggeler, *Der Denkweg Martin Heideggers* (163–88).

10. Marlène Zarader affirms a covert reliance on a notion of tradition when she associates Heidegger's thought of thinking with a "Hebraic frame" that starts with a covenant and follows with "calling and listening, memory and fidelity, gratitude and thanksgiving" (73).

11. A succinct explanation of "one-track" thought (*Vorstellen*) and its alternative for Heidegger, *Besinnung* or *Andenken*, is given by Joan Stambaugh in her article "Die Aufgabe des Denkens."

12. As a substitute for Husserl's intentional structure of consciousness, *Sorge* makes more facets of existence available for philosophy, including non-intellectual and quasi-intellectual modes, like striving, loving, and so on. As the meaning-structure in which Dasein acts, *Sorge*—which we must still define more precisely—opens the existent human being to non-intellectual objects, to its own death, for example, or to being with others. Everything that is posited in the analytic will be reinterpreted in Division Two as a modality of *Sorge*.

13. Theodore Kisiel traces the emergence of care in Heidegger's lectures on Augustine in *The Genesis of Heidegger's Being and Time* (200–203). On the trajectory of care in Heidegger's Christian readings, see van Buren (179). A thorough explication of the temporality of care, as well as the central role care has in determining Heidegger's notion of temporality in Division Two of *Sein und Zeit*, can be found in Dastur (28–38).

14. Drew Hyland registers some doubt about this reasoning when he examines Heidegger's "ambivalence" toward the myth in §42 (93). What Hyland argues on the basis of this, however, is hard to accept. He suggests that Heidegger finds the myth of cura pre-ontological "precisely because it is a *myth*" (94); how-

ever, it is not only "myths" that Heidegger adduces as pre-ontological testimony to ontological truths. Poems are another kind of testimony. In *Being and Time*, C. F. Meyer's "der römische Brunnen" operates in this way. *Gerede* does as well. The ontic is in fact full of half-understandings of the being of beings that could be taken as pre-understandings, and this makes sense since existence is interpretation through and through. There is no reason for Heidegger to be skeptical of myth in particular. Moreover, for something to be "pre-ontological" is no slur.

15. Given Heidegger's refusal of the term's history, it is perhaps not wise to implicate him in a longer tradition—one going back past the New Testament and Seneca even, reaching at least to Plato's image of Socrates. If he bumped into care along his own trajectory, it is perhaps not important that Augustine's Neoplatonism—which Heidegger elsewhere denigrates, while praising his Christian anthropology—has an antecedent in Plato. In the *Apology* Socrates describes his philosophical activities as attempts to persuade Athenians "epimelesthai tēs psuchēs," to care for the soul, and not for their bodies (*somatōn*) or their possessions (*chrēmaton*) (Apologia 30a–b p. 47). While elsewhere Heidegger is only too happy to return to Greek sources, the well-known association of care, *epimelea* or *merima*, with one of the historically most originary acts of philosophizing is too obviously ontical for his purposes, and at the same time too metaphysical. *Sorge* is not the highest anthropic activity producing the highest value in a scheme of values rising toward virtue. Likewise, *Sorge* cannot be found in the classroom, the agora, or the courts. It is certainly not the movement away from the physical toward a transcendent core, but names the structure of transcendence per se. "Minding," one way to say *Sorge* in English, is not above all philosophical, but belongs to Dasein in general. Care is the principle not only for its involvements in the world but also for its primary involvement with itself, from which the question of being derives—as the question of its own being, care for its being, minding its being, minding, not thinking. Here a similarity between Socrates' and Heidegger's concerns catches our attention. Somewhat like *epimelea* for Socrates, *Sorge* is for Heidegger the non-mental disposition that allows philosophy to be the most natural or essential activity for *anthrōpos*. Philosophy participates in Dasein's basic care-structure, as one of its modes of concern, and specifically as the concern for the self as that which cares.

With this in mind it is interesting that Heidegger should admit that he "bumped into" the phenomenon of care, as if it was before anything else an existential phenomenon and not a term with a history in metaphysics, one that, above all, drew into question the ontic-ontological relationship, the relationship between a philosopher and the capacity for philosophizing. Heidegger's admission is a highly rhetorical moment in the 1925 lectures, *Prolegomena zur Geschichte des Zeitbegriffs*. He has introduced the care-structure as the final foundation of Dasein, associated it with temporality, and extolled its virtue for being able to explain every "vor"—"Vorhabe," "Vorsicht," "Vorgriff"—in Dasein's make-up, all the ways in which Dasein is already in the world as interpreter and participant in its structures. Care has to be something outside the history of philosophy, at the innermost point of existence. Just as "das Dasein im Sichaussprechen immer schon aus einer vorgegebenen Ausgelegtheit spricht und notwendig aus ihr heraus spricht," so *cura* must lie in Dasein's unmediated relationship to itself, unmediated by anything other than its own movement of self-interpretation. At once, this puts care above and beyond the merely interpreted. It is not part of an interpretation, a projection, or a historically delimited understanding; it is instead the ahistorical, non-hermeneutic basis for interpretation. This is why Heidegger, although he mentions philosophical sources, prefers a care with which he unwittingly collides. Rather than admit that it is, like phenomenology, the product of intellectual-historical work, thinking, or even imaginative collage, the philosopher encounters the source of existence in existence. The encounter is accidental, and also necessary. It is ontically accidental, insofar as, since in care the self is displaced from itself, it moves in ignorance of care. It is ontologically necessary insofar as, since care is its self-interpretation, the philosopher who traces Dasein's self-interpreting movement will undoubtedly come across this word or concept, movement or structure that transcends each and every concrete interpretation and makes them all possible. It came before him—it is the self-identical ground of being-ahead-of-himself in which the philosopher is caught. There is another genealogy of care in Heidegger, an expressly Christian, theological one. On the trajectory of the concern for care across Heidegger's readings of expressly Christian theological texts, see van Buren (179).

16. What came to be known as *Fabularum Liber* contains a compendium of highly abbreviated myths drawn from many sources from the classical past and was widely consulted by authors in imperial Rome. The current text is regarded as faulty in numerous respects. According to a review by Wilfred E. Major of the latest published edition, it derives from a work originally entitled *Geneologiae*, which by ancient and modern reports was written by a freedman of Augustus named Gaius Julius Hyginus and was used by authors as illustrious as Ovid. The extant text frustrates scholars because of its obvious crudeness, lack of style, abundant errors, and simplification of more complex stories. For these reasons, it is assumed that the manuscript that forms the basis for the one modern edition is not the book Hyginus wrote. In addition, the manuscript of these problematic fables was itself notoriously difficult to read and was promptly destroyed after the *editio princeps* was made from it in 1535. This edition and two small fragments of the original medieval manuscript form the basis of the Teubner edition by Marshall.

None of this is particularly damning for Heidegger's inclusion of fable number 220 in §42 of *Being and Time*. But the status of the text might put his contentions about its power to illuminate Dasein in a different light. "Das im Dasein selbst liegende Seinsverständnis," in this very fable, "spricht sich vorontologisch aus" (*SuZ* 197). The interpretation of being that lies already in existent human being enunciates itself pre-ontologically in this exemplary fable. But Heidegger sees here a fabulum passed like *Gerede* among the people, and not a text edited and corrupted and corrected. When does the *already* of the pre-ontological take place? With the people, who passed around this story, presumably in oral form? With Hyginus, to whom the writing down of the fable is attributed? With Herder or Goethe, who adapt the cura story? Or with the obscure, probably Christianizing forces of preservation that protected the text and surely affected its contents over fifteen hundred years? Rather than the realm of Dasein here, we are in the realm of philology. That scribes and clerics preserved the fable in whatever form, despite the vicissitudes of transmission, means something, to be sure. And yet this one fable is one of two hundred seventy-seven preserved in the *editio princeps*, each of which is a tiny part of the attempt to write a universal genealogy of all that existed. Along the way, more than one fable provides a *genesis hominorum*. Deucalion and Pyrrha, famous from Ovid's retelling, also appear in Hyginus's version. In that myth, humans derive from stones.

17. The persistence of *Geist* (*spiritus, pneuma*) in Heidegger's writings, despite his will to avoid these terms and topoi, is the subject of Jacques Derrida's *Of Spirit: Heidegger and the Question*. Closely linked to the 1983 essay "Geschlecht: Sexual Difference, Ontological Difference," *Spirit* brings to writing a rhetorical complex of motifs, such as nationalism, blood and soil, the conjunction of Germanness and Greekness, flame, and so forth, mainly in Heidegger's works of the 1930s. The refusal of a *geistarme* Cura in the fable also belongs to this complex. On the more direct association of *Ungeist* with Americanism on one side and communism on the other, and as a consequence, of *Geist* with National Socialism, see Otto Pöggeler, *Heidegger in seiner Zeit* (207–13).

18. In the essay "The Passion of Facticity," Giorgio Agamben confirms that transcendental *Zerstreuung* in the Leibniz lectures is the source for Dasein's facticity, what Agamben calls "the figure of an original facticity" (195). His interest in the essay is the absence of love as an element of existence, and so he does not follow *Zerstreuung* past facticity to freedom and time.

19. Derrida analyzes the questionable subtraction that turns *Zerstreuung* into *Streuung*, suggesting that it is a movement of concealment, rather than deconcealment. To Derrida, *Zerstreuung* is positioned as a "corruption of pure originary possibility (*Streuung*)," and the distinction between the two is thus an avoidance or possibly even a purification of corruption or contamination, a privation that preserves an empirical bias toward binary sexual difference and

genetic production within supposedly "neutral" fundamental ontology ("Geschlecht" 76).

20. The interest in logic is not new, nor is the desire to bring logic back to its metaphysical grounds. To trace the origins of this desire in Heidegger's early writings, Steven Galt Crowell's "Making Logic Philosophical Again (1912–1916)" in Kisiel and van Buren, *Reading Heidegger From the Start,* is essential reading (55–72).

21. Such a devaluation of not-thinking, carried over from *Being and Time,* is emphasized in the *Beiträge.* In the preparatory "Vorblick," section 18, "Die Ohnmacht des Denkens," Heidegger sums up his anti-anti-intellectual program: "Deshalb ist die 'Ohmacht' noch nicht sogleich ein Einwand gegen das 'Denken', sondern nur gegen sein Verächter" (*Beiträge* 47).

CHAPTER 5

1. In a much more recent treatment of the topic, Howard Eiland notes the "peculiarly slippery manner" with which the "notion of distraction . . . operates" in Benjamin's writings. I would suggest that this slipperiness, which Eiland rightly identifies, has a source in the slipping operation of distraction itself, in which *noēsis,* the process in which any "notion" comes to be, slips away from itself. Although he takes *Zerstreuung* as a "concept" toward which Benjamin has an "attitude," his analysis of Benjamin's uses of the word is quite instructive. But *Zerstreuung* calls conceptuality into question for Benjamin, posing deep paradoxes for the understanding of thought, and gesturing toward a breakdown in the normal relations between perception and apperception. In addition, because he confines his analysis to the writings of the 1930s, Eiland misses the crucial significance of the term in the work on color and in the baroque book. In the baroque book, distraction is the a priori of concepts "überhaupt," when it comes to designating the relationship between art, theory, and the idea, whose proper name is "history." Furthermore, when he divides Benjamin's "attitude" toward distraction into "negative" and "positive," *Zerstreuung* is abandoned to a moralism that Benjamin assiduously avoids (51–52). Benjamin admits its "verrufene Gestalt" but indicates that it is precisely not for yet another condemnation that he will judge its effects—indeed, they cannot be subject to judgment at all—but for something else: "Lehrewerden," to become a doctrine. Until *Zerstreuung*'s antagonism to judgment, and, conversely, its openness to doctrine is understood, such moralism will continue to block its reception. Another recent example of moralism can be found in Bernhard Waldenfels' *Phänomenologie der Aufmerksamkeit,* where Benjamin's "inversion" of distraction is registered and then dismissed in one breath as "questionable" (105). For an analysis of the fear of distraction among media critics, see Schneider, "Kollekten des Geistes."

2. On Benjamin's interest in reproducibility across several texts of the 1930s, see the section "Der Titel.—Der Begriff: technische Reproduzierbarkeit" in Burkhardt Lindner's article on this essay in the *Benjamin-Handbuch*. Here Lindner equates reproducibility with temporal repeatability and geographical "Entortung" (235). On the role of "reproducibility" and other transcendentalizing words in Benjamin's thought, see Samuel Weber's *Benjamin's –abilities.*

3. Interest in this suffix probably derives from Benjamin's reading of the Jena romantics during work on his dissertation. See especially the section entitled "Die Idee der Kunst" in *Der Begriff der Kunstkritik in der deutschen Romantik* (*GS* I.1 87ff.). Schlegel and Novalis's *Athenaeum* fragments bring the prefix to the forefront of literary theory. The aim of literary criticism and theory, the raison d'être of the fragment form as well as the novel, is the "Poetisierung" of all relations. The gerund signals a movement toward the unity of all poetry—and all art—in a progressing, infinite confluence of genres.

4. The theory of coloring-experience does not only anticipate Heideggerian motifs; it also provides an anti-Hegelian solution to the Kantian distinction between experience and the absolute. Howard Caygill remarks on this intellectual context: "The proposal to break down the distinctions between intuition, understanding and reason has led historically either to a revival of pre-Kantian dogmatic metaphysics or to a form of Hegelianism." Yet he makes the mistake of thinking that Benjamin repeats a Hegelian gesture. "Benjamin, aware of both possibilities and of the traditional Kantian objections to them, nevertheless insists on a transformation of the transcendental philosophy of experience into a transcendental but speculative philosophy" (3).

5. A citation from Kierkegaard's journals makes the stakes of Benjamin's "experience" clear, through its contrary. "They say that experience makes a man wise. This is very unreasonable talk. If there were nothing higher than experience, experience would drive a man crazy" (*Journals and Papers* 469). It is this sort of craziness that Benjamin wants to think through.

6. According to the editors of the critical edition, Scholem reported that the essay on perception was written in 1914 or 1915 (*GS* VI 695). The editors reason that the rainbow dialogue would most likely have been written in the winter of 1915 (*GS* VII.2 561). The complex network of thoughts that gives rise to these early, esoteric reflections on color is laid out with special distinctness by Peter Fenves in "The Paradisal *Epochē*: On Benjamin's First Philosophy" (*Arresting Language* 174ff.). According to Fenves, Benjamin's early work on color forms not only a critique of Kant's theory of experience, but also a departure from Hermann Cohen's reading of that theory, as well as an overcoming of the latent subjectivity in Husserl's *Ideen*, plus a putting into practice of his study of Cantor's transfinite numbers, and, last but by no means least, a compliment to the language theory that Benjamin develops in the early reading of two poems by Hölderlin and in

his essay on language. For further developments of these readings, see Fenves's *The Messianic Reduction: Walter Benjamin and the Shape of Time* (especially chapters 3 and 5).

7. For an account of the discussion between Benjamin and Scholem on cubism during which this attitude toward painting was first adumbrated, see Brüggemann (125). Benjamin works out the details of his distinction between the beauty of art, which is spatial, and the beauty of nature, which isn't, in the fragment "Der Regenbogen oder die Kunst des Paradieses" (*GS* VII.2 562–63).

8. Half a century later Jean-Luc Nancy develops such a notion through a reading of works by a colleague and acquaintance of Benjamin's in Paris, Georges Bataille, in a theory of a community whose members have nothing in common (that is, with no shared mental goods). One can begin to follow the trail of this altered idea of community in Nancy's *The Inoperative Community*, especially chap. 1.

9. On the significance of this term "mass" in Benjamin: Samuel Weber interprets "the law of dispersion and collection that governs the ambivalent movement of the allegorical mass." Mass is allegorical because of its opaqueness to sight and the resulting resistance to manipulation as an entity. A mass comes together only in movement (and not merely in the reduced sense this term has in empirical politics), and more importantly out of a peculiar temporal pressure that Weber calls "coming-to-pass." Mass comes-to-pass, for Weber, and as such it corresponds to a Baudelairean figure that fascinated Benjamin, the *passante*. It also echoes one of the most esoteric writings of Friedrich Hölderlin, insofar as, in Weber's update of a Hölderlinian title, a mass, like the *passante*, "comes to be in passing by" (*Mass Mediauras* 84ff.).

10. See Weber, *Mass Mediauras* (102–4).

11. This refers to Kracauer's earlier, feuilletonistic writings on the new cult, as well as his even earlier writings on sociological method. A more complicated relationship to representation and the fragment can be found in *Zertrümmerte Fensterscheiben*, as it is interpreted by Inka Mülder-Bach in "Auf der Suche nach der Verlorenen Öffentlichkeit," in which Mülder-Bach tracks the development of the Kracauerian idea of the "zerstreute Masse" (131ff.).

12. It is worth noting that in the first line of his investigation into the foundations of sociology, Kracauer acknowledges *Die Theorie des Romans* as the source for the notion of history underlying his methodology. Lukács' concept "einer 'sinnerfullten Epoche'" that springs from "einer bestimmten metaphysischen Grundeinstellung" holds the position "eines erkenntniskritischen Grenzbegriffs" in his investigation. The difference, he later explains, lies in the protagonist. The "freischwebende[s] Subjekt" that, according to Kracauer, novels present and perpetuate ("Soziologie als Wissenschaft" 14) is replaced by a "gestaltlose Mannig-

faltigkeit" in sociology, a figure that he will soon place, on analogy with Lukács' theory of the novel, into a theory of film (19).

13. My understanding of *Gewohnheit* in Benjamin's writings differs from Carolin Duttlinger's in "Between Contemplation and Distraction: Configurations of Attention in Walter Benjamin." In an experience without transcendental guarantees, practices such as exercise (*Übung*) and accumulations of experience such as collections, texts, and *Gewohnheiten*—not to mention memory—are the sources for whatever duration experience may temporarily attain. For Duttlinger, however, *Gewohnheit* is a deteriorated form of attention—it is what happens to attention after its moment of presence, clarity, and force (37). In fact Benjamin sees *Gewohnheit*, as he does practice, lessons, and training, along with other repetitions, as positive modes of human experience in a detranscendentalized, historical arena.

14. Touch for Benjamin here seems to have little to do with touch in the history of philosophy, where the sense of touch stands for immediacy, intimacy, possession, and presence. Derrida gives a reading of the philosophical tradition for which touch has been the cornerstone, in *On Touching—Jean-Luc Nancy*. Although Benjamin does not come up in the book, one part of the analysis comes close to Benjamin's basic phenomenological insight that touch is a self-losing sense, and so contradictory to its philosophical reputation. Derrida demonstrates this by analyzing Nancy's equation of touch with weight, and weighing with thinking (71ff.). According to Derrida, Nancy shows touching-weighing-thinking to be an "appropriation of the inappropriable," and thus a relation to the untouchable. For Benjamin, touch almost immediately becomes a non-relation to the being that is supposed to be being touched.

15. For the most exacting reading of Benjamin's essay "Zur Kritik der Gewalt" in terms of his understanding of the revolutionary general strike, see Werner Hamacher, "Afformative, Strike."

16. A response notable for its departure from the usual terms of the debate surrounding Benjamin's call for an aesthetics that does not, when it becomes politicized, aestheticize politics is given by Peter Fenves in "Is There an Answer to the Aestheticizing of the Political?" The answer to the question posed in the title is no. Fenves's "no" corresponds to the different notion of the artwork in which the ground of politics shifts in an "epoch-making moment." "Artwork as a whole rests on the movement-in-place of its foundation." In other words, its political effects are directly proportional to the artwork's "Zerstreuungswert," its capacity to divert the world from a course in which "politics" could continue to mean the same thing (72).

17. Testimony to this conviction can be found much earlier. The ability to *see* similarities is the weak remainder of an ability to *become* similar, that is, to be-

come other than what one is. See the *"Zusatz"* to "Lehre vom Ähnlichen" (*GS* II.1 210).

1. In *Wild Materialism: The Ethic of Terror and the Modern Republic*, Jacques Lezra tracks "the movement from *res cogitans* to *res publica*" in Spain's Second Republic. He turns to another instructive baroque source for his analysis of a "Distracted Republic." The threat to the state of a sovereignty totally diffused among the people he finds articulated in Diego de Saavedra Fajardo's *Idea de un príncipe político Cristiano* (1640) (202–222).

2. "For where the union, or band of a commonwealth, is one man, there is no distraction; whereas in assemblies, those that are of different opinions, and give different counsel, are apt to fall out amongst themselves, and to cross the designs of commonwealth for one another's sake: and when they cannot have the honour of making good their own devices, they yet seek the honour to make the counsels of their adversaries to prove vain. And in this contention, when the opposite factions happen to be anything equal in strength, they presently fall to war" (Hobbes *Human Nature and De Corpore Politico* 140).

Works Cited

Adorno, Theodor W., and Walter Benjamin. *Briefe und Briefwechsel.* Ed. Lonitz, Henri. Vol. 1. Frankfurt am Main: Suhrkamp, 1994.

Agamben, Giorgio. "The Passion of Facticity." *Potentialities.* Stanford, CA: Stanford University Press, 1999. 185–204.

Anagnostopoulos, Georgios, ed. *A Companion to Aristotle.* West Sussex, UK: Wiley-Blackwell, 2009.

Anders, Günther. *Franz Kafka.* Trans. Steer, A. and A. K. Thorlby. London: Bowes and Bowes, 1960.

Anderson, Mark M. *Kafka's Clothes: Ornament and Aestheticism in the Hapsburg Fin de Siècle.* Oxford: Clarendon, 1992.

Aquinas, St. Thomas. *Commentary on Aristotle's De anima.* Trans. Foster, Kenelm and Silvester Humphries. Notre Dame, IN: Dumb Ox Books (Reprint), 1994.

Arendt, Hannah. *The Life of The Mind.* San Diego: Harcourt Brace Jovanovich, 1978.

Aristotle. *Aristotle's De anima, Books II and III.* Trans. Hamlyn, D. W. Oxford: Clarendon, 1993.

———. *The Complete Works.* Ed. Barnes, Jonathan. Vol. 2. Princeton, NJ: Princeton University Press, 1984.

———. *De anima.* Ed. Hicks, Robert Drew. Cambridge, UK: Cambridge University Press, 1907.

———. *De anima.* Ed. Ross, Sir David. Oxford: Clarendon, 1956.

———. *De caelo.* Eds. Stocks, J. L. and Harry Bernard Wallis. Oxford: Clarendon, 1922.

———. *Ethica Nicomachea.* Ed. Bywater, Ingram. Oxford: Clarendon, 1957.

———. *Metaphysics.* Ed. Ross, W. D. 2 vols. Oxford: Clarendon, 1997.

———. *Physics.* Ed. Ross, Sir David. Oxford: Clarendon, 1998.

"ARTFL Project." n.d. Web. *Dictionnaire de l'Académie Française, first edition (1694).* University of Chicago. July 29, 2009. http://artfl-project.uchicago.edu/node/17.

Attali, Jacques. *Noise: The Political Economy of Music.* Minneapolis: University of Minnesota Press, 2003.

Augustine. *Confessions.* Vol 1. Ed. O'Donnell, James J. Oxford: Clarendon, 1992.
———. *Confessions.* Trans. Chadwick, Henry. Oxford: Oxford University Press, 1991.

Barkley, Russell A. *Attention-Deficit Hyperactivity Disorder: A Handbook for Diagnosis and Treatment.* New York: Guilford, 2006.

Barthes, Roland. *Critical Essays.* Evanston, IL: Northwestern University Press, 1972.

Bay, Hansjörg. "Kafka's Tinnitus." *Odradeks Lachen: Fremdheit bei Kafka.* Eds. Bay, Hansjörg and Christof Hamann. Freiburg i. Br.: Rombach, 2006. 41–68.

Beistegui, Miguel de. *Thinking with Heidegger: Displacements.* Bloomington: Indiana University Press, 2003.

Bénichou, Paul. *Man and Ethics: Studies in French Classicism.* Garden City, NY: Anchor, 1971.

Benjamin, Walter. *Gesammelte Briefe.* Eds. Gödde, Christoph and Henri Lonitz. Frankfurt am Main: Suhrkamp, 1995.

———. *Gesammelte Schriften.* Eds. Tiedemann, Rolf and Hermann Schweppenhäuser. Frankfurt am Main: Suhrkamp, 1991.

Bergson, Henri. "Laughter." *Comedy.* Ed. Sypher, Wylie. Baltimore: Johns Hopkins University Press, 1980. 61–192.

Binder, Hartmut. *Motiv und Gestaltung bei Franz Kafka.* Bonn: H. Bouvier, 1966.

Blanchot, Maurice. *The Infinite Conversation.* Minneapolis: University of Minnesota Press, 1993.

Block, Irving. "The Order of Aristotle's Psychological Writings." *American Journal of Philology* 82 1 (1961): 50–77.

Blumenberg, Hans. *Die Sorge geht über den Fluß.* Frankfurt am Main: Suhrkamp, 1987.

Boulby, Mark. "Kafka's End: A Reassessment of the Burrow." *The German Quarterly.* March 1982: 175–85.

Bremmer, Jan N. *The Early Greek Concept of the Soul.* Princeton, NJ: Princeton University Press, 1983.

Brentano, Franz. *Deskriptive Psychologie.* Eds. Chisholm, Roderick M. and Wilhelm Baumgartner. Hamburg: Meiner, 1982.

———. *Psychologie vom empirischen Standpunkt.* Hamburg: Meiner, 1974.

———. *The Psychology of Aristotle: In Particular His Doctrine of the Active Intellect.* Trans. George, Rolf. Berkeley: University of California Press, 1977.

Brod, Max. *Der Prager Kreis.* Stuttgart: W. Kohlhammer, 1966.

Brüggemann, Heinz. "Fragmente zur Ästhetik / Phantasie und Farbe." *Benjamin-Handbuch: Leben–Werk–Wirkung.* Ed. Lindner, Burkhardt. Stuttgart: Metzler, 2006. 124–33.

Budgell, Eustace. "Spectator No. 77." May 29, 1711. *The Spectator Project.* Ed. Chaves, Joseph. Montclair Electronic Text Archive. Montclair State University. July 30, 2009. http://meta.montclair.edu/spectator.

Burnyeat, Myles. *Aristotle's Divine Intellect.* Milwaukee: Marquette University Press, 2008.

Caygill, Howard. *Walter Benjamin: The Colour of Experience.* London: Routledge, 1997.

Clearchus. "Fragment 7." *Die Schule des Aristoteles.* Heft III. 2. Aufl. Ed. Wehrli, Fritz. Basel: Benno Schwabe, 1969.

Coetzee, J. M. "Time, Tense, and Aspect in Kafka's 'The Burrow.'" *MLN* April 1981: 556–79.

Crary, Jonathan. *Suspensions of Perception: Attention, Spectacle, and Modern Culture.* Cambridge, MA: MIT Press, 2001.

Cristin, Renato. *Heidegger and Leibniz: Reason and Path.* Trans. Parks, Gerald. Dordrecht: Kluwer, 1998.

Crowell, Steven Galt, and J. E. Malpas. *Transcendental Heidegger.* Stanford, CA: Stanford University Press, 2007.

Cuche, François-Xavier. *Une Pensée Social Catholique: Fleury, La Bruyère et Fénelon.* Paris: Cerf, 1991.

Dagen, Jean, Elisabeth Bourguinat, and Marc Escola, eds. *La Bruyère, le métier du moraliste: actes du Colloque International pour le Tricentenaire de la Mort de La Bruyère (Paris, 8–9 Novembre 1996).* Paris: Champion, 2001.

Dahlstrom, Daniel O. *Heidegger's Concept of Truth.* Cambridge, UK: Cambridge University Press, 2001.

Dastur, Françoise. *Heidegger and the Question of Time.* Trans. Raffoul, François and David Pettigrew. Atlantic Highlands, NJ: Humanities Press, 1998.

Deleuze, Gilles, and Félix Guattari. *Kafka: Toward a Minor Literature.* Minneapolis: University of Minnesota Press, 1986.

De Ley, Herbert. *The Movement of Thought: An Essay on Intellect in Seventeenth-Century France.* Urbana: University of Illinois Press, 1985.

Derrida, Jacques. "Geschlecht: différénce sexuelle, différence ontologique." *Martin Heidegger.* Paris: L'Herne, 1983. 419–30.

———. "Geschlecht: Sexual Difference, Ontological Difference." *Research in Phenomenology* 1983: 65–83.

———. *Of Spirit: Heidegger and the Question.* Chicago: University of Chicago Press, 1989.

———. *On Touching—Jean-Luc Nancy.* Trans. Irizarry, Christine. Stanford, CA: Stanford University Press, 2005.

"Diatribe of a Mad Housewife." *The Simpsons.* Fox Broadcasting Company. Season 15, Episode 10. January 25, 2004.

Duttlinger, Carolin. "Between Contemplation and Distraction: Configurations of Attention in Walter Benjamin." *German Studies Review* 30 1 (2007): 33–54.

Eiland, Howard. "Reception in Distraction." *boundary 2* 30 1 (2003): 51–66.

Enders, Markus. *Transzendenz und Welt.* Frankfurt am Main: Peter Lang, 1999.

Escola, Marc. *La Bruyère/ 1, Brèves questions d'herméneutique.* Paris: Champion, 2001.

———. *La Bruyère/ 2, Rhétorique du discontinu.* Paris: Champion, 2001.

Fenves, Peter. *Arresting Language: From Leibniz to Benjamin.* Stanford, CA: Stanford University Press, 2001.

———. "Is There an Answer to the Aestheticizing of the Political?" *Walter Benjamin and Art.* Ed. Benjamin, Andrew. London: Continuum, 2005. 60–72.

———. *Late Kant: Towards Another Law of the Earth.* New York: Routledge, 2003.

———. *The Messianic Reduction: Walter Benjamin and the Shape of Time.* Stanford, CA: Stanford University Press, 2010.

Ferreira, Boris. *Stimmung bei Heidegger: Das Phänomen der Stimmung im Kontext von Heideggers Existenzialanalyse des Daseins.* Dordrecht: Kluwer Academic Publishers, 2002.

Foucault, Michel. *History of Madness.* Trans. Khalfa, Jean and Jonathan Murphy. London: Routledge, 2006.

Freud, Sigmund. *Gesammelte Werke.* Frankfurt am Main: Fischer, 1999.

Gasché, Rodolphe. "Über das Wegsehen: Aufmerksamkeit und Abstraktion bei Kant." *Aufmerksamkeit.* Eds. Haas, Norbert, Rainer Nägele, and Hans-Jörg Rheinberger. Eggingen: Klaus Isele, 1998. 129–60.

Haight, Jeanne. *The Concept of Reason in French Classical Literature, 1635–1690.* Toronto: University of Toronto Press, 1982.

Hamacher, Werner. "Afformative, Strike." *Cardozo Law Review* 13 4 (1991): 1133–57.

———. "Bogengebete." *Aufmerksamkeit.* Eds. Haas, Norbert, Rainer Nägele, and Hans-Jörg Rheinberger. Eggingen: Klaus Isele, 1998. 11–44.

———. "Des contrées des temps." *Contretemps* 1995: 60–69.

Hamann, Christof. "Roßmanns Zerstreuung." *Odradeks Lachen: Fremdheit bei Kafka.* Eds. Bay, Hansjörg and Christof Hamann. Freiburg i. Br.: Rombach, 2006. 115–44.

Hegel, Georg Wilhelm Friedrich. *Werke in Zwanzig Bänden.* Suhrkamp Taschenbuch Wissenschaft. Ed. Reinicke, Helmut. Vol. 10. Frankfurt am Main: Suhrkamp, 1986.

Heidegger, Martin. "Bauen Wohnen Denken." *Vorträge und Aufsätze.* Stuttgart: Neske, 1954. 139–56.

———. *Beiträge zur Philosophie: Vom Ereignis*. Frankfurt am Main: Vittorio Klostermann, 1989.

———. *Die Grundbegriffe der Metaphysik: Welt–Endlichkeit–Einsamkeit*. Frankfurt am Main: Vittorio Klostermann, 1983.

———. *Metaphysische Anfangsgründe der Logik im Ausgang von Leibniz*. Gesamtausgabe. Vol. 26. Frankfurt am Main: Vittorio Klostermann, 1990.

———. *Prolegomena zur Geschichte des Zeitbegriffs*. Frankfurt am Main: Vittorio Klostermann, 1979.

———. *Sein und Zeit*. Tübingen: Max Niemeyer, 1993.

———. *Was heißt Denken?* Tübingen: Max Niemeyer, 1997.

Heidsieck, Arnold. *The Intellectual Contexts of Kafka's Fiction: Philosophy, Law, Religion*. Columbia, SC: Camden House, 1994.

Heller, Paul. *Franz Kafka: Wissenschaft und Wissenschaftskritik*. Tübingen: Stauffenburg, 1989.

Hobbes, Thomas. *Human Nature and De Corpore Politico*. Oxford: Oxford University Press, 2008.

———. *Leviathan: Parts I and II*. Ed. Martinich, A. P. Ontario, Canada: Broadview, 2005.

Homer. *Iliad*. Homeri Opera. Eds. Munro, David B. and Thomas W. Allen. 2 vols. Oxford: Clarendon, 1920.

Husserl, Edmund. *Ideen zu einer reinen Phänomenologie und phänomenologischen Philosophie: Allgemeine Einführung in die reine Phänomenologie*. Tübingen: Niemeyer, 2002.

Hyland, Drew A. "Caring for Myth: Heidegger, Plato, and the Myth of Cura." *Research in Phenomenology* 27 (2001): 90–102.

Jaspers, Karl. *Psychologie der Weltanschauungen*. Berlin: Springer, 1960.

Jean Paul. *Sämtliche Werke. Abteilung II. Jugendwerke und Vermischte Schriften*. Eds. Miller, Norbert and Wilhelm Schmidt-Biggemann. Vol. 2. München: Carl Hanser, 1976.

Johnson, Monte Ransome. *Aristotle on Teleology*. Oxford: Oxford University Press, 2005.

Kafka, Franz. *Beschreibung eines Kampfes: Novellen, Skizzen, Aphorismen*. Gesammelte Schriften. Ed. Brod, Max. Vol. 5. Prag: Heinr. Mercy Sohn, 1936.

———. *Das Schloß*. Ed. Pasley, Malcolm. Frankfurt am Main: Fischer, 2002.

———. *Drucke zu Lebzeiten*. Eds. Koch, Hans-Gerd, Wolf Kittler, and Gerhard Neumann. Frankfurt am Main: Fischer, 1994.

———. *Nachgelassene Schriften und Fragmente*. Ed. Pasley, Malcolm. Vol. 1. Frankfurt am Main: Fischer, 1993.

———. *Nachgelassene Schriften und Fragmente*. Ed. Schillemeit, Jost. Vol. 2. Frankfurt am Main: Fischer, 1992.

————. *Tagebücher.* Eds. Koch, Hans-Gerd, Michael Müller, and Malcom Pasley. Frankfurt am Main: Fischer, 1990.

Kahn, Charles H. "Aristotle on Thinking." *Essays on Aristotle's De anima.* Eds. Nussbaum, Martha C. and Amélie Oksenberg Rorty. Oxford: Clarendon, 1992. 359–80.

Kant, Immanuel. *Kants handschriftlicher Nachlaß.* Akademie Ausgabe. Vol. 2. Berlin: Walter de Gruyter, 1923.

————. *Kritik der reinen Vernunft.* Ed. Timmermann, Jens. Hamburg: Felix Meiner, 2003.

Kierkegaard, Søren. *Søren Kierkegaard's Journals and Papers.* Trans. Hong, Howard V. and Edna H. Hong. Vol. 1. Bloomington: Indiana University Press, 1967.

Kirk, G. S., J. E. Raven, and M. Schofield. *The Presocratic Philosophers.* 2nd ed. Cambridge, UK: Cambridge University Press, 1983.

Kisiel, Theodore. *The Genesis of Heidegger's Being and Time.* Berkeley: University of California Press, 1993.

Kisiel, Theodore J., and John van Buren, eds. *Reading Heidegger from the Start: Essays in His Earliest Thought.* Albany: State University of New York Press, 1994.

Kleist, Heinrich von. *Sämtliche Werke und Briefe.* Ed. Sembdner, Helmut. München: Deutscher Taschenbuch Verlag, 1993.

Kovacs, George. "The Ontological Difference in Heidegger's *Grundbegriffe.*" *Heidegger Studies* 3/4 (1987–1988): 61–74.

Kracauer, Siegfried. "Kult der Zerstreuung." *Das Ornament der Masse.* Frankfurt am Main: Suhrkamp, 1963. 311–17.

————. "Soziologie als Wissenschaft: Eine erkenntnistheoretische Untersuchung." *Schriften.* Vol. 1. Frankfurt am Main: Suhrkamp, 1971. 7–102.

Kraus, Karl. *Aphorismen.* Ed. Wagenknecht, Christian. Frankfurt am Main: Suhrkamp, 1986.

Kudzus, Winfried. "Verschüttungen in Kafkas 'Der Bau.'" *Probleme der Moderne: Festschrift für Walter Sokel.* Eds. Bennett, Benjamin, Anton Kaes, and William J. Lillyman. Tübingen: Max Niemeyer, 1983.

La Bruyère, Jean de. *Characters.* Trans. Stewart, Jean. Baltimore: Penguin, 1970.

————. *Les caractères de Théophraste traduits du grec avec Les caractères ou Les moeurs de ce siècle.* Ed. Escola, Marc. Paris: H. Champion, 1999.

La Rochefoucauld, François. *Maxims.* Trans. Tancock, Leonard. London: Penguin, 1959.

Levi, Anthony. *French Moralists: The Theory of The Passions, 1585 to 1649.* Oxford: Clarendon, 1964.

Lezra, Jacques. *Wild Materialism: The Ethic of Terror and the Modern Republic.* New York: Fordham University Press, 2010.

Lindner, Burkhardt. "Das Kunstwerk im Zeitalter seiner technischen Reproduzier-barkeit." *Benjamin-Handbuch: Leben–Werk–Wirkung.* Ed. Lindner, Burkhardt. Stuttgart: Metzler, 2006. 229–51.

Lyons, John D. *Before Imagination: Embodied Thought from Montaigne to Rousseau.* Stanford, CA: Stanford University Press, 2005.

Magee, Joseph M. *Unmixing the Intellect: Aristotle on Cognitive Powers and Bodily Organs.* Westport, CT: Greenwood, 2003.

Major, Wilfred E. "P. K. Marshall, Hyginus: Fabulae. Editio altera." *Bryn Mawr Classical Review* 2003.6.37 (2003). http://bmcr.brynmawr.edu/2003/2003-06-37.html (accessed May 12, 2011).

Marek, Johann Christian, and Barry Smith. "Einleitung zu Anton Martys 'Elemente der deskriptiven Psychologie.'" *Conceptus* 1987: 33–47.

———. "Elemente der deskriptiven Psychologie." *Conceptus* 1987: 49–66.

Mesnard, Jean. *Les Pensées de Pacal.* Paris: Société d'Édition d'Enseignement Supérieur, 1993.

Montaigne, Michel de. "De la diversion." *Essais.* Vol. 3. Ed. Tournon, André. Paris: Imprimerie National, 1998.

———. *The Complete Essays of Montaigne.* Trans. Frame, Donald Murdoch. Stanford, CA: Stanford University Press, 1976.

Mülder-Bach, Inka. "Auf der Suche nach der Verlorenen Öffentlichkeit: Siegfried Kracauers Kultursoziologie der Angestellten." *Working Girls: Zur Ökonomie von Liebe und Arbeit.* Eds. Biebl, Sabine, Verena Mund, and Heide Volkening. Berlin: Kadmos, 2007. 126–37.

Nancy, Jean-Luc. *The Inoperative Community.* Trans. Connor, Peter et al. Minneapolis: University of Minnesota Press, 1991.

Nietzsche, Friedrich. *Kritische Studienausgabe.* Eds. Colli, Giorgio and Mazzino Montinari. 15 vols. München: Detuscher Taschenbuch Verlag, 1999.

Ogden, Daniel. *Greek and Roman Necromancy.* Princeton, NJ: Princeton University Press, 2001.

Opilik, Klaus. *Transzendenz und Vereinzelung: Zur Fragwürdigkeit des transzendentalen Ansatzes im Umkreis von Heideggers "Sein und Zeit."* Freiburg: Karl Alber, 1993.

Parmenides. *Fragments: A Text and Translation with an Introduction.* Trans. Gallop, David. Toronto: University of Toronto Press, 1984.

Pascal, Blaise. *Pensées.* Trans. Krailsheimer, A. J. New York: Penguin, 1995.

———. *Pensées.* Ed. Ferreyrolles, Gérard. Paris: Librairie générale de France, 2000.

Pascal, Roy. *Kafka's Narrators: A Study of His Stories and Sketches.* Cambridge, UK: Cambridge University Press, 1982.

Pasley, Malcolm. "The Burrow." *The Kafka Debate: New Perspectives for Our Time.* Ed. Flores, Angel. New York: Gordian, 1977. 418–25.

Philoponus. *On Aristotle on the Intellect (De anima 3.4–8).* Trans. Charlton, William and Fernand Bossier. Ithaca, NY: Cornell University Press, 1991.

Pöggeler, Otto. *Der Denkweg Martin Heideggers.* Pfullingen: Neske, 1990.

———. *Heidegger in seiner Zeit.* München: Wilhelm Fink, 1999.

Polansky, Ronald. *Aristotle's De anima.* Cambridge, UK: Cambridge University Press, 2007.

Polignac, Francois de. *Cults, Territory, and the Origins of the Greek City-State.* Chicago: University of Chicago Press, 1995.

Politzer, Heinz. *Franz Kafka: Parable and Paradox.* Ithaca, NY: Cornell University Press, 1962.

Ricord, Marine. *"Les Caractères" de La Bruyère ou les exercises de l'esprit.* Paris: Presses Universitaires de France, 2000.

Rist, John M. *The Mind of Aristotle: A Study in Philosophical Growth.* Toronto: University of Toronto Press, 1989.

Robertson, Ritchie. *Kafka: Judaism, Politics, Literature.* Oxford: Oxford University Press, 1985.

Ronell, Avital. *Stupidity.* Urbana: University of Illinois Press, 2002.

Roubach, Michael. *Being and Number in Heidegger's Thought.* London: Continuum, 2008.

Schestag, Thomas. "geteilte Aufmerksamkeit." *"geteilte Aufmerksamkeit": Zur Frage des Lesens.* Ed. Schestag, Thomas. Frankfurt am Main: Peter Lang, 1997. 7–28.

Schneider, Manfred. "Kollekten des Geistes: Die Zerstreuung im Visier der Kulturkritik." *Neue Rundschau* 110 2 (1999): 44–55.

Septuaginta: Id Est Vetus Testamentum Graece Iuxta LXX Interpretes. Ed. Rahlfs, Alfred. 2 vols. Stuttgart: Deutsche Bibelstiftung, 1935.

Simplicius. *On Aristotle's Physics 4.1–5, 10–14.* Trans. Urmson, J. O. Ithaca, NY: Cornell University Press, 1992.

Smith, Barry. "Brentano and Kafka." *Axiomathes* 1997: 83–104.

Sorabji, Richard. *The Philosophy of the Commentators, 200–600 AD: A Sourcebook.* Vol. 1. London: Duckworth, 2004.

———. *Time, Creation, and the Continuum: Theories in Antiquity and the Early Middle Ages.* Ithaca, NY: Cornell University Press, 1983.

Stambaugh, Joan. "Die Aufgabe des Denkens." *Zur philosophischen Aktualität Heideggers.* Vol. 1. Frankfurt am Main: Vittorio Klostermann, 1990. 141–48.

Stiegler, Bernard. *Prendre soin: de la jeunesse et des générations.* Paris: Éditions Flammarion, 2008.

Sussman, Henry. "The All-Embracing Metaphor: Reflections on Kafka's 'The Burrow.'" *Glyph* 1977: 100–131.

Taminiaux, Jacques. *Heidegger and the Project of Fundamental Ontology*. Trans. Gendre, Michael. Albany: State University of New York Press, 1991.

Themistius. *On Aristotle's On the Soul*. Trans. Todd, Robert B. Ithaca, NY: Cornell University Press, 1996.

Turner, Margaret. "The Influence of La Bruyère on the 'Tatler' and the 'Spectator.'" *Modern Language Review* 48 1 (1953): 10–16.

Vail, Loy M. *Heidegger and Ontological Difference*. University Park: Pennsylvania State University Press, 1972.

van Buren, John. *The Young Heidegger: Rumor of the Hidden King*. Bloomington: Indiana University Press, 1994.

Vernant, Jean-Pierre. *The Origins of Greek Thought*. Ithaca, NY: Cornell University Press, 1984.

Vernay, Robert. "Dissipation." *Dictionnaire de Spiritualité Ascétique et Mystique, Doctrine et Histoire*. Ed. Viller, M. Vol. 3. Paris: Beauchesne, 1957. 1346–47.

Waldenfels, Bernhard. *Phänomenologie der Aufmerksamkeit*. Frankfurt am Main: Suhrkamp, 2004.

Weber, Samuel. *Benjamin's -abilities*. Cambridge, MA: Harvard University Press, 2008.

———. *Mass Mediauras: Form, Technics, Media*. Stanford, CA: Stanford University Press, 1996.

Wedin, Michael V. *Mind and Imagination in Aristotle*. New Haven, CT: Yale University Press, 1988.

———. "Tracking Aristotle's Nous." *Aristotle's De Anima in Focus*. Ed. Durrant, Michael. London: Routledge, 1993. 128–61.

Winkler, Markus. "Kulturkritik in Kafkas 'Der Bau.'" *Zeitschrift für Deutsche Philologie* 1999: 144–64.

Witt, Charlotte. "The Evolution of Developmental Interpretations of Aristotle." *Aristotle's Philosophical Development: Problems and Prospects*. Ed. Wians, William. Lanham, MD: Rowman & Littlefield, 1996. 67–82.

Zarader, Marlène. *The Unthought Debt: Heidegger and the Hebraic Heritage*. Trans. Bergo, Bettina. Stanford, CA: Stanford University Press, 2006.

Index